Past Law,
Present Histories

Past Law,
Present Histories

edited by DIANE KIRKBY

Australian
National
University

E PRESS

ANU
E PRESS

Published by ANU E Press
The Australian National University
Canberra ACT 0200, Australia
Email: anuepress@anu.edu.au
This title is also available online at http://epress.anu.edu.au

National Library of Australia Cataloguing-in-Publication entry

Title: Past law, present histories / edited by Diane Kirkby.

ISBN: 97819222144027 (pbk.) 9781922144034 (eBook)

Notes: Includes bibliographical references.

Subjects: Law--History.
                Law--Research.
                Law--Social aspects.
                Law--Philosophy.

Other Authors/Contributors:
                Kirkby, Diane.

Dewey Number: 340.09

Cover design and layout by ANU E Press

Contents

III. Law as Theory and Practice

Introduction: Interdisciplinarity in the Study of Law's History

Diane Kirkby

Understanding law, its development, implementation and subsequent trajectory, requires empirical research that is both interdisciplinary and critical. The complex interplay between the timing, socio-political context and purpose of lawmaking in any specific instance calls for historical analysis through which we can engage with both narrow and broader definitions of law. Through historical analysis we can account for the often unpredictable direction of specific laws, and explain particularities as these change over time with each set of new circumstances. Informed by a critical theoretical and interdisciplinary approach, we can more deeply investigate the conceptual underpinning of law's meaning.

This collection is a contribution to scholarship historicising and critically examining different instances of lawmaking that also contributes to understanding the broader meaning of law. The essence of the collection is its interdisciplinarity. Contributors bring methods and questions from humanities, law and social science disciplines to highlight problems that are both national and international in their implication. From different disciplinary backgrounds and theoretical positions, they illustrate how diverse and complex the study of law's history has become.

The book had its genesis in the Australian and New Zealand Law and History Conference sponsored by La Trobe University and the Australia and New Zealand Law and History Society (ANZLHS) in Melbourne in December 2010. The theme of the conference, Owning the Past: Whose Past? Whose Present?, was designed to stimulate discussion around conflicting interpretations of the past in the present, and to highlight the continuing dialogue that exists between past and present and the contradictions inherent in the historical process. The conference attracted well over 100 speakers, all of whom were invited to submit their paper for publication; through a process of selection and refereeing, the papers published here were chosen.

The organising principle of the book is the relationship and interaction between the disciplines of law and history. This is not legal history as traditionally understood and practiced, as a self-perpetuating discrete area with its own logic of development and chronology. That view has been under sustained attack from critical studies scholars for over three decades, and was the basis for calling the first law and history conference in Australia back in 1982. Instead, this collection is one of interdisciplinary scholarship that draws on the strengths of different approaches to carve out new ways of knowing. Law is consistently subject to a historicised social and cultural context, which is specific to the time and place of its occurrence, and is similarly specific to time and place in its present significance and the meanings to be drawn from it. The contributors to this book explore the problematic of past law in history's present across indigenous Australia and New Zealand, from post-Franco Spain to current international law and maritime regulation, from settler colonial humanitarian debates and efforts to end cruelty to children and animals, to postcolonial legal proceedings in the stolen generation cases.

The book is organised into three distinct parts around the concepts that frame the interdisciplinary study of law's history: law and colonialism, law in community, law as theory and practice. Part I includes chapters dealing with the impact of a slavery trial on the development of international law and the challenges posed for the rule of law over questions of indigenous people giving testimony in colonial courts in both Australia and New Zealand. Emily Haslam reminds us that slave-trading was one of the first international crimes as she seeks to expand the field of international criminal law with a close study of nineteenth-century anti-slavery cases in Sierra Leone. Shaunnagh Dorsett takes us to colonial New Zealand for an examination of the particularities of that colony in relation to Māori giving unsworn testimony. Her argument endorses the need for detailed knowledge of local circumstances when assessing the larger imperial framework in which colonial laws were enacted. In her chapter, too, Anna Johnston concentrates on the imperial–colonial nexus as illustrated by the work of a single individual from early New South Wales whose actions and writings on Aboriginal people and the law courts exemplifies the formation of settler and indigenous identities, both enabling and simultaneously limiting Aboriginal legal subjectivity.

Part II concentrates on law's role in its community context and includes the evolution of animal protection law, issues of accessing the remedies available in law by working-class communities, the vexed question of the parental right to discipline children and the colonial context for violence against women in Aboriginal communities, all of which are issues of continuing relevance today. Stefan Petrow and Debra Powell in their individual chapters draw out continuities between past and present practice in explicit considerations of cruelty laws in Australia and New Zealand. Jenny Anderson advances knowledge of working-class use of legality as a means of regulating sexual activity, with a concentration on sexual assault cases in the state of Victoria. Libby Connors provides an invaluable corrective to Sydney-centric histories of post-contact Aboriginal law with new insights that are based on research relevant to the history of Queensland.

Part III explores law theoretically in Ann Genovese's important chapter on ways of doing feminist history of law with a specific focus on family law. This is followed by Aleksandra Hadzelek's examination of the theoretical problem of memory-making through law in an exploration of the national dilemma of remembering the unpopular regime of General Franco and Spain's civil war. Diane Kirkby, in the third chapter in this section, examines the Australian *Navigation Act 1912* as labour law in practice, changing its meaning and application with political and economic circumstances. The section is completed with a fourth chapter in which Thalia Anthony and Honni van Rijswijk explore a specific example of law in practice for families as they address the issue of parental consent for Aboriginal families whose children were removed by state policies.

All these papers examine past law, and present histories, in ways that illuminate and provide a valuable resource for continuing discussions. They demonstrate how diverse — and important — interdisciplinarity is to understanding law's meaning.

Acknowledgments

Many colleagues have been generous with their time reading these papers and making very valuable suggestions. First and foremost I am particularly grateful to Lee-Ann Monk for her invaluable help with the editing of individual papers, a task requiring time-consuming attention to detail. Catharine Coleborne offered insightful assistance at key moments; Rosemary Hunter and Margaret Thornton were unfailingly generous with their time and expertise; Janine Rizzetti stepped in when needed and undertook the hard work of conference organisation with great efficiency and cheerfulness; and all of them provided friendship and collegiality. I also have to thank Glenn Patmore for first suggesting this project and to John Wanna of ANZSOG for encouraging the idea. In addition there is a very long list of colleagues who acted as referees of individual chapters but who must remain anonymous to protect the process of academic confidentiality. To them and their professionalism, I am deeply indebted.

Lastly, I must thank the members of my family who, over many years, have uncomplainingly tolerated my absences from home while I undertook my research and who always give me unqualified loving support. They know how much that means.

I. Law and Colonialism

Redemption, Colonialism and International Criminal Law: The Nineteenth Century Slave-Trading Trials of Samo and Peters

Emily Haslam

You are the first convicted under this act, and England will anxiously look for such an example to be made, as will infuse terror and dismay into the minds of every remaining slave factor on these coasts.[1]

My Lord, and Gentlemen of the Jury, reflect for a moment on the miseries of slavery, what is it that the poor African does not endure? Think of the separation of husband and wife, father and mother, children, brothers, sisters, kindred, and friends; think of the cold, the heat, the labour and the lash, that unfeeling custom has doomed to the condition of the slave; and to whom shall he apply for redress? I glory in knowing that he can apply to British law …[2]

Introduction

In April 1812 in the Vice Admiralty Court of Sierra Leone, Chief Justice Robert Thorpe dramatically convicted and then pardoned Samuel Samo for slave-trading. The courtroom was crowded and the atmosphere was highly charged. The attorney-general, James Biggs, opened the prosecution with the expansive claim that the case 'embraces the essential concerns of one quarter of the globe we inhabit, and involves the security and morals, the happiness and liberty, of millions yet to live'.[3] In announcing Samo's pardon, Thorpe proclaimed, 'You have received the mercy of the royal pardon — May your future conduct deserve that of our Father who is in heaven'.[4] After this homily, Samo is said to have withdrawn in a 'death like silence' whilst others wept in the courtroom.[5]

---

1 Robert Thorpe CJ in *The Trials of the Slave Traders, Samuel Samo, Joseph Peters and William Tufft Before the Hon. Robert Thorpe, L.L.D. with Two Letters on the Slave Trade From a Gentleman Resident at Sierra Leone to an Advocate for the Abolition in London* (*The Trials of the Slave Traders*) (London: Sherwood, Neeley, and Jones, 1813) 33, Anti-Slavery Recovered Histories at http://www.recoveredhistories.org/pamphlet1.php?catid=50 last accessed 17 October 2011.
2 Mr Biggs, in *The Trials of the Slave Traders*, 27.
3 ibid., 13.
4 Thorpe, in *The Trials of the Slave Traders*, 39.
5 ibid.

At the time, Samo's case attracted widespread interest and generated political controversy and debate beyond the colony. And yet, this case and the subsequent trials of Charles Hickson, Joseph Peters, William Tufft and Thomas Wheeler, have been overlooked in accounts of the development of international criminal law. As the first tranche of proceedings brought under the British *Slave Trade Felony Act 1811*, which made slave-trading a felony,[6] they represent a handful of the criminal and civil law cases from the early nineteenth century dealing with the slave trade and abolition. These have been largely overlooked by international legal scholars. Whilst it is true that there is a significant body of literature related to the United States,[7] the literature dealing with the English context has tended to focus on a few key cases,[8] to emphasise the activities of a narrow group of abolitionists,[9] and to overlook (international) criminal law.[10] Present-day approaches overwhelmingly trace the origins of contemporary international criminal law to the Nuremberg and Tokyo Trials.[11] The neglect of this earlier litigation is disappointing.[12] Slave-trading was one of the first international crimes.[13] Legal and institutional responses to the slave trade gave rise to many similar controversies that face the international community today, including the limits of international intervention and the extent of criminal responsibility. This chapter begins the process of exploring what international criminal law looks like when slavery litigation is brought back into the picture by examining some of the early slave-trading trials before the Vice Admiralty Court of Sierra Leone. In particular the focus is on

---

6   An Act for Rendering More Effectual an Act made in the Forty Seventh Year of His Majesty's Reign, entitled *An Act for the Abolition of the Slave Trade*, 51 Geo III C 23, 14 May 1811 (Slave Trade Felony Act).

7   For example, Robert Cover, *Justice Accused: Antislavery and the Judicial Process* (New Haven: Yale University Press, 1975).

8   Most notably *Somerset v Stewart* (1772) 98 Eng. Rep. 499; *Gregson v. Gilbert* 99 Engl. Rep 629 and The Slave, Grace, (1827) 166 Eng. Rep. 179. See further, F.O. Shyllon, *Black Slaves in Britain* (London: Oxford University Press, 1974).

9   For example, William Wiecek, '*Somerset*: Lord Mansfield and the Legitimacy of Slavery in the Anglo-American World', *University of Chicago Law Review* 42, (1974–75): 86; Steven Wise, *Though the Heavens May Fall* (Cambridge, MA: Da Capo Press, 2005).

10   To the extent that literature deals with international law, it tends to focus on the struggles over search and seizure in relation to slave ships, see Leslie Bethell, 'The Mixed Commissions for the Suppression of the Transatlantic Slave Trade in the Nineteenth Century', *Journal of African History* VII, 1 (1966): 79–93; Holger Lutz Kern, 'Strategies of Legal Change: Great Britain, International Law, and the Abolition of the Transatlantic Slave Trade', *Journal of the History of International Law* 6, (2004): 233–58; Howard Hazen Wilson, 'Some Principal Aspects of British Efforts to Crush the African Slave Trade, 1807–1929', *The American Journal of International Law* 44 (1950): 505–26.

11   See, for example, Antonio Cassese, 'From Nuremberg to Rome: International Military Tribunals to the International Criminal Court', in *The Rome Statute of the International Criminal Court: A Commentary*, vol. I, eds, Antonio Cassese, Paola Gaeta and John R.W.D. Jones (Oxford University Press, 2002): 3–19; Madoka Fatumura, *War Crimes Tribunals and Transitional Justice: The Tokyo Trial and the Nuremberg Legacy* (Abingdon: Routledge, 2008); Dominic McGoldrick, 'Criminal Trials before International Tribunals: Legality and Legitimacy', in *The Permanent International Criminal Court: Legal and Policy Issues*, eds, Dominic McGoldrick, Peter Rowe and Eric Donnelly (Oxford: Hart, 2004): 9–46.

12   And, perhaps inevitable given 'the singular focus on Nazi war criminals' as 'the exemplification of evil', Gerry Simpson, 'Didactic and Dissident Histories in War Crimes Trials', *Albany Law Review* 60 (1996–97): 811.

13   Piracy is widely considered to be the first international crime, Gerry Simpson, *Law, War and Crime* (Cambridge: Polity Press, 2007) 161–62.

two of the trials, that of Samo and, to a lesser extent as a point of comparison, that of Peters. This contribution focuses less upon the doctrinal significance that this body of litigation had in the development of international criminal law. Rather, its focus is on the didacticism that emanated from the courtroom in Samo's case and its similarities to that occurring in contemporary international criminal trials. It argues that, in Samo's case, a religiously accented adjudicative logic of redemption was deployed in the service of a broader colonial project. The chapter suggests that this redemptive framework continues to exert influence in contemporary international criminal law. Today, these narratives are for the most part secularised with transition to democracy and the rule of law replacing emancipation and reconciliation replacing redemption. By suggesting the deployment of this narrative for a colonial project, this chapter seeks to contribute to a richer history of the development of international criminal law and more specifically its redemptive trope.[14]

The chapter begins by setting out the legal, institutional and political context of these cases by exploring the *Slave Trade Felony Act 1811* and the significance of Sierra Leone to abolitionists at institutional and symbolic levels. Whilst the cases examined here are essentially 'British' rather than 'international', they are relevant to international criminal law because of the leading role that Britain played in developing strategies and tools to abolish the slave trade at the international level,[15] and because participants in the Vice-Admiralty hearings engaged with thorny international legal questions of jurisdiction and nationality. Whilst the aim of the chapter is to contribute to a more expansive account of the development of international criminal law, it does not intend by focusing on British cases, to gloss over other, particularly non-European, contributions to the development of international criminal law.[16] The third section explores the cases before moving on to examine the contestation to which they gave rise. Such contestation demonstrates that abolitionists understood law's potential to contribute to the construction of public memory and the importance of the trial as a show.[17] This final section explores the logic of redemption that ran through

---

14   For criticisms of this redemptive trope see, for example, Thomas Brudholm, *Resentment's Virtue: Jean Amery and the Refusal to Forgive* (Philadelphia: Temple University Press, 2008).

15   See, for example, Suzanne Miers, *Britain and the Ending of the Slave Trade* (London: Longman 1975); Ethan Nadelmann, 'Global Prohibition Regimes: The Evolution of Norms in International Society', *International Organisation* 44, (1990): 479–526.

16   For the criticism that non-Eurocentric origins are all too often overlooked in international legal histories see, for example, Upendra Baxi, *The Future of Human Rights* (Oxford University Press, 2002); Balakrishnan Rajagopal, *International Law from Below: Development, Social Movements and Third World Resistance* (Cambridge University Press, 2003).

17   For an excellent account of the construction of memories of abolition (which however does not deal with law and litigation) see J.R. Oldfield, *'Chords of Freedom': Commemoration, Ritual and British Transatlantic Slavery* (Manchester University Press, 2007). On remembering the slave trade and abolition see further, Catherine Hall, 'Remembering 1807: Histories of the Slave Trade, Slavery and Abolition', *History Workshop Journal* 64, (2007): 1–5; Elizabeth Kowaleski Wallace, *The British Slave Trade and Public Memory* (Chichester: Columbia University Press, 2006).

Samo's case and the political usage made of it. The chapter concludes by positing Samo's case as evidence of how the redemptive trope of international criminal law has been implicated in a colonial project.

Background to the cases

Shortly after Britain abolished the slave trade in 1807,[18] it became apparent that the penalties provided by the Abolition Act were insufficient.[19] The potential profits that slave-trading could generate made the financial penalties far too derisory to deter the practice. On 14 May 1811, the Slave Trade Felony Act was passed, instigated within parliament by Henry Brougham, Member of Parliament for Camelford. By section 1, removal, or assisting in the removal, transportation and shipment of slaves by British subjects, or in British territory, became a felony; and the legislation also provided increased penalties of imprisonment and hard labour for between three and five years or transportation for 14 years, thereby degrading slave factors, in the words of Thorpe CJ, to 'pickpockets and swindlers'.[20]

In terms of the numbers of prosecutions, the impact of the Act was negligible.[21] This may explain the lack of attention that has been paid to the cases by (international) legal scholars. Nonetheless, this does not mean that the Act's significance should be underestimated in assessing how it helps further our understanding of the development of international criminal law. The limited numbers prosecuted (whilst revealing) should not be allowed to obscure the messages participants attempted to deliver through litigation and how these prosecutions were 'read' at the time, both inside and outside the courtroom.

---

18   *An Act for the Abolition of the Slave Trade* 47 Geo. III c 3, 25 March 1807 (Abolition Act). On abolitionism more generally see further, Roger Anstey, *The Atlantic Slave Trade and British Abolition 1760–1810* (London and Basingstoke: Macmillan, 1975); Robin Blackburn, *The Overthrow of Colonial Slavery, 1776–1748* (London and New York: Verso, 1996); Adam Hochschild, *Bury the Chains: The British Struggle to Abolish Slavery* (Basingstoke and Oxford: Macmillan, 2005).

19   See, for example, Mr Brougham, House of Commons Debate, 5 March 1811, vol. 19, cc 233–40. See further Monroe H. Freedman, 'Henry Lord Brougham — Advocating at the Edge for Human Rights', *Hofstra Law Review* 36 (2007): 311–22.

20   *The Trials of the Slave Traders*, 11.

21   Marika Sherwood, *After Abolition: Britain and the Slave Trade since 1807* (London: I.B. Tauris, 2007), 301. See further, Old Bailey Proceedings Online (http://www.oldbaileyonline.org) February 1817, Trial of John Bean Hannay (t18170219-123); Old Bailey Proceedings Online (http://www.oldbaileyonline.org), February 1819, Trial of Philippe Caday, alias Phillibert Armand Clerensac, Joseph Ann Tresgrose (t18190217-36); Old Bailey Proceedings Online (http://www.oldbaileyonline.org), January 1820, Trial of Jaques Alexandre Carrol, Alexandre Villemont (t18200112-66). See further, Proceedings under the Slave Trade Felony Act in the Island of Ceylon, Admiralty Commission of Oyer and Terminer, May 17 1813 and Proceedings under the Slave Trade Felony Act in the Island of Java, 2 October 1813, reported in *Ninth Report of the Directors of the African Institution*, 12 April 1815 (London: Ellerton and Henderson, 1815) (Google books last accessed 10 November 2011).

Sierra Leone was an institutionally prominent site in slave trade abolition, the 'centre of the government's efforts to suppress the wider trade'.[22] As home, first to Vice Admiralty and then to mixed commission courts at Freetown, Sierra Leone was the location in which much early jurisprudence relating to abolition was decided. Beyond that, it played a central symbolic role for abolitionists. Well-known British abolitionists had played a pivotal part in each of the attempts to establish Sierra Leone as a colony, including in 1787, 1790, and then, finally, in 1808 when it became a Crown Colony. Its origins can be traced from Granville Sharp's plan to establish a home for poor black Londoners to those abolitionists who invested in the Sierra Leone Company. Many of these became influential in the African Institution, which was established after abolition with the professed objective of promoting civilisation and happiness in Africa.[23]

Sierra Leone was beset with a series of problems, including the controversial practice of enlisting and apprenticing former slaves.[24] Partly as a result of raising these concerns the previous governor, Thomas Thompson, was replaced in 1810 by Edward Columbine. This was the volatile political context in which Thorpe was appointed Chief Justice of Sierra Leone in 1808, although he was not allowed to travel to Sierra Leone until 1811. Thorpe was no stranger to controversy, having previously been removed as a judge in Upper Canada.[25] Thorpe's criticisms of the management of Sierra Leone drew him into a bitter conflict with the African Institution. He was relieved of his post in 1815, for reasons which included the complaints that he made against that institution, some of which featured in the pamphlet debate over Samo's pardon.[26]

The trials of Samo, Peters, Tufft, Wheeler and Hickson

The trials of Samo, Peters, Tufft, Wheeler and Hickson took place between April and June 1812. A detailed account of the trials was written by a 'gentleman resident at Sierra Leone to an advocate for the abolition in London'. These reports were made public, with the view of affording:

---

22   David Lambert, 'Sierra Leone and Other Sites in the War of Representation over Slavery', *History Workshop Journal* 64, (2007): 105.

23   ibid., 105.

24   Section 7 of the Abolition Act permitted 'slaves taken as prizes or forfeitures' to be 'enlisted for the land or sea-service' or 'bound as apprentices, whether of full age or not, for a term of 14 years'. Section 17 provided for the renewal of such apprentices at the end of their term.

25   John McLaren, '"Men of Principle or Judicial Ratbags? The Trials and Tribulations of Maverick Colonial Judges in the 19th Century" or "A Funny Way to Run An Empire"', *Windsor Review of Legal & Social Issues* 27 (2009): 150.

26   ibid., 149–50.

the British Legislature, the Government, and the people in general, an early and correct view of the operation of the recent slave felony act of parliament: an act which reflects the highest honour on those whose humanity was so determined and conspicuous in conducting to a happy issue the long and strenuously contested question of African emancipation.[27]

The pamphlet is not an official account. The identity of the author is not declared. Yet, in the debates that followed Samo's pardon, the African Institution suggested that it was published either by Thorpe or by his friends.[28] In the absence of an official report, this document is the source from which the following account of the trials of Samo and Peters is drawn. The account was clearly influenced by the pamphlet writer's broader objectives as noted above. Even so, the way in which he told the story of the trials, even if not a verbatim record, is revealing. Assuming the African Institution was correct that Thorpe approved of publication, the account can be seen as strong evidence of how the judge framed the role of law in abolition.

Samo was indicted for five counts of slave-trading between August 1811 and January 1812. Samo's twofold plea in response to the substantive offences appeared to be that he was respectable, an assessment supported by a number of witnesses, and that he had been working towards abolition.[29] Samo was found guilty. However, Samo had also raised a more fundamental procedural objection to the jurisdiction of the court, which he renewed at the sentencing stage. He maintained that the *Slave Trade Felony Act 1811* only applied to British subjects. Further he argued that as he was Dutch and, moreover, residing outside British jurisdiction in the Rio Pongas (now Guinea), the Act did not apply to him. Thorpe rejected these legal objections with the observation that the chiefs of the Rio Pongas treated white men living there as British.[30] Although dismissed at this stage, these jurisdictional objections return to centre stage in the debates that followed.

When it came to sentencing, as Thorpe observed, there was not any obvious mitigating evidence on Samo's behalf. Nor was this a case where the jury had recommended his sentence to be reduced.[31] Despite this, he deferred sentencing Samo 'in the hope of finding such exertions made by your friends to extirpate this trade, as will in a great measure diminish, though they may not be able to

---

27   *The Trials of the Slave Traders*, v.
28   *Special Report of the Directors of the African Institution Made at the Annual General Meeting on the 12 of April 1815 Respecting the Allegations Contained in A Pamphlet Entitled 'A Letter to William Wilberforce'* (African Institution, Special Report), (London: Ellerton and Henderson, 1815), 93 (Google books last accessed 11 November 2011).
29   *The Trials of the Slave Traders*, 21–22.
30   ibid., 31.
31   ibid., 33.

eradicate it'.[32] In this way the judge opened his determination of sentence to external influences, making a pardon conditional on the willingness of others to show penitence by renouncing the slave trade. He continued:

> And in proportion to the contrition exhibited, and the zeal for its destruction manifested, the discretion which the law gives to the Court shall be extended to you; and if it appears evidently the intention of the other slave factors, in the vicinity of this colony, to lead a new life, and turn benevolent and industrious, I will use my influence with the amiable personage at the head of this Government to extend the royal mercy to you on this laudable salutary and necessary repentance.[33]

The Chief Justice's call seems to have received favourable answers. As a result of the respect in which Samo was apparently held, the court received several petitions from such eminent persons as the king of Mandingo and the king at Isles de Loss. Petitioners promised to renounce the trade if Samo were granted a pardon.[34] Thorpe claimed, 'it is not the individual victim of the law that is the most valuable' but 'the annihilation of the diabolical traffic is the victim the law demands',[35] and this was an action of which the gentleman letter writer thoroughly approved.[36]

Other defendants fared better. Days after Samo's trial ended, Charles Hickson was tried for the same offence and acquitted. A short while later, Thomas Wheeler, the acting agent at Bance Island, was also acquitted — the principal witness having returned home for fear of offending neighbouring kings.[37] Some defendants, however, met with less lenient treatment. William Tufft, a black, English-educated, former servant, essentially pleaded that he was acting under the orders of others, which was not accepted on the evidence. He was sentenced to three years hard labour on public works at Sierra Leone, but his sentence was commuted on condition that he join the Marine Corps for life. Tufft's associate, Joseph Peters, who was tried in June 1812, found the court in a particularly unforgiving mood. His conduct, Biggs said, was compounded by ungratefulness, *because he was in receipt of British pay 'for attendance on British troops'*.[38] Central to Peters's case was a narrative of both resistance and complicity. Peters had rewarded Chief Dallamoodoo and King Murra Brimer with slaves because they had helped him secure the recapture of fugitive slaves. Peters's trial is also

---

32   ibid., 35.
33   ibid.
34   ibid., 36.
35   ibid., 34–35.
36   'To have the "father of the trade", converted into its avowed enemy, and all his African connexion solemnly pledged to assist him in the humane work of abolition, was a great point gained, and infinitely preferable to sacrificing an individual slave trader to the rigour of the law.' ibid., 37.
37   ibid., 49.
38   ibid., 41.

notable for the part played by Africans in testifying against him.[39] Peters was sentenced to seven years transportation. He remained in prison until he was pardoned by the governor on the condition that he left Africa for ever.[40]

Samo's case contested

Samo's case became a point of bitter contestation amongst prominent abolitionists. This debate formed part of a broader pamphlet dispute in which Thorpe made a series of damaging accusations about the Sierra Leone Company and the African Institution in a public letter to William Wilberforce,[41] some of which resonated with those made earlier by Governor Thompson.[42] Whilst Samo's case was not the primary focus of this contestation, concerns that Thorpe raised about the allegedly oppressive exercise of jurisdiction against slave-traders by the authorities in Sierra Leone brought his own treatment of Samo into the frame.

For, amongst the many criticisms he levelled, Thorpe railed against the treatment of individuals apprehended outside the jurisdiction of Sierra Leone and convicted of slave-trading, in a manner that he considered to be both illegal and heavy-handed. In one such extra-territorial expedition in June 1813, HMS *Thais* arrested Robert Bostwick and John M'Queen, destroyed their factory and released over 240 slaves to Sierra Leone and condemned them as slavers.[43] Bostwick and M'Queen were sentenced to 14 years transportation but were freed following a successful petition to the Prince Regent. Other extra-territorial expeditions organised by Lieut-Colonel C. W. Maxwell who had been appointed Governor in July 1811, came under Thorpe's fire. Thorpe criticised the resulting sentencing in his absence by his non-lawyer deputy, Robert Purdie, of Malcolm Brodie, George Cooke and James Dunbar to transportation for slave trading and of Charles Hickson to hard labour on public works. Thorpe's concerns about jurisdiction were justified in so far as Brodie, Cooke and Dunbar were pardoned

---

39   He appears to have been convicted almost solely on the testimony of Africans, including former slaves. The evidence of at least 14 Africans (Banta, Dallamoodoo, Tom Krooman, Duboo, Yangyaraa, Adam, Bondoo, Quiepa, Saree, Borega and Boree) including three women (Monday, Foosingbag, Katta) is reported, in addition to that of Kenneth Macaulay 'Esq'. The court's treatment of African testimony of complicity and resistance in this case is explored in a further article in draft with the author.

40   *Report of the Committee of the African Institution*, vol. 8 (London: Ellerton and Henderson, 1814), 15 (Google books last accessed 11 November 2011).

41   Robert Thorpe, *A Letter to William Wilberforce, ESQ. M.P. Vice President of the African Institution Containing Remarks on the Reports of the Sierra Leone Company, and African Institution with Hints Respecting the Means by Which An Universal Abolition of the Slave Trade Might Be Carried into Effect* (*Letter to William Wilberforce*) (London: Law and Gilbert, 1815) Anti-Slavery Recovered Histories at http://www.recoveredhistories.org/ last accessed 11 November 2011.

42   Including the enlistment and apprenticeship of freed slaves, a practice Thorpe compared to slave-trading, 'involuntary servitude for life, established by an Act of Parliament, purporting to abolish slavery'. ibid., 46.

43   ibid., 19.

as a result of being tried in the wrong court.[44] However, his criticism of his deputy, Purdie, forced him to justify his own conduct in Samo's case because Samo had also been apprehended outside the jurisdiction of Sierra Leone.[45] Thorpe explained:

> to my great surprise and annoyance, Samuel Samo, and Charles Hickson were brought before me, as British subjects trading in slaves; they were seized by Governor Maxwell's orders at the Isles de Loss, for selling slaves in the Rio Pongas, neither of which places were ever considered as belonging to Great Britain, nor did British jurisdiction ever extend over them in any shape ... I found, however, so many insurmountable difficulties (for I was bound to protect the legal rights of the prisoner), that I informed the Governor, that I could not pronounce the sentence directed by the Act on Samo; and to prevent my reasons from being publickly known (lest they might affect the Abolition cause,) I advised the Governor to send to the Rio Pongus [sic], induce the Chiefs to ask for Samo's pardon, and influence them to promise, that if their petition was granted, they would allow no more Slave trading in their dominions.[46]

In this way Thorpe challenged the idea that it was his actions in Samo's case that constituted a precedent for Purdie in the cases of Brodie, Cooke and Dunbar. He claimed, 'I rebuked the outrage, and refused to adjudge any punishment, having declared to the Governor, I was not authorised to do so'.[47]

In revealing that he suggested the pardon because his court did not have jurisdiction in the case, Thorpe displayed both a concern for adherence to the law coupled with an understanding of the potential for its strategic deployment. Thus, he appears to have understood the value of clothing his potentially unpalatable verdict in the international legal idea of jurisdiction, even when earlier in the trial he had rebuffed Samo's challenge to the court's jurisdictional competence. This understanding of the importance of law was also reflected in broader debate, showing how protagonists understood the contribution

---

44 According to the opinion of the Crown Office lawyers. *They could only have been tried in the colonial court of Sierra Leone had a special commission been issued* to permit such a trial. To the African Institution's charge that Thorpe was primarily responsible for obtaining such a commission, Thorpe responded that he had been unaware of the impending extra-territorial actions planned by the governor. African Institution, Special Report, 96; Robert Thorpe, *Postscript to the Reply 'Point by Point' Containing an Exposure of the Misrepresentation of the Treatment of the Captured Negroes at Sierra Leone and Other Matters Arising From the Ninth Report of the African Institution* (London: R. & R. Gilbert, 1815) (Google books last accessed 10 November 2011), 44 (discussing the actions against Samo and Hickson). In fact Cooke was awarded damages of £20,000 in an action against Maxwell before the King's Bench in 1817, which the government assumed responsibility for paying. Brodie died although he also instituted proceedings and Bostock agreed an out of court settlement, see Christopher Fyfe, *A History of Sierra Leone* (Oxford University Press, 1962) 123.

45 See further, African Institution, Special Report, 98.

46 *Letter to William Wilberforce*, 18–19.

47 Robert Thorpe, Postscript, 38.

law could make to the public memory. For example, the African Institution claimed that it was vital that the 'proper' interpretation should be placed on the pardon, a position echoed by William Wilberforce. Wilberforce's concern, as expressed in the House of Commons debate following his unsuccessful motion to institute an inquiry on Brodie, Cook and Dunbar, was that 'considerable error had crept into the world' because people believed that their pardon was granted on the merits rather than on a legal technicality.[48] These struggles show how abolitionists appreciated the capacity of the law to contribute to collective memory and the importance of the didactic potential of the law. This can be seen from the lengths Thorpe went to inside the courtroom to create a show of pardoning Samo, notwithstanding his concerns about lack of jurisdiction and notwithstanding that his verdict apparently rested on the basis of a negotiated compromise. It is to this show that this contribution now turns.

The logic of redemption and international criminal law

Samo's trial was a spectacle, in which a religiously inflected logic of redemption at the individual and collective levels was used to legitimise a colonial project,[49] central to which was the idea of Britain as an abolitionist state.[50] This logic was manifested in an implicit and sometimes explicit discourse of sin and redemption at the individual and collective levels.[51] Stories of individual redemption and its relationship to the collective were played out in the context of witnesses, the defendant and a broader community. These stories served a wider political project and were deployed to exculpate as much as to implicate. This logic continues to resonate in contemporary international criminal law,

---

48   British Parliamentary Debates (*Hansard*), House of Commons Debates, vol. 30, 14 April 1815. In the debate that followed regarding the establishment of a parliamentary inquiry, concern was expressed 'when they recollected all that was necessary for furthering the great work of abolition, it could not be unimportant to have all the aspersions and calumnies which had been cast upon the Government removed; and to show that it had not taken any part against the abolitionists, but that the sentence had been remitted through a mere defect of form in the trial', Mr Whitbread, *Hansard*, vol. 30, 14 April 1815.

49   Thorpe CJ made frequent references to the divine, for example, 'crime against God or man', *The Trial of the Slave Traders*, 34. These references to religion are matched outside the courtroom by the judge's view of the law of nations. Thorpe claimed that the 'law of nations is built on the unerring rules of justice, which unchangeably direct every law, human or Divine, for individual man, or collective empire; it is founded on the law of nature, directed by the law of God' (Thorpe, *A Letter to William Wilberforce*, 61).

50   On the well documented 'moral pressure' that abolitionists lent to the imperial project see David Rieff, *A Bed for the Night: Humanitarianism in Crisis* (London: Vintage, 2002), 59; Miers.

51   On the role of religion in abolitionism, see Christine Bolt and Seymour Drescher, *Anti Slavery, Religion and Reform* (Kent: William Dawson and Sons, 1980); Huw T. David, 'Transnational Advocacy in the Eighteenth Century: Transatlantic Activism and the Anti-Slavery Movement', *Global Networks* 7, 3 (2007): 367–82; David Turley, *The Culture of English Antislavery, 1780–1860* (London and New York: Routledge, 1991).

albeit in a secularised version. It is hoped that tracing this logic of redemption and its usage will contribute to a richer account of the history and politics of international criminal law.

Biggs — and the pamphlet writer — saw the trial as a fundamental step to emancipation. However, in Samo's case, this transition did not necessarily require the conviction and punishment of the accused. If conviction and punishment were not central to transition, pardon and redemption were. The courtroom provided a space in which the sin, pardon and redemption of the accused and others could be theatrically performed. Thus, whilst Samo was ostensibly central to proceedings, his case was used to create a show of publicly exonerating and blaming others.

Witnesses did not only testify for the purposes of giving evidence but, by participating in the trial, they were able to redeem themselves, even if their redemption was achieved after a personal struggle. Take Samo's clerk, William Skelton, who on Biggs's persuasion became convinced of the 'exceeding wickedness and cruelty of the slave trade' to testify against his former master. Biggs compared his conduct favourably with that of other named slave-traders who refused to 'renounce the monstrous traffic'.[52] Biggs lamented the death of one of the principal witnesses by noting his remorseful atonement:

> Mr David James Lawrence fell a victim to disease and a broken heart, in consequence of the vile treatment and persecution of the slave traders, who hated him because he had renounced their fellowship and business, and complied with the laws of his country.[53]

In the pamphlet debate, Thorpe was particularly critical of the conviction of Brodie, who had testified in Samo's case, promising to renounce the slave trade.[54] Thorpe saw no evidence that Brodie had broken this promise.[55] This redemptive framing found its apogee in the pardon that was granted to Samo. Thorpe proclaimed:

> let that baneful commerce which has so long retarded the civilization, diminished the population, and dimmed the glory of Africa, be destroyed — let it be shattered to atoms in a storm of benevolent charity for mankind — it will be an immolation acceptable to the Deity — it will

---

52 *The Trials of the Slave Traders*, 24.

53 ibid., 24–25.

54 Robert Thorpe, Postscript, 36–37.

55 Although the testimony, as reported was hardly expansive, 'he does not know of Mr Samo supplying any slaves; the slave dealers trade as secretly as possible, to evade the acts' (*The Trials of the Slave Traders*, 18).

be a sacrifice of human viciousness on the altar of Divine compassion —
it will be death until sin — and a new birth unto righteousness — it will
plead your pardon in this life, and plead for mercy in life everlasting.[56]

This redemptive logic lent support to the idea of Britain as an abolitionist state
and was deployed to buttress a colonial imperative. First, take the reporting of
the case. In accordance with the logic of what Makau Mutua has described as
a 'savage-victim-savior' metaphor in human rights law,[57] the pamphlet writer's
aim was to inform of the 'beneficial effects arising from their disinterested zeal
in behalf of those thousands of enslaved Africans who could do nothing for
themselves'.[58] Further, driven as it may have been by his concerns about legal
jurisdiction, the pardon gave Thorpe an opportunity to exercise leverage over
powerful individuals outside the court's jurisdiction. In this way redemption
in the form of pardon could be mobilised to buttress other imperial ambitions.
Thorpe saw Samo's case as providing an opportunity to extend Britain's
territorial rights on the coast.[59] Writing to Governor Maxwell about Attorney
General Biggs, Thorpe wrote:

> I am convinced you are too deeply indebted to him by his extricating
> you from a most severe difficulty; the friends of the Abolition are too
> deeply indebted to him for his exertions in the slave trade; and Great
> Britain is too deeply indebted to him *for the extra territorial he has
> established on the coast for her.*[60]

Third, the hearings made a show of absolving the British public and the British
state from guilt. As is widely observed, international criminal hearings make
partial histories, despite their avowed archival functions. Not only is the
production of history constrained by the demands of the legal process[61] but,

---

56 ibid., 35.
57 'The human rights corpus is driven — normatively and descriptively — by … the savage-victim-
savior metaphor, in which human rights is a grand narrative of an epochal contest that pits savages against
victims and saviors. In this script of human rights, democracy and western liberalism are internationalized
to redeem savage non-Western cultures from themselves, and to alleviate the suffering of victims, who are
generally non-western and non-European' (Makau Mutua, 'Terrorism and Human Rights: Power, Culture, and
Subordination', *Buffalo Human Rights Law Review* 8 (2002): 5).
58 *The Trials of the Slave Traders*, v.
59 On the deployment of humanitarian concerns in the interests of empire in a contemporary context see,
for example, Amy Bartholemew, ed., *Empire's Law: The American Imperial Project and the 'War to Remake the
World'* (London: Pluto Press, 2006); Costas Douzinas, *Human Rights and Empire: The Political Philosophy of
Cosmopolitanism* (Abingdon: Routledge-Cavendish, 2007).
60 As quoted in the African Institution, Special Report, 103.
61 Marie-Bénédicte Dembour and Emily Haslam, 'Silencing Hearings? Victim-Witnesses at the ICTY',
European Journal of International Law 15, no. 1 (2004): 151–77.

as Gerry Simpson argues, all too often those histories are consciously deployed as part of a broader legitimising,[62] or state building function.[63] Of the British public, Thorpe observed in Samo's case:

> Could the animated skeletons that are landed here, imploring death for relief, be visible in England, an universal exclamation would involuntarily burst from that inestimable people — 'Without ocular demonstration, we could not have believed that human depravity could have extended to these enormities — extirpate these monsters!'[64]

As regards the British state, Biggs in opening Samo's prosecution observed:

> the humane and anxious desire of the Parliament of the British empire to abolish the barbarous traffic in slaves is universally known, the remotest tribe on the face of the earth are apprized long ere this of the benevolent desire of every good mind in England, that however savage might be the race of distant climes, their land should not contain a single slave.[65]

Biggs portrayed Britain's support of the slave trade as provisional and reluctant:

> through the unwise and tyrannical system of Dutch, Portuguese, Danish, Spanish and French colonization, England was obliged unwillingly to acquiesce in the temporary policy of an iniquitous slave trade, yet she never for a moment lost sight of the grand and ultimate determination of effecting its radical and signal prostration.[66]

The individualising of the slave-traders' guilt also operated to disassociate them from their national state, notwithstanding the role that Britain had played in the slave trade more generally.[67] Thus, Biggs maintained that Peters was daily violating the Slave Trade Felony Act and 'acting with practical ingratitude

---

62   For example, the Nuremberg and Tokyo trials can be seen as 'attempts to vindicate the superiority of Western civilisation and the conduct of the Allied war'; Gerry Simpson, 'Didactic and Dissident Histories', 830.

63   ibid., 827. Notably, the Eichmann trial was at least partly about the legitimacy of the establishment of the state of Israel (ibid., 826). So too is it argued that a driving force behind the establishment of the International Criminal Tribunal for the former Yugoslavia was the need for the West to affirm its 'own fundamental morality' (Pierre Hazan, *Justice in a Time of War: The True Story behind the International Criminal Tribunal for the Former Yugoslavia* (Texas: A & M University Press, 2004), 19).

64   *The Trials of the Slave Traders*, 11.

65   ibid., 14.

66   ibid.

67   See, for example, David Brion Davis, *The Problem of Slavery in the Age of Revolution 1770–1823* (Ithaca and London: Cornell University Press, 1975); Kenneth Morgan, *Slavery and the British Empire From African to America* (Oxford University Press, 2007); Hugh Thomas, *The Slave Trade: The History of the Atlantic Slave Trade 1440–1870* (London and Basingstoke: Picador, 1997); James Walvin, *Black Ivory: A History of British Slavery* (London: Harper Collins, 1992). On British involvement in the slave trade after abolition, see Sherwood. On the 'fiction of detachability' in international criminal law according to which 'the state ... is imagined as an entity distinct from its bad apples and rogue statesmen' see Gerry Simpson, *Law, War and Crime*, 63.

towards the country from which he derived his subsistence'.[68] At the same time, redemption provided an opportunity for British slave-traders to reconcile with abolitionism; compare Biggs's elaborate description of the 'redemption' of Skelton and Lawrence to the absence of the themes of pardon, sin and redemption in Peters's case, notwithstanding the centrality to that case of the resistance of runaway slaves and the complicity of those recapturing them. Whilst in Samo's case evidence is given as to how the court came by the evidence of former slave-traders and how Biggs persuaded some of them to testify and thereby 'atone' their guilt,[69] in the account of Peters's case there is no information as to how the African witnesses came into contact with the court and the legal process.[70] In Peter's case it is the very absence of this trope that contributes to the erasure by the trial of Africans in redemption/emancipation, notwithstanding their extensive testimony in the courtroom. This is consistent with the logic of the 'savage-victim-savior' metaphor mentioned above.

Contemporary war crimes trials exhibit many similarities to the adjudicative framework adopted in Samo's case. There is a striking similarity between the optimism displayed by many contemporary international criminal lawyers in the transformative potential of the law and the claim that the slave-trading trials marked the first stage of emancipation.[71] Typically, war crimes trials are show trials in so far as they direct their didactic gaze beyond the courtroom,[72] and look to the future as much as to the past.[73] Compared to other transitional justice mechanisms, such as truth commissions, contemporary international criminal hearings adopt a more retributive approach to the accused, allowing little space for amnesties.[74] Despite this, international criminal hearings are permeated with ideas about individual and collective redemption. This can be seen in the claim, which is all too often made, that testifying is curative[75] and avoids revenge.[76]

---

68   *The Trials of the Slave Traders*, 41.

69   ibid., 23.

70   This is a narrative framework that left little room for the participation — let alone agency — of Africans in processes of redemption, and for the replacement of stories of suffering with stories of resistance exemplified by the act of running away.

71   Biggs claimed, 'This day will live in history, that will record this trial as the ground-work of that "universal emancipation" which it appears to be the will of the Almighty to spread, in process of time, throughout the world' (*Trial of the Slave Traders*, 27).

72   Hannah Arendt, *Eichmann in Jerusalem: A Report on the Banality of Evil* (London: Penguin Books, 1994); David Hirsh, *Law Against Genocide: Cosmopolitan Trials* (London: Glasshouse Press, 2003); Mark Osiel, *Mass Atrocity, Collective Memory and the Law* (New Jersey: Transaction Publishers, 2000); Simpson, 'Didactic and Dissident Histories', 804.

73   See, for example, Dembour and Haslam; Ruti Teitel, *Transitional Justice* (Oxford University Press, 2000).

74   See, for example, Diane Orentlicher, 'Settling Accounts: The Duty to Prosecute Human Rights Violations of a Prior Regime', *Yale Law Journal* 100 (1991): 2537–615.

75   See further, for example, Osiel, 273.

76   This approach also operated to defer, that is to control vengeance in Samo's case. Thorpe claimed: '"There is a God, all nature cries aloud," that marks the movements of this world, and brings us to account; when you are summoned before that great tribunal for judgment, and those unfortunate Africans, whom you branded on the thigh with burning implements of torture, shall arise in evidence against you, what can you expect from the seat of Supreme Justice?' (*The Trials of the Slave Traders*, 34).

Whilst this framing dominates much of the literature, it is problematic. First, international criminal hearings have revealed a significant dislocation between the reality and promise of healing, for the courtroom is not a therapeutic forum — at least not for all. Stories of redemption have been shown all too often to instrumentalise survivors for the sake of the international criminal process.[77] Although better practice and legal innovations can go some way towards mitigating some of the negative aspects of courtroom experiences,[78] the redemptive framing of survivor testimony all too often instrumentalises victims in the service of a broader political project. This may include the construction of a political or international community[79] and the expression of 'political contrition'.[80] Thus, redemption at the individual level is expected to contribute to redemption at a broader societal level. Notably, those who are 'saved'[81] by participating in international criminal hearings rarely have a role in determining the broader agenda to which their participation avowedly contributes. In Samo's case this logic of redemption operated to buttress Britain's extra-territorial rights on the coast[82] and to minimise the role of Africans in their own emancipation. Bringing slavery and abolition back into the picture of international criminal law, shows how this redemptive trope was driven less by a curative imperative than by an imperial project.

Conclusion

As 'the point in the constellation from which all legal discussion of war crimes trials proceeds or reverts', histories of international criminal law typically point to the Nuremberg and Tokyo trials as foundational.[83] And yet, particular narrative framings of international criminal law have a longer trajectory than the

---

77 Dembour and Haslam.
78 For example, the establishment of victim participation at the International Criminal Court, widely seen as one response to the failure of the United Nations Tribunals for Yugoslavia and Rwanda to make adequate provision for the involvement of survivors in legal proceedings (Claude Jorda and Jérôme de Hemptinne, 'The Status and Role of The Victim', in Cassese, Gaeta and Jones, 1387–419).
79 On the appropriation of women's stories of sexual violence for the sake of 'post-conflict national identity' see Katherine M. Franke, 'Gendered Subjects of Transitional Justice', *Columbia Journal of Gender and Law* 15 (2006): 823. For Steinitz it is the international community which is the real subject of transition in the Milosevic trial (Maya Steinitz, 'The Milošević Trial Live!', *Journal of International Criminal Justice* 3 (2005): 107).
80 In the case of the establishment of the United Nations Security Council's International Criminal Tribunal for Rwanda see Ralph Zacklin, 'The Failings of Ad Hoc International Tribunals', *Journal of International Criminal Justice* 2 (2004): 542.
81 This language is taken from Anne Orford who writes of the challenge of how to respond to the 'victim who refused to be saved, the subject who will not speak her suffering in the time and place and languages offered to her by the mechanisms of transitional justice'. This indicates the ongoing rhetoric of saving in international criminal law (Anne Orford, 'Commissioning the Truth', *Columbia Journal of Gender and Law* 15 (2006), 883).
82 Letter from Thorpe to Governor Maxwell quoted in African Institution, Special Report, 101–02.
83 McGoldrick, 9–46.

mid-twentieth century. This chapter does not trace an unbroken historical path. It does, however, suggest striking similarities between the narratives running through some of the first trials under the British Slave Trade Felony Act and contemporary international criminal hearings. In Samo's case, the deployment of redemption supported an imperial mission — inside and outside the courtroom. The implication of redemption in a colonial project challenges us to reflect upon the origins and use of narratives of redemption today. Admittedly, narratives of imperialism and colonialism in international criminal law play out differently in the contemporary context.[84] However, Samo's case shows how this redemptive trope was tied up with a imperial project to which a politicised discourse of sin and redemption lent weight.

Acknowledgments

My thanks go to Kate Bedford, Rod Edmunds, Toni Williams and to the anonymous reviewer for their helpful comments.

---

84   As epitomised, for example, by the controversy surrounding the International Criminal Court's focus to date on the global south. See further Mahmood Mamdani, *Saviours And Survivors: Darfur, Politics and the War On Terror* (London: Verso, 2009).

Linguistics, Religion and Law in Colonial New South Wales: Lancelot Threlkeld and Settler-Colonial Humanitarian Debates

Anna Johnston

Reverend Lancelot Threlkeld was a familiar face in the Sydney law courts during the late 1820s and 1830s. The missionary — the sole London Missionary Society (LMS) representative in the Australian colonies during this period — was regularly accompanied by an Aboriginal man, Biraban, who served as dual translator and advisor to Threlkeld. The presence of the two men dramatised questions about Aboriginal legal status and humanitarian interests in the colonial legal system, connecting local affairs with broader imperial concerns. Attending many of the key cases during the 1830s, Threlkeld was instrumental in raising uncomfortable questions about how legal processes dealt with Aboriginal people. His prolific and provocative writing on such issues circulated settler colonial controversies pertaining to the law around the British empire. Neither simply a cross-cultural hero nor a self-aggrandising bigot, Threlkeld exemplifies the complexity of settler identities and societies in formation.

In recent years, studies of settler societies have come to the fore in a variety of interdisciplinary contexts, as historians, sociologists, and literary/cultural theorists seek to account for Anglo-American hegemony from the nineteenth century onwards, and to question the self-congratulatory narratives that settler nations typically promulgate about their origins. Legal questions are particularly interesting ones to pose in this context, because they provide a fascinating framework through which to explore the circulation of ideas and discourse related to race, identity, and colonialism. Jennifer Hamilton argues that modern Anglo-American systems of law were significantly influenced by settler encounters with indigenous peoples. How law courts understood indigenous people — whether their ethnic identity was recognised by the court or not, and when and how that identity counted — was central not only to establishing relationships between settlers and indigenes, but also to the very formation of both those identities. In the western United States and Canada, Hamilton suggests, law was central to colonising projects and it had effects beyond legal institutions: these colonial legacies 'are key discursive elements in social and political life in settler states'.[1] Problems of communication continue to trouble twenty-first-century Australian courts, particularly in relation to the provision of interpreting services and, because of the prevalence of ear disease and hearing loss in Aboriginal communities, assistance for defendants with profound speech and hearing disabilities. In these current debates, we can hear echoes of the colonial courts in trying to account for Indigenous difference and in assessing the role of non-Indigenous intermediaries in accessing justice.[2]

The mutually constitutive nature of these relationships — in which not only Indigenous identities but also settler identities were forged (in part) in terms of legal rights and responsibilities — is particularly instructive in historicising contemporary relationships between settler and Indigenous Australians, and between Aborigines and the law. Accounting for the complexity and contradiction within those relationships also attempts 'to make the past less predictable'.[3] Threlkeld's role as translator in the nineteenth-century courts — and more broadly in the colonial community — effectively worked to provide Aboriginal defendants with a way to have their voices heard within a system that struggled to account for them as legal subjects. Yet, in his legal work, Threlkeld also crafted a position for himself that was dependent on his exclusive right to speak on behalf of Aborigines: his translation of Aboriginal evidence about crime was almost always contextualised by his adamant testimony that Indigenous people were incapable of swearing oaths, understanding a higher being (by which they could have sworn), or being converted to Christianity. His conflicted position both enabled and limited Indigenous legal subjectivity. Threlkeld's well-meaning interventions provide a lens through which to examine how white colonists' legal rights and responsibilities (and indeed, their roles within a courtroom) were formed often in conflict with, or contrast to, Indigenous entitlements, in ways that were crucial to settler identity formation.

Threlkeld's Lake Macquarie Mission was one of the LMS's unsuccessful colonial ventures: within two years of its commencement, the society refused to endorse Threlkeld's bills and, in 1829, he was dismissed.[4] Nevertheless, and with funding from the colonial government (until 1841), Threlkeld persisted and continued to pursue not only evangelising but also two interlinked projects about which he

1   Jennifer A. Hamilton, *Indigeneity in the Courtroom: Law, Culture, and the Production of Difference in North American Courts* (New York and London: Routledge, 2009), 2.
2   See Damien Howard, Sue Quinn, Jenny Blokland and Martin Flynn, 'Aboriginal Hearing Loss and the Criminal Justice System', *Aboriginal Law Bulletin* 58 (1993), online; 'Specific Hearing Health Issues Affecting Indigenous Australians', in *Hear Us: Inquiry into Hearing Health in Australia*, Community Affairs References Committee, http://www.aph.gov.au/senate/committee/clac_ctte/hearing_health/report/index.htm accessed 18 October 2011.
3   Nicholas Thomas, 'Against Heritage: An Afterword', in *Reading Robinson: Companion Essays to Friendly Mission*, eds, Anna Johnston and Mitchell Rolls (Hobart: Quintus, 2008), 187.
4   This chapter draws on research material that is discussed in greater detail in my recent book *The Paper War: Morality, Print Culture, and Power in Colonial New South Wales* (Crawley: UWAP, 2011).

was passionate: collecting Aboriginal language and translating for Aborigines called before the court. Threlkeld's linguistic skills were a central part of his LMS inheritance: language collection, in order to translate scripture and preach in local languages, was fundamental to Protestant mission work. Experience in Polynesia, prior to his arrival in New South Wales in 1824, ensured that Threlkeld quickly began recording the Aboriginal language that surrounded him at Lake Macquarie.[5] His first linguistic efforts were collated in 1825, and his major publications appeared intermittently between 1834 and 1850. Posthumously, his individual works were published as *An Australian Language as Spoken by the Awabakal …* (1892). This was not simply an intellectual project. Threlkeld saw his language facility as crucial in intervening between Aborigines and the colonial courts. In this work, as in other arenas, the missionary chose a controversial position that placed him directly at odds with many powerful settler colonial interests. He had written to the LMS in 1825 that, although his appointment was initially to minister to settlers and Aborigines, he could not represent both parties: 'No man, who comes to this Colony and has ground and cattle and Corn, can dispassionately view the subject of the blacks, their interest says annihilate the race'.[6] Threlkeld chose to represent Indigenous interests and his earliest letters to the LMS resound with news of unreported and unprosecuted violence against Aborigines.

Much recent colonial legal history focuses on the period from the 1820s up to the late 1830s and a series of important cases that show the legal system grappling with the question of Aboriginal legal rights and responsibilities.[7] Threlkeld attended, participated in, or was discussed during many of these cases. From his first appearance in 1827 for *R v Tommy*, Threlkeld appeared at 11 subsequent trials in the next decade, including the multiple Brisbane Water trials in 1835 and the important *inter se* case *R v Murrell* (1836). In his annual Report of the Mission to the Aborigines at Lake Macquarie, New South Wales, Threlkeld regularly discussed matters pertaining to Aboriginal negotiations with the colonial courts, becoming increasingly frustrated with the anomalous position in which Indigenous people found themselves and, eventually, explicitly calling for imperial intervention for humanitarian ends. In written accounts of his court work, Threlkeld explicitly and politically advocated for Aboriginal civil rights. The contradictions between Threlkeld's role within the

---

5   For a comparison of Threlkeld's service in Polynesia and Australia, see Anna Johnston, 'A Blister on the Imperial Antipodes: Lancelot Edward Threlkeld in Polynesia and Australia', in *Colonial Lives across the British Empire*, eds, David Lambert and Alan Lester (Cambridge University Press, 2006), 58–87.
6   L.E. Threlkeld to Rev. George Burder and W.A. Hankey, 10 August 1826, 'Letter', Council for World Mission (CWM), Australia Box 2, School of Oriental and African Studies (SOAS).
7   Amongst others, see Lisa Ford, *Settler Sovereignty: Jurisdiction and Indigenous People in America and Australia, 1788–1836* (Cambridge, Mass., and London: Harvard University Press, 2010); Bruce Kercher, *Outsiders: Tales from the Supreme Court of NSW, 1824–1836* (Melbourne: Australian Scholarly Publishing, 2006).

court — as recorded in the court reports appearing in local newspapers — and his written representations about that role reveal the complex and contradictory position he occupied.

Language collection preoccupied Threlkeld from his earliest days in New South Wales.[8] From his arrival in Newcastle, waiting for a road and a dwelling to be built at Lake Macquarie, Threlkeld erected a tent that Chief Justice Francis Forbes had donated, and conducted interviews with local Aborigines. Forbes's gift reveals the interconnections between linguistics and law from the outset. The missionary sent Forbes a copy of his first printed language study, *Specimens of a Dialect of the Aborigines of New South Wales: Being the First Attempt to Form their Speech into a Written Language* (1827), and the judge was delighted that his 'very humble contribution … has derived a value from the work performed beneath its shelter which nothing else could have given it'.[9] Like other legal men in the colony, Forbes was very interested in Threlkeld's linguistic work and wanted to provide assistance to him. Arguably, this was in part due to the empire-wide interest in collecting indigenous languages — as the century proceeded, language study became something of a gentlemanly pursuit, akin to the burgeoning interest in amateur natural history — but also because there were obvious implications for the colonial legal system in establishing effective formal modes of communication between settlers and indigenes. Men such as Forbes did not operate in a vacuum — his previous experience in Bermuda and Newfoundland clearly informed his New South Wales tenure — and questions about indigenous subjects in colonial law were formulated in transnational and comparative contexts. The shared interest also reveals the imbrication of legal and religious identities in this period.

During his tenure as New South Wales attorney-general, Saxe Bannister regularly corresponded with and sought information from Threlkeld; the two men arrived in Sydney within months of each other in 1824. The connection was instrumental for Threlkeld: Bannister solicited his social calls, introduced him to the newly arrived governor Lieutenant-General Ralph Darling and Archdeacon Thomas Hobbes Scott, and regularly sought his opinion on current affairs. Bannister was fascinated by the missionary's linguistic project, regularly enquiring about and commenting upon Threlkeld's methods. Threlkeld wrote to him frankly, in 1825:

> With respect to seeing my system, it can be seen and known in two minutes, namely, first obtain the language, then preach the Gospel,

---

8 For an excellent overview of Threlkeld's linguistic work, see David A. Roberts, '"language to save the innocent": Reverend L. Threlkeld's Linguistic Mission', *Journal of the Royal Australian Historical Society* 94, no. 2 (2008): 107–25.

9 Niel Gunson, ed., *Australian Reminiscences and Papers of L.E. Threlkeld, Missionary to the Aborigines, 1824–1859* (Canberra: AIAS, 1974), quoted at 229.

then urge them from Gospel motives to be industrious at the same time becoming a servant to them to win them to that which is right. This is the sum and substance of our practice. We persuade Men.[10]

Bannister's education lent him insight into linguistic study. On reading his personal manuscript copy of Threlkeld's first linguistic work, *An Orthography and Orthoepy of a Dialect of the Aborigines of New South Wales Part 1* (1825), Bannister warmly congratulated the author, asked for extra copies to send to friends in London and Oxford, and recommended that the LMS should send a copy to Lord Bathurst (then colonial secretary) in order to shore up the approval of the New South Wales land grant for the mission. Although supportive, he clearly questioned some of Threlkeld's methodology and, in so doing, revealed his assessment of Aboriginal capabilities:

> I have always thought that the greatest care should be taken not to apply the complications of grammar as established in books to the expressions of a simple people — and perhaps your present pursuit, if confined rightly to an examination of the mere actual modes of speech in use here by the uncorrupted, will exhibit a very curious and instructive stage of the human mind.[11]

Despite his reservations about the sophistication of Aboriginal languages, Bannister directly solicited Threlkeld's assistance for the new court system established in 1824. Threlkeld declined Bannister's request to train interpreters for the courts in 1826 as he felt his linguistic knowledge was not yet adequate.

The following year, Bannister was replaced as attorney-general by Alexander Macduff Baxter, and Threlkeld was directed to attend *R v Tommy* as an interpreter: he demurred 'on account of my little knowledge of the language' but was told that he would have Bungaree, probably one of the best-known Aboriginal figures in Sydney at the time, to assist and that he must 'do [his] best'.[12] Baxter's enlistment of Bungaree was largely symbolic, and his placatory words either naive or cynical. Unless able to prove that they understood English and had a belief in a higher being in order to demonstrate the meaning of an oath, Aborigines were not able to be sworn as witnesses; neither, as Threlkeld and Biraban repeatedly found, could Aboriginal advisors be sworn as official translators. Without an acceptable translator who could swear an oath, Aboriginal voices were effectively silenced by the legal system. Men such as Bungaree and Biraban were crucial to the communicative acts taking place between the missionary and defendants — their role as cultural and legal

10   L.E. Threlkeld to Rev. George Burder, 10 October 1825, CWM, Australia Box 2, SOAS.
11   L.E. Threlkeld to Rev. George Burder, 22 October 1825, CWM, Australia Box 2, SOAS, quoting Bannister.
12   L.E. Threlkeld, 'Memoranda of Events at Lake Macquarie: Journal Extracts and Annual Reports to 1841', in Gunson, 97.

intermediaries is highly suggestive and would bear further analysis than is possible here. Sometimes Biraban needed a second intermediary to assist his advice to Threlkeld. In 1837, in *R v Wombarty*, Biraban found a Port Macquarie man who could communicate with the accused (who was from 'the interior near Port Macquarie') but because 'the Black could not be sworn with myself as assistant interpreter' Wombarty was discharged.[13] These moments in court represent very complex cross-cultural negotiations. Even though the records are partial (and often problematic in their bias), the glimpses that we can reconstruct reveal just how nuanced and troubled was the contemporary debate.

Threlkeld's first court appearance was unprepossessing: neither he nor Bungaree succeeded in communicating with the Aboriginal defendant Tommy, who made his defence in his own language with rare phrases of broken English. Neither Bungaree nor Threlkeld seem to have had a working knowledge of that language, which presumably pertained to the Bathurst region where the alleged crime occurred: despite his linguistic study, Threlkeld (like many others) was slow to realise that separate regional languages existed which could be mutually incomprehensible. Forbes, the presiding judge, is reported in the *Sydney Monitor* as summarising the case as 'fully made out'; and the jury found Tommy guilty.[14] He was sentenced to death and was hanged on the last day of 1827. Threlkeld declared that Tommy was 'found guilty on the clearest evidence',[15] and attended the execution as part of the religious presence that commonly accompanied condemned men. Threlkeld's attendance subsequently generated an unbecoming spat between Protestant and Catholic clergy in the colonial newspapers — Tommy's Catholic baptism on the scaffold infuriated the Protestant attendants — but usually religious attendance imbued the public spectacle of English and colonial executions with moral authority and sober religious import, as Randall McGowen demonstrates.[16] Threlkeld's presence in court worked similarly to impart a sense of moral order to the unsettling presence of Aborigines, particularly given the fissures in law that their presence

---

13   L.E. Threlkeld, 'Report of the Mission to the Aborigines at Lake Macquarie, New South Wales' (1837), in Gunson, 136.

14   'R v Tommy', Supreme Court of New South Wales, 1827, Decisions of the Superior Courts of New South Wales, 1788–1899, the Division of Law, Macquarie University, http://www.law.mq.edu.au/scnsw/Cases1827-28/html/r_v_tommy__1827.htm accessed 31 August, 2004.

15   L.E. Threlkeld, 'Reminiscences of the Aborigines of New South Wales' (1853–55), in Gunson, 97.

16   Randall McGowen, 'The Changing Face of God's Justice: The Debates over Divine and Human Punishment in Eighteenth-Century England', *Criminal Justice History* 9 (1988): 63–98; see also V.A C. Gatrell, *The Hanging Tree: Execution and the English People, 1770–1868* (Oxford University Press, 1994) and, on execution in colonial Australia, Michael Sturma, 'Death and Ritual on the Gallows: Public Executions in the Australian Penal Colonies', *OMEGA* 17, no. 1 (1986): 89–100; Libby Connors, 'The Theatre of Justice: Race Relations and Capital Punishment at Moreton Bay, 1841–59', in *Brisbane: The Aboriginal Presence, 1824–1860*, ed. Rod Fisher (Brisbane History Group Papers, 1992), 48–57; John McGuire, 'Judicial Violence and the "Civilizing Process": Race and the Transition from Public to Private Executions in Colonial Australia', *Australian Historical Studies* 29, no. 111 (1998): 187–209.

revealed, and it certainly foregrounded the importance of Christianity to the workings of English law. Arguably, though, the missionary's presence also focalised the incongruity of Aborigines as legal subjects.

When charged, Aborigines, like settlers, entered a process that inscribed them within legal discourse. The Information for each charge inaugurated a process of textual inscription and subject formation. The language of the Information is bureaucratic and formulaic: the particulars of each charge were entered by a law clerk on pre-printed forms. So, to take the instance of *R v Jackey* in 1834, the accused is described in a routine fashion: 'Jackey an Aboriginal native of the said Colony not having the fear of God before his eyes but being moved and seduced by the instigation of the Devil …' The language of the charge and its reading — a performative speech act — dramatises the interdependence of religious and legal discourses, and immediately reveals the peculiar position of non-Christians brought before the court. If white colonials could be temporarily seduced by the devil into criminal acts then, logically, Aborigines were especially vulnerable to moral turpitude given their ignorance of Christianity. From this moment onwards, Jackey's non-Christian status proved a major hurdle to him accessing English justice. Threlkeld attended Jackey's trial as interpreter. On the one hand we can imagine Threlkeld's role as enabling Jackey to assert some limited legal rights, yet Threlkeld's role as religious representative and gatekeeper complicates any such easy assessment. Despite his lengthy evangelical career in New South Wales, Threlkeld did not baptise any Aboriginal people, even Biraban whom Threlkeld knew was educating other Aborigines about Christianity. In 1837, Judge William Westbrooke Burton concluded that — after nearly 15 years involvement with Threlkeld and after nearly a decade assisting him in the courts — Biraban was 'not yet aware of the nature of an oath'.[17]

Threlkeld's role in all the cases in which he appeared as translator and ethnographic expert is thus ambiguous. Whether we understand his work as enabling Aboriginal testimony or speaking on behalf of Aborigines, as fighting for Aboriginal civil rights or as an ineffectual salve to the consciences of concerned citizens and legal personnel, Threlkeld's presence in the court (like that of Bungaree or Biraban) dramatises the conflicted position of English law in a colonial setting. Edward Broadhurst, appearing for another Aboriginal defendant in *R v. Billy* (1840), decried the impossible position in which Christian linguistic and ideological framing placed Indigenous people. Reading out 'that part of the indictment which stated that the prisoner had been excited and moved by the instigation of the devil', Broadhurst expostulated that this was 'a being whom the aborigines have no more knowledge of than they have of the

---

17   'R v Wombarty', Supreme Court of New South Wales, 1837, Decisions of the Superior Courts of New South Wales, 1788–1899, the Division of Law, Macquarie University, http://www.law.mq.edu.au/research/colonial_case_law/nsw/cases/case_index/1837/r_v_wombarty/ accessed 31 August 2004.

existence of the true God'.[18] Ironically, Threlkeld was directly responsible for imparting that knowledge at precisely the same time that he regularly testified to Aboriginal ignorance of religion.

Threlkeld joined an international network of humanitarian figures who were concerned about indigenous welfare under settler colonialism, and troubled by the morality of colonisation more generally. Much recent scholarship has considered this 'imperial network' and provided imperial history with finely nuanced analysis of the multiple voices and issues at stake in the second British empire, connecting metropolitan debates with colonial concerns.[19] Yet, much of this scholarship works from the Colonial Office down, or from Clapham outwards: understanding what humanitarianism looked and felt like in the colonies is rare, particularly from the antipodean perspective. Threlkeld's work across a range of humanitarian/evangelical activities provides an excellent vantage point to consider such issues, not least because he was largely ineffective in bringing about change during his career. His voluminous writings, impassioned and informed, failed to make the impact they could have, in part because of his difficult personality and fractured relationship with the LMS, but also because the colonial setting meant that he recognised contentious issues well before they registered on metropolitan agendas. In terms of legal rights for Aborigines, Threlkeld was at the vanguard of humanitarian interest. It was just at the point that the Lake Macquarie Mission lost colonial government funding that Threlkeld's representations could have had real effects.

Threlkeld's work translating for Aboriginal defendants at the New South Wales Supreme Court resonated well beyond King Street, Sydney. The reports of the Lake Macquarie Mission were sent annually to the archdeacon, the colonial secretary, and the governor, and Threlkeld often sent copies to members of his wide international correspondence network. The missionary regularly infuriated local colonial officials with his contentious claims about Aboriginal disadvantage and settler violence: to be fair, his reports were sometimes ill-advised and imprecise in detail, and thus had the potential to be as damaging to genuine efforts to curtail settler aggression as they were to the reputations of

---

18 'R v Billy', Supreme Court of New South Wales, 1840, Decisions of the Superior Courts of New South Wales, 1788–1899, the Division of Law, Macquarie University, http://www.law.mq.edu.au/research/colonial_case_law/nsw/cases/case_index/1840/r_v_billy/ accessed 31 August 2004.
19 See Alan Lester, *Imperial Networks: Creating Identities in Nineteenth-Century South Africa and Britain* (London and New York: Routledge, 2001); Alan Lester, 'Humanitarians and White Settlers in the Nineteenth Century', in *Missions and Empire*, ed. Norman Etherington (Oxford University Press, 2005), 64–85; Catherine Hall, *Civilising Subjects: Metropole and Colony in the English Imagination, 1830–1867* (Cambridge: Polity, 2002); Anna Johnston, *Missionary Writing and Empire, 1800–1860* (Cambridge University Press, 2003); Elizabeth Elbourne, *Blood Ground: Colonialism, Missions, and the Context for Christianity in the Cape Colony and Britain, 1799–1852* (Montreal: McGill Queen's University Press, 2002).

figures of colonial authority.[20] Eventually, however, metropolitan sympathisers and organisations — who needed colonial evidence to support their humanitarian campaigns — eagerly sought such accounts.

On his return to London, Bannister was among the earliest metropolitan activists to call for law reform to enable Aboriginal testimony. Like Threlkeld, Bannister vociferously agitated for improving Aboriginal status through legal means. Bannister's *Humane Policy* (1830), which focused mainly on conflict in the Cape Colony, was explicit about the state of law in New South Wales:

> The English rules of evidence, the absence of interpreters, and the ill-conduct of the people (both settlers and convicts, with special exceptions,) render it exceedingly difficult to cause the law to be put in force against murderers and other heinous wrong-doers towards the natives; and when, by any concurrence of favourable circumstances, conviction has been obtained, the government has sympathised too much with the oppressing class, and too little with the oppressed, to permit justice to have its course.[21]

Threlkeld's influence is clear in Bannister's advocacy for active philanthropic exertions proportionate to the scale of colonial populations. Of the new Swan River colony, he exhorts: 'It is, therefore, exceedingly to be hoped that at least an attempt will be made to save them, through the means by which at Sydney the London Missionary Society tried with considerable effort in 1826, in defiance of extraordinary obstacles'.[22]

Bannister's service in New South Wales was relatively brief, and he was rarely lauded by his contemporaries for his legal work. He departed under contentious conditions, and spent most of his voyage home writing a lengthy defence of his colonial service, in part spurred by attacks in the colonial press just prior to his departure.[23] Bannister was determined to establish the fact of his scrupulous treatment of Aborigines, both in terms of his legal concerns about their status and, somewhat paradoxically, his effort to suspend his humanitarian politics to allow for the appropriate conduct of his role. His key principle was 'to carry the

---

20   Roger Milliss expresses his frustration with Threlkeld's typically elliptical and imprecise accounts of events surrounding the Myall Creek massacre: Roger Milliss, *Waterloo Creek: The Australia Day Massacre of 1838, George Gipps and the British Conquest of New South Wales* (Melbourne: McPhee Gribble, 1992), 101–2.
21   Saxe Bannister, *Humane Policy; Or Justice to the Aborigines of New Settlements Essential to a Due Expenditure of British Money, and to the Best Interests of Settlers, with Suggestions How to Civilise the Natives by an Improved Administration of Existing Means* (1830) (London: Dawsons of Pall Mall, 1968), ccxl.
22   ibid., ccliv.
23   A document full of self-justification — reprinting much of his correspondence with Governor Darling (with whom he often quarrelled) and the colonial press — Bannister's *Statements and Documents Relating to Proceedings in New South Wales, in 1824, 1825, and 1826, Intended to Support an Appeal to the King by the Attorney General of the Colony* (Cape Town: printed by W. Bridekirk, 1827) bears intriguing similarity to Threlkeld's own justification to the LMS, *A Statement Chiefly Relating to the Formation and Abandonment of a Mission to the Aborigines of New South Wales* (Sydney: printed by R. Howe, Government Printer, 1828).

law into effect wherever, and in whatever way these people [Aborigines] came into contact with us', and to encourage any effort to improve their condition. Concerned with the ethics of cross-cultural contact prior to his appointment (a '"problem" as difficult as it is interesting'), Bannister insisted that the very fact that the Colonial Office was aware that he had 'formed something like decided opinions on the subject' ensured that he was 'most cautious not to attempt setting up "theories" on it'.[24]

Yet Bannister did not have a good reputation for discretion, and his preferences were evident in his correspondence with Threlkeld, for example. The two men were drawn together by scepticism about Rev. Samuel Marsden — the controversial magistrate–chaplain of the Church of England — and other prominent religious figures in New South Wales whose involvement in settler capitalism and politics dimmed their advocacy for Aboriginal affairs. The internecine tensions between evangelical and established Protestantism sharpened their critique and strengthened their shared assumptions. Bannister and Threlkeld were highly critical of the phrenological studies of Aborigines conducted by visiting medical officers on the French exploration voyages of Captain Bougainville in mid 1825, and were well aware of the dangerous potential of pseudo-science to affirm settler prejudice. Bannister sarcastically notified Threlkeld that the 'French medical gentleman has confirmed his opinion of the innate deficiency of these poor people by a careful examination of many heads'. Threlkeld suggested that, 'Perhaps the Aborigines think that there is an innate deficiency in the bulk of white men's sculls [sic] which prevents their attainment of the native language'. Dismissive of craniological studies, Threlkeld hotly asserted that his evangelical work:

> lies wholly and solely with an organ that has escaped their notice namely the heart, but had they even searched and found an innate deficiency in that organ, I would then have smiled and retorted my trust is in him who has said 'A new heart will I create within them'.[25]

This kind of deeply affective evangelical language and reasoning was familiar to both Bannister and Threlkeld; their writings resound with intense emotion, which may also account for their similar reputations for immoderate behaviour.

Bannister's *Humane Policy* contains trenchant critiques of imperial expansion, which reveal both his passionate humanitarian beliefs, and his refreshing lack of political caution: 'It is impossible to justify our present course of destroying every where those, whose only crime is, that they precede us in the possession of lands, which we desire to enjoy to their exclusion'.[26] While recognising the

---

24 Bannister, *Statements and Documents Relating to Proceedings in New South Wales*, 123.
25 L.E. Threlkeld to Rev. George Burder, 10 October 1825, CWM, Australia Box 2, SOAS.
26 Bannister, *Humane Policy*, vi.

work of those (like Threlkeld) who attempted to leaven imperial expansion with 'humane policy' towards indigenous communities, Bannister argued that such advocates were thwarted at every step because imperial policy and colonial governments had strongly supported opponents of humanitarianism. In New South Wales, he exhorted, 'Common right, in matters of life and death, is constantly outraged, by our neglecting the plainest principles of equity', laws that have 'for many years been known to be of the first necessity'.[27]

Bannister was one of few witnesses to the British parliament's 1837–38 Select Committee on Aborigines in the British Settlements who had held colonial office in New South Wales, and his testimony drew on his personal experience across New South Wales and the Cape Colony, and his persistent research about other settler colonies. Although the committee was dominated by the turbulent state of the Cape Colony, the Australian colonies make for a repeated — if muted — comparison throughout the monumental *Report from the Select Committee on Aborigines (British settlements); Together with the Minutes of Evidence, Appendix and Index*. Threlkeld's Lake Macquarie Mission was mentioned by several witnesses, and in written submissions, although the influence of powerful enemies such as John Dunmore Lang substantially discredited the mission. Bannister referred to the translation work Threlkeld performed (although he did not name the missionary). He advocated an empire-wide 'system of publicity' to bring colonial news to the attention of the British public and to readers in the colonies. Frequent publication of the reports of 'functionaries' would be crucial, he suggested, as would 'a very careful report of all trials of all sorts'.[28] Threlkeld's annual reports must have been foremost in his mind. Legal reform was his main platform: the current state of affairs not only 'constantly stopped justice' in New South Wales but also effectively 'stops the civilisation of these people at the threshold'. The failure of the justice system led to indigenous dissatisfaction and their 'impunity encourages the colonists to hold the lives of the natives cheap'.[29]

Zoe Laidlaw compellingly describes the production of the final report of the select committee as a collaborative effort of Thomas Fowell Buxton's family, especially Anna Gurney. Late intervention by Sir George Grey (coincidentally, a keen supporter of Threlkeld's linguistic studies) resulted in considerable compromises and radical re-editing, such that the 'cuts produced a broadly imperial report, rather than the explosively Cape-focused document the

---

27   ibid., 7.
28   *Report from the Select Committee on Aborigines (British Settlement) With Minutes of Evidence Appendix and Index (1837)*, British Parliamentary Papers, VII, 175.
29   ibid., 176.

Buxtons had planned'. Laidlaw also notes that Bannister — a close associate of the Buxtons — was considered too indiscrete to share in the knowledge of the collaborative authorship.[30]

Bannister's response to the published select committee report lacked subtlety. Dedicated to Buxton as the chair of the committee, *British Colonization and Coloured Tribes* (1838) was intemperate in tone and frank in its disappointment. The report is internally inconsistent, Bannister insisted: 'when good, [it] is almost a dead letter; and its bad passages, grossly inconsistent wit [sic] its evidence, are of a most dangerous tendency'. Bannister was highly critical of many who gave evidence at the select committee, including Major Dundas, acting Governor Wade, and the former Cape Colony governors Benjamin D'Urban and Sir Lowry Cole. Such are the men, Bannister fulminated, 'with memories as infirm as their judgments, to whom the colonial-office is in the habit of confiding the interests of our remote possessions, and the fate of the coloured people'.[31]

The Select Committee on Aborigines in the British Settlements and its report galvanised many. In 1838, the inaugural annual meeting of the Aborigines Protection Society (APS) in London noted that they already had correspondents sympathetic to their cause in New South Wales but sought to establish a network of 'well-informed gentlemen' resident in all the colonies to which the APS directed its attention. They requested communications, 'conveying the most specific and authentic intelligence of all circumstances connected with the Aborigines, as the most effectual means of guiding the Society to the adoption of wise and appropriate measures on their behalf'.[32] Threlkeld was a regular writer to the APS, in part through his earlier association with Bannister, who was involved in the establishment of the APS with Thomas Hodgkin, and served as one of its founding honorary secretaries. Threlkeld's involvement in the New South Wales Auxiliary Aborigines Protection Society (also established 1838) — where he served on the inaugural management committee — cemented the links between New South Wales and London, Threlkeld and Bannister. The APS noted their 'most lively satisfaction' at the New South Wales initiative: it was the first auxiliary society established.[33] Threlkeld's speech to the Auxiliary APS reflected on his 22 years' colonial residence, and a lengthy abstract appeared in the second annual report of the APS (1839). He retold narratives of colonial violence against Aborigines that had shocked him on arrival, and strongly restated his key principle 'that the Aborigines were entitled to protection and

---

30   Zoe Laidlaw, '"Aunt Anna's Report": The Buxton Women and the Aborigines Select Committee, 1835–37', *The Journal of Imperial and Commonwealth History* 32, no. 2 (2004): 18, 19; see also Laidlaw, *Colonial Connections, 1815–45: Patronage, the Information Revolution and Colonial Government* (Manchester and New York: Manchester University Press, 2005).

31   Saxe Bannister, *British Colonization and Coloured Tribes* (London: William Ball, 1838), 253, 244.

32   *First Annual Meeting of the Aborigines Protection Society* (London: Aborigines Protection Society, 1838), 12–13.

33   *Second Annual Report of the Aborigines Protection Society* (London: Aborigines Protection Society, 1839), 25.

compensation from those who had forcibly deprived them of their patrimony'.[34] The APS regularly published Threlkeld's Annual Report of the Lake Macquarie Mission, and other correspondence, in their reports and extracts from their papers and proceedings. Reform of Aboriginal evidence laws was one of the first and most important goals for the APS: Threlkeld's experience made him a significant informant for the London committee.

The late 1830s saw an acceleration of Threlkeld's concern with court processes and Aboriginal rights. His 1837 annual report exploded with frustration. It was, Threlkeld wrote, 'a mere Legal Fiction' to claim that Aborigines were 'subject to and under the protection of British Law' when their evidence could not be heard in court. '[T]he strictness of the administration of the law becomes the height of injustice to all', he posited, and cast this as a moral failing not just of the colony but of Britain. The value of Aboriginal land, he reminded his readers, 'fills the coffers of our Exchequer with Gold, exalts Britain amongst the nations'. Britons accrued a debt by establishing colonies based on 'the destruction of the native inhabitants thereof, and thus presents a powerful claim to the tender sympathies of our Christian Charities'. Surely, in 'this age of Intellect', he pleaded, the British constitution could be amended to take account of circumstances that it could never have foreseen: if not, the consequence would be that 'year after year, the Aborigines [would] be frittered away from the land by private vengeance for injuries publicly sustained'. Generally, Threlkeld suggested, there was 'a kindly feeling, a friendly disposition manifested towards the Blacks by the Colonists', but the 'private vengeance of injured Europeans' would, he warned, with steady purpose 'surely, secretly, and speedily annihilate the Aborigines from the face of this Land'.[35] Threlkeld's provocative warning about the effects of neglecting Aboriginal testimony joined other more sober efforts to engender change.[36] The APS extracted from the 1837 report Threlkeld's explosive comments about the 'Legal Fiction' of colonial law, and his story about Wombarty's trial, for reprinting in their *Extracts from Papers and Proceedings* (1839).

Other personal connections linked Threlkeld to metropolitan debates. Burton had requested a copy of Threlkeld's personal records as part of the evidence he collected to take back to Britain on his two-year leave in 1839. Burton had been the presiding judge at five of the 1835–36 cases at which Threlkeld had appeared as translator (and also at the libel trial Threlkeld brought against John Dunmore Lang in 1836); in 1838, he sentenced the seven settlers convicted of the Myall Creek massacre. Threlkeld was keenly interested in the Myall Creek trials, as they brought to a head many of the rumours and evidence about settler

---

34   ibid., 15.
35   Threlkeld, 'Report 1837', 136.
36   See Nancy Wright's excellent analysis of the Aboriginal Evidence acts. Nancy E. Wright, 'The Problem of Aboriginal Evidence in Early Colonial New South Wales', in *Law, History, Colonialism: The Reach of Empire*, eds, Diane Kirkby and Catharine Coleborne (Manchester University Press, 2001), 140–55.

aggression to which he had long been privy. During the long process of copying his records, Threlkeld wrote to Burton with further evidence about violence taking place on the Liverpool Plains and seeking his advocacy with Governor George Gipps:

> such things ought to be made known to his Excellency that he may be enabled to judge betwixt man and man in the unequal warfare with the Blacks, and I could not rest satisfied to let the matter rest until my annual report to the Governor.[37]

Threlkeld's careful copperplate transcription of his lengthy *Memoranda Selected from 'Twenty Four Years of Missionary Engagements in the South Sea Islands and Australia'* bears a respectful and personal autograph for Burton. Roger Milliss notes that Burton failed to produce the formal submission about the treatment of Aborigines — to be titled 'Memoranda of Outrages against the Aborigines' — that he had intended, but that his notes towards the project contain much material drawn directly from Threlkeld's *Memoranda* and his 1837 and 1838 reports.[38] Burton carefully assessed Threlkeld's testimony about mass slaughter of Aborigines and the culpability of police and military officials (Sergeant Temple and Major James Nunn, in two separate instances that Threlkeld described in his 1837 report). The missionary's frank and fulsome explanations to Burton's subsequent queries indicate a considerable level of trust in Burton (for many years, Threlkeld had been very circumspect about what evidence he made public). Comments in personal correspondence between the two men also suggest a personal connection.

Burton published *The State of Religion and Education in New South Wales* (1840) during his short absence from New South Wales, and his book bears some evidence of Threlkeld's perspectives, amongst many others. His characterisation of Australia as 'a great Moral Wilderness'[39] recalls Threlkeld's dire description of the poverty of the antipodean religious mission in 1827: 'all dry, dry, very dry scattered bones, in the midst of a waste howling wilderness'.[40] Burton condemns the absence of religion in outlying areas, and specifically situates this as a causal factor for the Myall Creek atrocities: these crimes, 'of almost unheard

---

37   L.E. Threlkeld to Judge Burton, 20 July 1838, Original Documents on Aborigines and Law, 1797–1840 (Sydney: The Centre for Comparative Law, History and Governance of Macquarie University, and State Records NSW), http://www.law.mq.edu.au/scnsw/Correspondence/74.htm see also Gunson, 267–68.
38   Milliss, 612.
39   William Westbrooke Burton, *The State of Religion and Education in New South Wales* (London: J. Cross, 1840), 310.
40   L.E. Threlkeld, *A Statement Chiefly Relating to the Formation and Abandonment of a Mission to the Aborigines of New South Wales; Addressed to the Serious Consideration of the Directors of the London Missionary Society* (Sydney: R. Howe, Government Printer, 1828), 29. See Meredith Lake, 'Protestant Christianity and the Colonial Environment: Australia as a Wilderness in the 1830s and 1840s', *Journal of Australian Colonial History* 11 (2009): 21–44, for an analysis of the trope of wilderness for Protestant clergy writing about Australia, although Threlkeld's usage predates her examples.

of depravity', were the 'consequences of Men living unawed by, because far out of the reach of the laws, and uninfluenced by Religion'.[41] Interestingly, Burton also makes clear his contempt for John Dunmore Lang, Threlkeld's long-term adversary, and the 'Internal Animosities' in which Lang and his *Colonist* newspaper revelled.[42]

Those internal animosities motivated many of the mixed messages that emerged from colonial New South Wales. Ultimately they ensured that Threlkeld's evidence was itself something of a dead letter at the time of the select committee. Lang had an ongoing feud with Threlkeld and a predilection for undermining religious competitors, so his written testimony to the committee repeated his libellous comments that Threlkeld had mismanaged the Lake Macquarie Mission from the outset and, consequently, little had been achieved in the decade since its formation. Marsden was so exasperated with Threlkeld's independence and quarrelsome behaviour that his submission made no mention of missions in New South Wales at all. Instead, as is typical of Marsden's abrupt dismissal of Australian Aborigines, his letter resonates with indignation on behalf of the Māori and exclusively details his humanitarian efforts in New Zealand. Only the LMS missionary John Williams (soon to depart for Erromanga where he would be killed by islanders) lauded Threlkeld's active employment amongst Aborigines.

By 1840, Threlkeld's annual reports were receiving the publicity that Bannister had advocated in the select committee. One phrase in particular resonated across many different media in colonial and metropolitan sites: 'Christian laws will hang the aborigines for violence done to Christians, but Christian laws will not protect them from the aggressions of nominal Christians, because aborigines must give evidence only upon oath'.[43] Yet 1841 saw the end of colonial government funding for the Lake Macquarie Mission.

Threlkeld's involvement in legal settings implicates him in the messy, inchoate operations of colonial governmentality, even while his work was motivated by a desire to force the system to confront its own limitations, as in the case of Aboriginal testimony. Threlkeld's legal representations were bound with the efforts of the nascent settler state to govern its most challenging subjects, even though attempts at control were frequently unstable and insecure. Connecting local Supreme Court trials with the broader work of British parliamentary committees emphasises the ways in which colonial knowledge moved across

---

41 Burton, *State of Religion*, 279.
42 See ibid., Appendix, cxviii.
43 The phrase originated in Threlkeld's 1840 Report: 'Report of the Mission to the Aborigines at Lake Macquarie, New South Wales' (1837), in Gunson, 166. It was reprinted, with various abridgements and commentary, by the *Sydney Herald*, *Sydney Gazette*, in the *APS Extracts*, and by the London Quakers' *Report from the Meeting for Sufferings*.

geographical boundaries while also providing the motor for governing both locally and trans-imperially. Threlkeld himself linked specific instances of colonial law to broader philosophical questions about the relationship between European and colonial peoples, between imperial policy and colonial governance. He brought to bear his ethnographic, evangelical knowledge upon issues germane to constitutions and sovereignty. Yet, the complexity of his own writing, and the awkward slippage between his good intentions and the consequences of his representations, provide evidence that continues to trouble simple narratives about Australia's colonial past.

'Destitute of the knowledge of God': Māori Testimony Before the New Zealand Courts in the Early Crown Colony Period

Shaunnagh Dorsett

In 1843 the imperial parliament passed the *Colonial Evidence Act*.[1] Its purpose was to allow colonial legislatures to pass acts or ordinances to allow their indigenous inhabitants to give unsworn testimony before the courts. Unsworn testimony was testimony given by those who were not able to take the oath. At common law the rule was that evidence could only be given on oath, rendering those devoid of religious belief incompetent to testify. In British colonies, therefore, this rule resulted in most of the indigenous inhabitants being unable to give evidence before English courts. This was particularly problematic in the Australian colonies. The imperial Act of 1843 was the outcome of various ineffectual attempts to allow for such evidence by way of local act or ordinance, particularly in New South Wales and, more latterly, Western Australia. While some attention has been paid to the politics and processes of law reform concerning unsworn testimony in empire, and the ways in which such reforms formed part of broader disputes about the shape of colonial governments,[2] these discussions have almost entirely revolved around the Australian colonies.[3] New Zealand has received comparatively little attention. To the extent to which New Zealand has been considered, it has been in the context of the overall matrix of imperial reform and therefore much of the particular politics and processes of reform within New Zealand still await consideration.[4] Although New Zealand promptly took advantage of the imperial legislation and passed a local Ordinance under its auspices, the history of the interaction between Māori and the courts, and their ability to testify before them, prior to the passing of that Ordinance diverges significantly from that of the Australian colonies. The particular history of New Zealand in respect of unsworn testimony illustrates

---

1 *Colonial Evidence Act* 6 Vic. c. 22 (1843) (Imp).

2 See in particular Damen Ward, 'Imperial Policy, Colonial Government and Indigenous Testimony in South Australia and New Zealand in the 1840s', in *Law and Politics in British Colonial Thought: Transpositions of Empire*, eds, Shaunnagh Dorsett and Ian Hunter (New York: Palgrave Mcmillan, 2010); Russell Smandych, 'Contemplating The Testimony of "Others": James Stephen, The Colonial Office, and The Fate of Australian Aboriginal Evidence Acts, circa 1839–1849', *Australian Journal of Legal History* 8 (2004): 237.

3 See also Nancy Wright, 'The Problem of Aboriginal Evidence in Colonial New South Wales', in *Law, History, Colonialism: The Reach of Empire*, eds, Diane Kirkby and Catharine Coleborne (Manchester University Press, 2001), 140–55.

4 For New Zealand and imperial reform see Ward.

the interplay of local micro-politics with imperial imperatives, as well as the ways in which the colonial office sought to accommodate the needs of specific colonies within the often constrictive bounds of imperial constitutional law.

Local dictates and imperial imperatives: The *Land Claims Ordinances*

Unlike other indigenous groups around the empire, prior to the passing of the imperial Act, Māori already had some limited ability to give unsworn testimony. In the 1840 *New Zealand Land Claims Act* (NSW) provision was made for unsworn testimony to be given by Māori.[5] The *New Zealand Land Claims* bill was introduced into the New South Wales Legislative Council in May 1840.[6] Its purpose was to institute a process for investigating lands acquired from Māori pre 1840 and the conditions under which those lands were acquired. The official position was that only titles derived from the Crown itself would be recognised, and a proclamation to this effect had been issued by Governor George Gipps, prior to the signing of the *Treaty of Waitangi*. A proclamation to similar effect was issued by (then) New Zealand Lieutenant Governor William Hobson in early 1840.[7] Prior to this time, however, significant land had changed hands, purchased directly from Māori by pākehā (non- Māori, in this period generally white settlers). Land acquisitions from Māori, therefore, were to be investigated and those which were 'founded on equitable principles, and not in extent or otherwise prejudicial to the present or prospective interests of Her Subjects in New Zealand' were to be allowed and confirmed.[8] Such a process had no parallel in other Australasian colonies, where the possibility of indigenous ownership of land was not even acknowledged. In New Zealand, however, the land claims investigations were critical to settlement of the new colony.

The bill was modelled on the *Claims to Land Act 1835* (NSW), under which a Court of Claims was established to investigate claims to grants essentially where the Crown had made multiple promises to grants and the documentary records

---

5   *New Zealand Land Claims Act* 4 Vic. No. 7 (1840) (New South Wales). New Zealand was a dependency of New South Wales for 18 months between late 1839 and 1841. During this period the New South Wales Governor, Sir George Gipps, and the Legislative Council passed laws for New Zealand.

6   Votes and Proceedings of the Legislative Council 1840 No. 1, copy in Gipps to Russell, Despatch No. 40/66, 29 May 1840, The National Archives (TNA), CO 201/297, fol 190a/b. For a full account see *The New Zealand Land Claims Act of 1840*, Evidence of Dr Donald M. Loverage for the Crown, WAI 45 #I 6 (Muriwhenua Claim), 1993 [revised version 2002] (Waitangi Tribunal, Wellington).

7   On 30 January 1840 Hobson read two proclamations, the first declaring the boundaries of New South Wales to include New Zealand; the second stating the Crown's intention to only recognise titles derived from the Crown itself: Issued 30 January 1840, Hobson to Gipps, TNA, CO 209/7, fol. 23–24.

8   Votes and Proceedings of the Legislative Council 1840 No. 1, 29 May 1840, TNA, CO 201/297, fol. 190a/b.

were insufficient to establish the entitled grantee.[9] Under both land claims acts, determinations were to be guided by 'real justice and good conscience'. Of course, the stark difference between the New South Wales and New Zealand acts was the New South Wales Act did not mention, or allow for the possibility of, indigenous owners. Nevertheless, it provided a convenient template that, in form, complied with Normanby's instructions to Gipps for the preparation of the Act.[10] Section VII of the *New Zealand Land Claims Act*, generally dealing with the calling of witnesses, recording of evidence, and penalties for perjury, was derived from s 6 of the 1835 New South Wales Act. However, cl. VII included provisions for the evidence of 'Aboriginal Natives', a provision obviously absent in the original Act. The evidence of the Māori vendors was critical to the functioning of the Act. As in any investigation to title, it was necessary to receive the evidence of the seller as to the nature of the transaction.

At this time, unsworn testimony was still not permitted in any courts either in England or around empire.[11] As noted above, unsworn testimony was testimony given by those who were not able to take the oath. At common law the rule was that evidence could only be given on oath, rendering those devoid of religious belief incompetent to testify. However, it had been accepted since the decision in *Omichund v Barker* that the oath could be taken by 'infidels' who believed in *a* god and that they would be punished if they swore falsely. Chief Justice Sir Edward Willes noted that while the common law is a Christian institution, the substance of an oath predates Christianity, and has 'nothing to do with Christianity, only that by the Christian religion we are put still under greater obligations not to be guilty of perjury ...'.[12] While the forms of oaths may vary, the substance is the same: God in all of them is called upon as a witness to truth.[13] Thus, it followed that 'a man is not to be questioned as to his particular opinions, (as, whether he believes the gospels,) but, whether he believes in the

---

9   *An Act for Appointing and Empowering Commissioners to Examine and Report upon Claims to Land under the Great Seal of the Colony of New South Wales*, 5 Wm IV No. 21 (1835) (New South Wales), in turn based on an earlier Act of the same name: 4 Wm IV No. 9 (1833) (New South Wales).

10   Loverage, *New Zealand Land Claims Act*, 43.

11   A possible exception to this was the resolution of the Council of Assiniboa on 2 February 1837 allowing for the admittance of native testimony in all courts in the District of Assiniboa: 'Several Objections Having Been Made By Many Of The Colonists To The Validity Of Indian Evidence; It Is Resolved 1st. That The Evidence Of An Indian Be Considered Valid, And Be Admitted As Such In All Courts Of The Settlement'. The resolution is reproduced in E.H. Oliver, *The Canadian North-West: Its Early Development and Legislative Records* (Ottawa: Government Printing Bureau, 1914), vol. 1, 278. The resolution was of doubtful legal validity as it was likely repugnant to the common law. The earliest legislative endeavour to provide for such evidence was the 1764 draft legislation prepared by the British Parliament to supplement the *Royal Proclamation of 1763*. It was intended to establish a system of superintendents within the territory reserved for Indian Nations. The legislation specifically provided for both the appointment of superintendents and interpreters, as well as the taking of evidence in both civil and criminal matters from Indians (presumably non-Christian Indians): E.B. O'Callaghan, ed., *Documents Relative to the Colonial History of the State of New York*, vol. VII (Albany, New York: Weed, Parsons & Co., 1856–61), 637. My thanks to Mark Walters for drawing this to my attention.

12   *Omichund v Barker* (1744) Willes 538, 547 (125 ER 1310, 1314).

13   ibid.

existence of a God, and a future state'.[14] The rule was developed in the context of India. Thus, it was designed to allow evidence from those who believed in a god, but were not Christians. 'Infidel' testimony was admitted in a number of trials at the Old Bailey, although never the testimony of atheists. For example, in 1765, John Morgan, prosecutor in an action for theft, and a 'Mohametan', was allowed to swear on the 'Alcoran' at the Old Bailey. According to Morgan, 'I touch the book, the Alcoran, with one hand, and put the other to my forehead; then I look upon it I am bound to speak the truth'.[15] In *R v Sayhead*, the prosecutor, Bonhalel, both a foreigner and a Mohametan, was able to give evidence through an interpreter,[16] while in *R v Boxo Colloso, Boxo Tindle*, Carder, a Mohametan originally from Bombay, swore on the 'forms of that religion', also giving evidence through an interpreter.[17] However, problematically, most indigenous peoples, particularly in the Australian colonies, did not adhere to any recognisable religion. They were entirely 'destitute of the knowledge of God' and therefore unable to swear any oath, even under the common law 'infidel' exception.

While the practical purpose of admitting unsworn testimony before the Land Claims Commission was clear, the legal validity of the measure was unclear. The *New Zealand Land Claims Act* was passed by the New South Wales Legislative Council at a time in which Gipps's policy was to make general provision for the admitting of unsworn testimony by Aborigines. In October 1839 the New South Wales Legislative Council passed an Act to allow unsworn testimony.[18] According to the despatch which accompanied the Act to London, the 'measure was introduced at the desire of the attorney-general in consequence of the difficulty of obtaining convictions which he experienced in several cases, wherein native blacks have been concerned, either as the accused or the injured party'.[19] The Act provided that evidence would be given 'so much weight as corroborating circumstances may entitle it to'. Further, it required evidence be corroborated by European witnesses. The Act, however, was disallowed.[20] Gipps, it seems, had overreached himself. According to the barristers, Campbell and Wilde, to whom it had been referred for a legal opinion:

---

14 Samuel March Phillips, *A Treatise on the Law of Evidence* (London: Butterworth and Son, 1814), 11. To the same effect see Sir Geoffrey Gilbert, *The Law of Evidence*, sixth edition, vol. 1 (London: James Sedgwick, 1801), 129; Thomas Peake, *A Compendium of the Law of Evidence*, fourth edition (London: Reed and Hunter, 1813), 154–57.

15 *R v John Ryan, Jeremiah Ryan, Mary Ryan*, 27 February 1765, *Proceedings of the Old Bailey* (http://www.oldbaileyonline.org), ref. no. t17650227-5 (theft) (*Morgan's Case* 1 Leach 53 (168 ER 129).

16 *R v Sayhead*, 12 April 1809, ibid., ref. no. t8090412-57 (theft).

17 *R v Boxo Colloso, Boxo Tindle*, 3 July 1822, ibid., ref. no. t8220703-20 (violent robbery).

18 *An Act to Allow the Aboriginal Natives of New South Wales to be Received as Competent Witnesses in Criminal Cases* 3 (*Aboriginal Evidence Act*) Vic. No. 16 (1839).

19 Gipps to Normanby, 14 October 1839, *Historical Records of Australia: Series I, Governors' Despatches to and from England* (Sydney: Committee of the Commonwealth Parliament, 1914–25), series I, vol. 20, 368 (*HRA*).

20 On this further, see Smandych.

[t]o admit in a Criminal proceeding the evidence of a witness acknowledged to be ignorant of the existence of a God or a future state would be contrary to the principles of British Jurisprudence; and the Act is loosely worded with respect to the admission of which evidence and the weight to be given to it that we do not think it could be attended with any advantage.[21]

Between the time that the New South Wales *Aboriginal Evidence Act* was sent to London, and notification of its disallowance received in New South Wales, over a year had elapsed. During this time, the New South Wales Legislative Council had passed the *New Zealand Land Claims Act*. The unsworn evidence provision in this Act was broader than that in the soon to be disallowed *Aboriginal Evidence Act*. Section VII asserted that:

Provided always, that in all cases in which it may be necessary to take the evidence of any Aboriginal Native who shall not be competent to take an Oath, it shall be lawful for the said Commissioners to receive in evidence the statement of such Aboriginal Native, subject to such credit as it may be entitled to, from corroborating or other circumstances.

The *New Zealand Land Claims Act* was disallowed, although not for reasons relating to the unsworn testimony provision. Section VII was not mentioned, either in correspondence, or by James Stephen in his minute on the Act. Rather, attention was directed to the issue of the effect of the separation of New Zealand from New South Wales on the Ordinance. Russell was set on disallowance.[22] He advised Hobson that the separation of New Zealand rendered 'obsolete and impracticable' generally arrangements 'which require the interposition of the governor of the old colony'.[23] The characterisation of the Act as 'obsolete and impracticable' was that of James Stephen, who advised that laws passed by one colony could still operate in another — Quebec laws in the Canadas for example — unless they became obsolete and impracticable. Stephen may have left matters as they were but, given Russell's determination to disallow the Act, he advised that disallowance could be achieved simply by despatch.[24] As a result, at the first session of the New Zealand Legislative Council, the New South Wales Act was replaced by the local *Land Claims Ordinance* (NZ).[25] Section 9,

---

21   The attorney-general and solicitor-general to Russell, 27 July 1840, *HRA*, series I, vol. 20, 756.

22   Russell, Minute, appended to Gipps to Russell, 16 August 1840, TNA, CO209/6, fol. 420.

23   Russell to Hobson, 16 April 1841, Despatch No 41/27 of 16 April 1841, *British Parliamentary Papers* (*BPP*) 1841 XVII (311), 60 and Russell to Gipps, 16 April 1841, *BPP* 1841 (311), 60. Both Hobson and Gipps were instructed to postpone notification of the disallowance of the Act, pending passing a new Ordinance.

24   Stephen, Minute, appended to Gipps to Russell, 16 August 1840, TNA, CO209/6, fol. 420.

25   *Land Claims Ordinance* 4 Vic. No. 2 (1841).

providing for unsworn evidence, was identical to s. 7 of the original Act. This Ordinance was allowed.[26] Again, the unsworn testimony provision received no obvious attention, either locally or at the Colonial Office.

Perhaps, as Gibbs was so certain that the original unsworn evidence Ordinance would be approved, he did not allude to this unusual provision. Neither did Hobson, who presumably had neither any idea of its unusual nature nor that the *Aboriginal Evidence Ordinance* had been disallowed. In neither Gipps's instructions to the commissioners on their appointment, nor Hobson's (substantially similar) instructions on their reappointment under the new Ordinance, was the matter of Māori evidence mentioned.[27] In both sets of instructions Edward Godfrey and Mathew Richmond were simply reminded that in summoning witnesses and recording evidence they were to be guided by the Act. Both sets of instructions, however, made it clear that a protector must be present at all proceedings, as must a competent interpreter. The protector could function as both.[28]

After the 1841 *Land Claims Ordinance* had been allowed, the law officers, Pollock and Pollett, recommended disallowance of the Western Australia *Aboriginal Evidence Act* (1841).[29] This Act had been passed in part on the urging of Russell, following the disallowance of an earlier Ordinance.[30] On 26 October 1842, some eight months after the New Zealand *Land Claims Ordinance* was allowed, they reported that the 1841 Western Australian Act suffered from the same defect as the earlier New South Wales Act. It was repugnant. They stated that: 'the two Acts are in fact, as far as regards the nature of these objections, substantially the same'.[31] This led Stephen to suggest the enactment of an imperial statute. It was obvious that the local legislatures did not have the constitutional power to override a principle that was, at least as far as the law officers were concerned, fundamental to the common law.[32]

---

26   Lord Stanley to Governor Hobson, Despatch No. 27/42, 18 March 1842, *BPP* XXVIII (569), 464.

27   Gipps to Commissioners, 2 October 1840, TNA, CO209/6, fol 407ff; Hobson to Godfrey and Richmond, *Instructions for the Commissioners*, Archives New Zealand (ANZ), OLC 5/4B, 4.

28   On the other hand, the final commissioner, Spain, appointed from London, received no specific instructions. William Swainson and Chief Justice William Martin (prior to their departure to New Zealand), suggested that it would be desirable to furnish Spain with a full set of instructions: Martin to Russell, 10 March 1841, TNA, CO209/13, fol. 185. James Stephen responded to Russell that, as there was a 'positive law prescribing his duties', his instructions would simply be to execute the Act. No further instructions were required: Stephen, Minute, 12 March 1841, TNA, CO 209/13, fol. 367.

29   *An Act to Allow the Aboriginal Natives of Western Australia to give Information and Evidence without the Sanction of an Oath* 4 & 5 Vic. No. 22 (1841). See generally Ann Hunter, 'The Origin and Debate Surrounding the Development of Aboriginal Evidence Acts in Western Australia in the Early 1840s', *University of Notre Dame Australia Law Review* 9 (2007): 115.

30   *An Act to allow the Aboriginal Natives of Western Australia to give Information and Evidence in Criminal Cases and to enable Magistrates to award Summary Punishment, for certain Offences* (1840) 4 Vic. No. 8. The terms of this Act were quite different to its New South Wales counterpart. For the reasons for the disallowance of this earlier Ordinance see generally Hunter, ibid.

31   Pollock and Pollett (Law Officers) to Stanley, 26 October 1842, TNA, CO 201/337, fol. 295, in Smandych, 270.

32   Stephen, Minute, 28 February 1842, TNA, CO18/31, fol 16 in Smandych, 271.

So, why was no comment made on the unsworn testimony provisions of either the original New South Wales *New Zealand Land Claims Act 1840* or the 1841 New Zealand *Land Claims Ordinance*? The New Zealand provisions were, after all, broader than those of either the New South Wales or Western Australian acts, which had been disallowed. The acts were scrutinised by James Stephen and it is impossible that he simply failed to notice the unsworn testimony provision. In 1813 Stephen, still a young lawyer, was appointed by the Colonial Office to scrutinise colonial laws on a fee basis.[33] He was paid three guineas per Act. In 1825 he was appointed as legal advisor to the Colonial Office and counsel to the Board of Trade, where he continued to scrutinise and comment on colonial legislation and, in 1836, he became permanent under-secretary. In this role he continued his previous task of reporting on colonial acts and ordinances. After 1813, on the advice of Stephen, it became required that all colonial laws were sent to London. It was in any case a requirement in most governors' standing orders that they do so. Failure to do so could, and did, lead to them being declared invalid.[34] Most acts and ordinances were reported on by the Colonial Office legal adviser (namely Stephen). Where the colonial law was potentially repugnant, however, the solicitor-general or attorney-general might, on advice from the Colonial Office, appoint Crown law officers to write an opinion.[35] This latter process had, of course, occurred in the case of both the New South Wales and the Western Australian Aboriginal Evidence acts. Stephen, most likely at the direction of the secretary of state for the colonies, The Hon Edward Stanley, referred the Western Australian Act to the law officers, aware of the advice that would come back. There seems little doubt, however, that as a matter of policy Stephen, as well as both Russell and Stanley, was in favour of allowing unsworn testimony. Stephen's recommendation to disallow the Western Australian Act was reluctant, and conveyed only because it seemed impossible not to make such a recommendation in light of the law officer's opinion that the Act was repugnant.[36]

What then constituted repugnancy? And in what circumstances and on what grounds were colonial ordinances and acts disallowed? Most problematic was where an act or ordinance was supposedly repugnant to the common law. The unsworn testimony provisions were enacted at a time of transition in the conventional meaning of 'repugnancy' and the way in which it was interpreted. In 1851, Rogers, Stephen's successor, noted that the unsworn testimony ordinances of the early 1840s had been one of the most obvious examples of the problems

---

33 Paul Knaplund, *James Stephen and the British Colonial System 1813–1847* (Madison: University of Wisconsin Press, 1953), 12.
34 ibid., 38–39.
35 D.B. Swinfen, *Imperial Control of Colonial Legislation, 1813–1865: A Study of British Policy towards Colonial Legislative Powers* (Oxford: Clarendon Press, 1970).
36 Stephen, Minute, 28 February 1842.

of determining the meaning of repugnancy to the common law.[37] Smandych records that Stephen was privately of the opinion that neither the New South Wales Act nor the Western Australian Act were repugnant as they were not, in his opinion, contrary to the 'principles of British Jurisprudence'. Indeed, admitting such evidence was neither opposed to divine law or to Englishmen's Birthright.[38] By contrast, the law officers took a narrower approach, whereby a statute was repugnant if it was in contravention of a rule of the common law, such as that of the requirement of taking the oath. For Stephen, no fundamental common law principle was at stake in the matter of unsworn evidence. To the contrary, to allow such evidence would have been in the best interests of justice.[39] By the late 1840s, Stephen's position was the accepted one and, by the time of the *Colonial Laws Validity Act*, the position had been reached that colonial legislatures could pass any law unless it directly contradicted with an imperial statute intended to apply to that colony.[40] Of course, this explanation assumes that repugnancy was always and only a question of law. As significant as the legal position, however, was the politics of disallowance, of which the Aboriginal Evidence acts are a key example.[41]

As a matter of speculation, there are two possible, not necessarily mutually exclusive, explanations for the failure to disallow the unsworn testimony provisions in the *Land Claims Act* and *Land Claims Ordinance*. The first is that Stephen simply determined as a matter of pragmatism that the matter should go ahead, aware of the result of referring the Ordinance to the law officers. Despite their opinions of both the New South Wales and Western Australian acts, Stephen was not of the opinion that unsworn testimony provisions were actually repugnant. Was then the provision simply ignored? While this is a simple explanation, problematically the *Land Claims Ordinance* was in fact referred to the law officers, who simply noted that they 'had no objection in point of law'.[42]

The second possible explanation lies in the nature of the Land Claims Commission itself.[43] The Land Claims Commission was to be guided by 'real justice and good conscience'. Consequently, the commissioners were to act 'without regard to legal forms and solemnities'.[44] The commission, therefore, was a species of

---

37 Swinfen, 61.
38 Stephen, Minute, 28 February 1842. An example of a fundamental common law principle might be found in the Picton incident, in which Governor Thomas Picton of Trinidad was brought to trial in 1806, charged with inflicting torture in order to extort the confession of Louisa Calderon, a British subject.
39 Minute, Stephen, ibid.
40 Swinfen, 65.
41 On repugnancy in all its guises see Damen Ward, 'Legislation, Repugnancy and the Disallowance of Colonial Laws: The Legal Structure of Empire and Lloyd's Case (1844)', *Victoria University of Wellington Law Review* 41 (2010): 381.
42 Pollock and Pollett (Law Officers) to G.W. Hope, 12 March 1842, TNA, CO 209/17, fol. 172.
43 My thanks to Damen Ward for suggesting this line of argument.
44 *Land Claims Ordinance* 1841, s. 6.

statutory court of 'equity and good conscience'. Thus, it was neither a court of common law nor equity,[45] and decisions were to be made according to the more discretionary norms of 'real justice and good conscience', although such courts could apply common law or equitable principles, or a modified version of them. The first courts of 'equity and good conscience' were small debt courts,[46] later more generally courts of request.[47] In England, such courts were designed to allow matters to be determined in a manner that was shorn of the need for technicalities, difficult pleading or even lawyers, and they were often run by laypersons. The *Land Claims Ordinance* further directed that the commissioners were to direct themselves by 'the best evidence they can procure, whether the same be such evidence as the law would require in such cases or not'.[48] Otherwise, the commissioners had similar powers to call witnesses and require documents to be produced as the Supreme Court.[49] Evidence, other than Māori evidence, was by oath. There is, however, no suggestion that the particular issue of Māori evidence in any way dictated the court's form. As noted above, that form was conveniently based on the 1835 New South Wales *Land Claims Act*, the form of which in turn had been suggested by the judges of the Supreme Court of New South Wales, based on (unspecified) 'American precedent'.[50] It may be, therefore, that it was considered by the Colonial Office that, as the land commission was not a common law court, its provisions could not be repugnant to the common law. Further, although not specified by the Ordinance, no appeal would be possible to the Supreme Court. This would include appeals on matters of competency (of either pākehā or Māori witnesses).[51] As a statutory jurisdiction, unique rules could be set as to who gave evidence, and under what circumstances. However, had this been the case, it is unclear whether the Ordinance would have been referred to the law officers for an opinion in the first place.

Importantly, the land claims process, one which was of profound significance to the colonisation of New Zealand (and one, given the agitations of the New Zealand Company, of profound political import — both in England and locally),

---

45   Courts of equity and conscience were neither courts of common law or of equity: *Becke v Wells* 1 C & M 76 (1832) (149 ER 321).

46   The first appears to have been *An Acte for the Recovering of Small Debt, and for relieving of the poore Debtors in London* 3 Jac I, c. 15 (1605).

47   On courts of request as courts of equity and conscience see Harry Arthurs, *Without the Law: Administrative Justice and Legal Pluralism in Nineteenth-Century England* (University of Toronto Press, 1985).

48   *Land Claims Ordinance* 1841, s. 6.

49   ibid., ss. 7, 10.

50   The Act was established on the advice of the Forbes Supreme Court. Sir Francis Forbes CJ, Sir James Dowling and William Westerbrook Burton JJ suggested that a court of equity and good conscience be established: Judges to Colonial Secretary, 18 May 1833, *Chief Justice's Letter Book, 1824–1835*, State Records of New South Wales, 4/6651, 331.

51   The Ordinance is silent as to appeals. However, the general rule was that no appeal lay to a common law court by writ of error or writ of false judgment from a court of equity and good conscience: *Scott v Bye* 2 Bing 344 (1824) (130 ER 338). Further, there is no record of any appeal ever having been made on any grounds.

could not have proceeded without such a provision.[52] In the end, imperial dictates and local need may simply have overridden strict legal requirements. The specific requirements of the colonisation of New Zealand could not perhaps be deferred to British imperial law. The answer may be all of the above, and may never be known.

Māori, the courts and the local ordering of law

While Māori were giving evidence before the specialist Land Claims Court, they were also giving evidence before the regular courts. In this case, however, it was not as a result of special statutory authority, but because the high level of Christianisation meant that, prior to the passing of the *Unsworn Testimony Ordinance*, many Māori were already able to give evidence before the regular courts, either swearing as Christians, or under the 'pagan' or 'infidel' rules. Just as the sale of land (and therefore the involvement of Māori in the process) was critical to the legal settlement of the colony, the participation of Māori in the regular courts was also crucial to that settlement, here through their participation in the establishment of the domestic legal order. Māori appeared in legal proceedings before all levels of court: magistrates courts; coroner's court; County Court; and the Supreme Court itself. They also appeared in criminal proceedings and those concerning commerce. Their high level of integration into the local fabric of law distinguished New Zealand from the other Australasian colonies. While in New South Wales, for example, Indigenous Australians were subjected to law (as defendants or victims), Māori were active participants in the legal process, not only subject to, but witnesses in, and initiators of, legal proceedings.[53] This level of engagement with law is undoubtedly one of the reasons why the passing of the Ordinance in 1844 was so uncontroversial. The high conversion rate of Māori to Christianity was a feature of the colony. Māori often described themselves in court as 'missionaries', or 'Mihinare', showing that they were Christian (and probably Anglican in particular). The editor of the *New Zealand Gazette* referred to those able to take the oath as missionaries: 'if any of the witnesses for the prosecution are not "Missionaries", the best way would

---

52   In practice, the commissioners would not proceed without the evidence of the Māori vendors. James Busby, the former British resident to New Zealand, had two claims rejected because of his refusal to call the relevant vendors as witnesses, although he did call other witnesses, mainly pākehā, but also one Māori, who had been present at the signing of the deeds of purchase. The result of this rejection was that the governor refused to allow him to re-file or proceed with these claims.

53   For an example of an action initiated by Māori see the prosecution of Steele for assault by a Māori woman, Caroline: *Caroline v Steele*, 8 September 1843, Police Magistrates Court, Auckland, reported in *Auckland Chronicle*, 13 September 1843, 2; or a civil action in the Supreme Court in contract for the value of 193 pigs: *Ropata Nuitone o Te Pakaru v Johnsone Wilkinson*, 7 September 1846, Supreme Court, Auckland, Martin CJ, Auckland civil minute book, 1844–56, ANZ, Auckland, BBAE 5635/1a, 47 reported in *New Zealand Spectator and Cook's Strait Guardian*, 26 September 1846, 4.

be to instruct them now in the sanctity of an oath and the existence of a Deity'.[54] Māori converted to Christianity in large numbers from the 1820s and, by the Crown Colony period, Christianity had spread to almost every *iwi* (tribe). There are differing explanations for this extent of conversion, all of which may have played a part.[55] Suggestions include a fatal impact to existing belief structures that was experienced from encountering European culture; that disadvantaged groups gained influence from the new religion; that missionaries were a source of *mana* (prestige); that Māori adapted by creating a Māori Christianity; and that they desired to learn the 'magic of writing'.[56] Religion was integrated into a worldview that was built around structured rules which fused physical and spiritual domains. As Raeburn Lange tells us, religious authority was integrated into the existing structure of local leadership as it was 'consistent with Māori understandings of power'.[57]

As a result, many Māori could give sworn testimony before both the county court and the Supreme Court, although it appears they were as frequently sworn under the 'pagan' or 'infidel' rules. At the first session of the Supreme Court in Wellington, held by Henry Samuel Chapman, first puisne judge of the Supreme Court, the grand jury was asked to find a true bill against John McCarthy for stealing some clothes which were the property of 'an aboriginal native'.[58] The only witnesses to the alleged crime were Māori. Chapman informed the grand jury of the circumstances in which 'pagan' (or 'infidel') witnesses could give evidence. When the witnesses came to be sworn, they were asked whether they were Christians. Two confirmed that they were, and were sworn. The others are reported to have 'answered with a shrug of the shoulders "au" [sic].'[59] However, Chapman declined to further question the beliefs of these potential witnesses, rather he asked the crown prosecutor if the trial could proceed without them, and it did. A true bill was presented and McCarthy was tried. He was convicted on the evidence of the two sworn Māori witnesses, Pukahu and Tokoiwa. In *McCarthy*, although in the end only taking sworn evidence,

---

54   *New Zealand Gazette and Wellington Spectator*, 26 July 1843, 3.

55   Lachy Paterson, 'Maori Conversion to the Rule of Law and Nineteenth-Century Imperial Loyalties', *Journal of Religious History* 32 (2008): 216, 220.

56   For a summary of these, from which this is taken, see Paterson, ibid.; see also Raeburn Lange, 'Indigenous Agents of Religious Change in New Zealand 1830–1860', *The Journal of Religious History* 24 (2002): 279; Gary Glover '"Going Mihinare", "Experimental Religion" and Maori Embracing of Christianity — A Reassessment', *Christian Brethren Research Fellowship Journal* 121 (1990): 44.

57   Lange, ibid., 288.

58   *New Zealand Gazette and Wellington Spectator*, 1 May 1844, 3, reporting on the Supreme Court session of 12 April 1844. Chapman arrived in Wellington in February 1844. Prior to this time there had been no permanent Supreme Court in Wellington. Martin CJ, on circuit, held the first Wellington session of the Supreme Court on 4 October 1842.

59   *R v McCarthy*, Supreme Court, Wellington, Chapman J, 17 April 1844, reported in the *New Zealand Gazette and Wellington Spectator*, 1 May 1844, 3; [HS Chapman], Notebook entitled 'Criminal trials No.1', 1844–45, MS-0411/009, Hocken Library, Dunedin, entry for 17 April 1844, 15–18. Rather than 'au' (meaning I), the witnesses presumably shrugged and said 'aua' — meaning I don't know, or no.

Chapman J nevertheless instructed the court generally on the rules of unsworn evidence so as to 'satisfy your minds on a point on which I know considerable misconception prevails'. According to Chapman:

> a pagan witness who believes in a supreme being, who will punish him for telling a lie, either in the next world or in this, is a good witness, provided he be sworn according to the ceremonial which he believes to be binding on his conscience.[60]

Further, according to Chapman, the fact that the imperial parliament had just passed a law to admit pagan witnesses without oath was 'proof that they could not now be admitted'.[61]

Prior to the 1844 Ordinance there are only three instances, other than *McCarthy*, of Māori giving evidence before the Supreme Court, all tried before Martin CJ: *R v Maketu*; *R v Leethart*; and *E Poti*.[62] Most of the interaction between Māori and the courts occurred at the lower level county courts, or even before magistrates. In *Maketu*, decided at the first sitting of the new Supreme Court, three Māori witnesses were called: Tohu, E Atohu and E Hoa. All three were examined by sworn interpreter, George Clarke Jr, who was later appointed sub-protector for Wellington. According to the newspaper report, Tohu, (commonly called Charley Penny) was asked if he was a Christian, to which he replied no. He was further asked if there was a God, to which he replied that he believed there was a God, and 'if he spoke falsely he would be punished'. He was sworn, 'but did not kiss the book'.[63] The latter two witnesses were also examined, but no comment is made as to how they were sworn. *Leethart* was tried at the same session. Leethart, annoyed at alleged trespass, deliberately shot at Pooterai.[64] He was tried for 'shooting to cause grievous bodily harm', and convicted of

---

60   *McCarthy*, ibid.
61   *McCarthy*, ibid. Chapman was generally in agreement with the need to reform these rules of evidence, and would have preferred non-Christian evidence to be by affirmation (ibid). He was not in favour of 'pagan oaths'. Most particularly, he was not in favour of non-Christian forms of swearing. In extra-judicial commentary he had previously condemned such practices, specifically including the practice by which 'Chinese' swore on cracked saucers or, in the West Indies, witnesses 'swore on the dirt of graves': H.S. Chapman, 'Legal Notes', c. 1858, Alexander Turnbull Library, Wellington (ATL) MS Papers-8670-047. The paper is undated. It is part of a collection of materials, including correspondence, which has been collated and designated c. 1858 by the ATL. However, the internal evidence points to this document having been written around 1845. On this, and Chapman's views on 'barbarous customs' generally see Shaunnagh Dorsett, '"Sworn on the Dirt of Graves": Sovereignty, Jurisdiction and the Judicial Abrogation of Barbarous Customs in New Zealand in the 1840s', *The Journal of Legal History* 30 (2009): 175.
62   *R v Maketu*, Supreme Court, Auckland, Martin CJ, 2 March 1842, reported in *New Zealand Herald and Auckland Gazette*, 5 March 1842, 2; *R v Leethart*, Supreme Court, Auckland, Martin CJ, 2 March 1842, reported in *New Zealand Herald and Auckland Gazette*, 5 March 1842; *R v E Poti*, Supreme Court Wellington, Martin CJ, 7 Oct. 1842, reported in *New Zealand Gazette and Wellington Spectator*, 19 October, 1842, 3.
63   *R v Maketu*, Supreme Court, Auckland, Martin CJ, 2 March 1842, reported in *New Zealand Herald and Auckland Gazette*, 5 March 1842, 2.
64   William Swainson, *New Zealand and its Colonisation* (London: Smith, Elder and Co., 1859), 58. Swainson was attorney-general at the time.

common assault. Of the three witnesses one, Tooke, was Māori. He was similarly asked if he was a Christian, and replied that he believed if he spoke falsely he would be punished.[65]

In *E Poti*, it was reported that a Māori, having been placed in the witness box, had the usual oath administered to him. Mr Clarke (the same George Clarke Jnr who had interpreted in *Leethart* and *Maketu*) translated the oath for him. Then, 'the Maori took the puka puka [book] and swore'. However, the report goes on to say that the swearing took place 'in a manner indicative of an entire unacquaintance with the real nature of an oath'.[66] In fact, the editor was entirely outraged by the trial, stating that:

> Not only was the prisoner a Moari [sic], but also the aggrieved person, and consequently the whole case constituted one of those acts, which might fairly have been tried by native laws and customs. Neither the accuser nor the accused knew a word of our language. An interpreter was required to translate the indictment to the prisoner, and to interpret the awfully responsible oath which an accuser takes in all cases of a criminal nature.[67]

Despite the brevity of the above descriptions, they are the best that can be discerned from the historical record. No case, for example, was appealed from a lower court to the Supreme Court on the grounds of inadmissibility of evidence. There are other instances of Māori giving evidence, before the Magistrates, the Court of Quarter Sessions and the County Court.[68] In these instances, the detail is missing. We might assume, therefore, that all Māori were sworn under the same common law rules as in the decisions of the Supreme Court. However, there is some evidence that this was not so. During the session at which McCarthy was tried, Chapman asked the Crown Prosecutor what the practice was concerning unsworn Māori testimony. The prosecutor replied that the practice in the County Court had been to allow evidence to be taken without oath and leave the weight to be given to it to the jury.[69] Presumably he could only speak for practice in the

---

65   *R v Leethart*, 2 March 1842, Supreme Court, Auckland, Martin CJ, reported in *New Zealand Herald and Auckland Gazette*, 5 March 1842, 2.

66   *R v E Poti*, Supreme Court Wellington, Martin CJ, 7 October 1842, reported in *New Zealand Gazette and Wellington Spectator*, 19 October 1842, 3.

67   Editorial, *New Zealand Gazette and Wellington Spectator*, 19 October 1842, 2. Interpreters had been provided at the trial. The role of interpreters has not yet been the subject of sustained inquiry. For example, what effect, if any, did the way in which interpreters asked questions as to religious belief impact on determinations as to the admissibility of testimony?

68   The County Court was created by 5 Vic. No. 2 (Ordinance passed 29 Dec 1841 and taking effect 1 March 1842). The same Ordinance abolished the Courts of General and Quarter Sessions. The court had criminal jurisdiction in all crimes except perjury that were punishable by fine, or imprisonment or both or transportation for a period not exceeding seven years. It had civil jurisdiction in all matters up to £20. The Court was abolished by 7 Vic. No. 8 (passed 27 June 1844 and taking effect 30 September 1844).

69   *New Zealand Gazette and Wellington Spectator*, 1 May 1844, 3, reporting on the Supreme Court session of 12 April 1844.

Southern District before Edmund Storr Halswell, Judge of the County Court. It appears from the report that Chapman's refusal to allow unsworn evidence in *McCarthy* was not expected by those in court.

An editorial in the *New Zealand Gazette and Wellington Spectator* sheds doubt on whether such testimony was given, at least as regards Halswell's practice. As noted above, the editor had called for an ordinance to admit unsworn testimony precisely because of an alleged refusal by Halswell to allow such testimony. While no record actually survives of Halswell refusing to allow unsworn testimony, in April 1844, Halswell did refuse to allow a juror to take part in proceedings who had refused to take the oath from 'conscientious scruples'. Having admitted to the court he was not a Quaker, but 'a member of the connexion of Wesleyan Methodists', he was excused. Halswell is reported as saying that he would refer the matter to the Supreme Court.[70] On the other hand, Halswell was not above unconventional procedure. On a number of occasions he invited others to sit on the bench with him. In *Te Kopo and E Pokai*, both charged with theft, Halswell allowed Turingha Kuri the 'Chief of Kai warra warra', to sit on the bench with him and to give his opinion on the matter,[71] while in *E Waho* both Bishop Selwyn (the first Anglican Bishop of New Zealand) and Moturoa (a Chief from the Wellington area) were invited to sit with him.[72] Similarly, by his own admission, in *Pakewa* 'several leading chiefs sat on the bench with me'.[73]

There is, in fact, little evidence of Māori being admitted as witnesses before the County Court without taking the oath. It may be that this happened before the Magistrate's Court, which was largely staffed by laypersons, but what records remain of County Court proceedings suggests that most Māori were sworn, either as Christians, or as believers in future punishment and reward. In *Lockwood*, for example, E. Hape told the court that:

> I am a missionary; I was induced to become a missionary because I believed in God, and that Christ was God; I know it to be wicked to tell lies, and if I do not speak the whole truth I shall be punished when I die.[74]

70   *R v Thompson*, 16 April 1844, County Court, Nelson, Halswell J, reported in *The Nelson Examiner and New Zealand Chronicle*, 20 April 1844, 3. There is no record of any referral of the matter to the Supreme Court.
71   *R v Te Kopo and E Pokai*, County Court, Wellington, Halswell J, 28 June 1842, reported in *New Zealand Gazette and Wellington Spectator*, 2 July 1842, 3.
72   *R v E Waho*, 19 December 1843, County Court, Wellington, Halswell J, reported in *New Zealand Gazette and Wellington Spectator*, 30 December 1843, 2; Journals of William Cotton, ATL, vol. 6, qMS-0566, entry for 19 December 1843, 39; Louis Ward, *Early Wellington* (Wellington: Whitcombe and Tombs, 1928), 125.
73   Halswell to Lord Lyttleton, 18 June 1846, in *Copies or Extracts of Correspondence between the Colonial Office and Mr Halswell, relating to the Discharge of his Duties whilst Protector of Aborigines in New Zealand*, ed. Barry Baldwin (House of Commons, London, 1846), 9. While Halswell does not mention the case, by description it must be *R v Pakewa*, Court of Quarter Sessions, Wellington, Halswell J (Chairman), 4 October 1841, reported in *New Zealand Gazette and Wellington Spectator*, 6 October 1841, 3; 9 October 1841, 3.
74   *R v Lockwood*, County Court, Wellington, Halswell J, 24 May 1842, reported in *New Zealand Gazette and Wellington Spectator*, 28 May 1842, 3.

Similarly, in *E Waho*, charged with stealing clothing, three witnesses, all Māori, appeared for the defence: Pomare, William E. Tako and Maria.[75] Pomare, who was described as 'Chief of the Chatham Islands' was examined by the court as to his belief in future rewards and punishments, while Maria described herself as a 'church of England missionary native'. William E. Tako (Wiremu Tako), the 'Chief of Kumu Toto', was also presumably sworn.[76]

Not only was the appearance of Māori as witnesses in trials reasonably common in the period, their failure to appear was commented on adversely on several occasions. In *R v Hastings*, a key witness, a Māori woman named Hannah, failed to turn up when called as witness. Halswell noted that this was the third case in which a Māori witness had not turned up and that two other cases had failed for this problem. While the defendant, Te Ito, gave evidence, it was insufficient in Hannah's absence to obtain a conviction. The impression is that Hastings was fortunate.[77] Similar comments were made by Halswell at the trial of Daniel Munroe.[78] Two Māori had informed the chief constable that they had received certain goods, found to be stolen, from Munroe in return for potatoes to eat. While two other witnesses were called, only the Māori witnesses could connect Munroe with the stolen goods. He was acquitted. Where possible, the courts would compel witnesses to appear.[79] However, *Munroe* is an example of how, in a limited way, Māori evidence could on occasion make its way before the courts, even in the absence of the witnesses themselves. In that case, the two pākehā witnesses recounted the story that they had been told by the missing Māori witnesses as to how they had acquired the stolen goods. Inclusion of these accounts in the trial was possible because the rule against hearsay did not emerge until later in the century, in part as a reaction by the courts to statutory reforms to competency.

---

75   *R v E Waho (Wahu, Awaho)*, County Court, Wellington, Halswell J, 19 December 1843, reported in *New Zealand Gazette and Wellington Spectator*, 30 December 1843, 2–3. E. Waho was committed in the Police Magistrates Court on 30 November 1843: *New Zealand Gazette and Wellington Spectator*, 6 December 1843, 3. Despite the prosecution calling ten pākehā witnesses, the jury initially returned a verdict of 'not guilty'. However, on being re-instructed by the judge the jury finally returned a guilty verdict.

76   A change in name can indicate that a particular Māori individual had been baptised or otherwise accepted Christianity, although it is by no means an entirely reliable indicator. There were many other reasons why Māori might adopt English names, and many Christian Māori who did not. Lyndsay Head notes that 'after conversion Māori were normally called by their baptismal name, which was usually an English or biblical name, transliterated into Māori'. The example she gives is that of Wi (or William/Wiremu) Tako (Lyndsay Head, 'Land, Authority and the Forgetting of Being in Early Colonial Maori History' (PhD thesis, University of Canterbury, 2006), 29). It is likely that Tako was a Christian in this period, and he died a Catholic. For more on Tako, see his obituary, *Evening Post*, 10 November 1887, 2.

77   *R v Hastings*, County Court, Halswell J, Wellington, 20 December 1843, reported in *New Zealand Gazette and Wellington Spectator*, 6 January 1844, 3.

78   *R v Daniel Munroe*, County Court, Halswell J, Wellington, 20 September 1843, reported in *New Zealand Gazette and Wellington Spectator*, 27 September 1843, 3.

79   At the inquest into the death of Archibald Milne the coroner, John Fitzgerald, was forced to adjourn proceedings and obtain a warrant to force Awaho to appear as a witness. *Milne*, 27 December 1841, Coroner's Court, Wellington, FitzGerald (Coroner) with Halswell and White JPs, reported in *New Zealand Gazette and Wellington Spectator*, 29 December 1841, 2.

Local law reform: The *Unsworn Testimony Ordinance* 1843

By the time the *Colonial Evidence Act* was passed, therefore, Māori had been giving evidence, at least before both the Land Claims Court and the regular courts, for over three years. The desirability, however, of further extending the ability of Māori to give unsworn testimony from the limited arena of the Land Claims Court to the general courts of the colony had been noted in a number of quarters. In July 1843, for example, the editor of the *New Zealand Gazette and Wellington Spectator*, commenting generally on the — as he saw it — fairly unimpressive legislative agenda of the Legislative Council, questioned why no ordinance had been passed to allow unsworn evidence? After all, it would be more immediately practicable than 'preparing enactments relating to "the rule in Shelley's Case" or "contingent remainders"'. He noted the necessity for such an ordinance as:

> [w]ithin the last six months, His Honor the Judge of the County Court of Wellington, did reject a Native witness because it appeared on examination that he did not acknowledge a Supreme being; but we understand that in other parts of this island the English rule of Law has been intrenched [sic] upon and such evidence admitted.[80]

The editor specifically noted that there was no excuse for such an omission, as such a provision was specifically provided for in the *Land Claims Ordinance*. Undoubtedly ignorant of the origins of that provision, and of the disallowance of the New South Wales *Aboriginal Evidence Act*, he sheeted home the failure to enact a local unsworn testimony ordinance to the change in attorney-general since the drafting of the *Land Claims Ordinance*.[81] In 1844 the editor of the *Wellington Spectator* returned to the matter and noted for the benefit of his readers that the imperial parliament had now enacted a measure to allow for pagan evidence to be admitted without oath, and that it was to be hoped that the governor and council would soon pass such a measure, as they understood that otherwise a gross crime might be committed in the presence of pagan Māori only, as it once could have been in England before Quakers.[82]

Almost immediately after the passing of the *Colonial Evidence Act*, Governor FitzRoy moved to enact a local measure, bringing the *Unsworn Testimony* bill

---

80   Editorial, *New Zealand Gazette and Wellington Spectator*, 26 July 1843, 3.
81   ibid. Francis Fisher, the first attorney-general, was appointed from Sydney as an interim measure, awaiting the arrival of William Swainson. Swainson was appointed attorney-general on 21 September 1841.
82   Editorial Note on the opening of a new session of the Supreme Court, *New Zealand Gazette and Wellington Spectator*, 1 May 1844, 3.

before the Legislative Council.[83] The imperial Act simply provided that the passing of any act or ordinance to make admissible in any Court of Justice the evidence of those who were 'destitute of the knowledge of God and of any religious Belief' would not be held null, void or invalid because thought repugnant.[84] Based on these words, and ignoring the clear limitation to 'tribes of barbarous and uncivilized People', Brown thought they could extend the reach of the Ordinance to all who had not had the benefit of religious education, a suggestion with which Sir Robert FitzRoy, Governor of New Zealand, at least initially agreed.[85] Brown, whose interpretations of the Act appear to have somewhat irritated William Swainson, the attorney-general (who noted that Mr Brown 'appears to have great confidence in this own judgment'), understood the Act to mean that if three or four persons whose opinion could not be trusted agreed on a thing that would 'establish a fact', and this could be so equally whether they were barbarian or white man who had not had the benefit of a religious education. Dr Martin agreed. That, however, was clearly beyond the licence of the imperial Act. The result was, therefore, as Brown pointed out, that the aborigines had the advantage of a while man in this regard.[86]

Mr Brown was correct in this regard. The *Colonial Evidence Act* was passed at a time when a range of reforms were being considered to the law of evidence. Throughout the nineteenth century generally, statutory reforms were introduced to widen the category of those who were competent, but such reforms were accompanied by the concurrent development by the courts of exclusionary rules of evidence. Reform took place in two waves: the first, 1828–54, was directed towards those who were incompetent because of defect of religious principle.[87] In 1828, statutory reform allowed Quakers and Morovians to affirm while, in 1833, similar reforms were introduced for Separatists.[88] Brougham also gave his famous speech on law reform in 1828. Among other reforms, he urged that the rules be relaxed to allow anyone who believed in a supreme being and future reward and punishment to affirm.[89] The second wave, in which reform was directed towards those with a lack of religious belief, was between 1854 and 1869.[90]

While proposals for a general right to affirm were placed before the British parliament as early as 1838, the broader matter of atheistic evidence took longer

---

83   *Unsworn Testimony Ordinance*, 7 Vic. No. 16 (1844).
84   *Colonial Evidence Ordinance* 6 Vic. c. 22 (1843) (Imp.), s. 1.
85   *The Southern Cross*, 13 July 1844, 3–4, reporting on the proceedings of the Legislative Council for Tuesday 9 July 1844.
86   ibid.
87   C.J.W. Allen, 'Bentham and the Abolition of Incompetency from Defect of Religious Principle', *The Journal of Legal History* 16 (1995): 172, 173.
88   9 George IV c.32; 3 & 4 William IV c. 82.
89   Henry Brougham, *A Speech on the Present State of the Law of the Country; delivered in the House of Commons, on Thursday, 7 Feb., 1828*, second edition (London: Henry Colburn, 1828), 4; Allen, 173.
90   Allen, 173.

to be addressed, and those with no religious belief were not finally permitted to give evidence until 1869.[91] Arguments against admitting evidence from unbelievers were diverse but, according to Allen, the most common opposition was based on a belief that to allow such evidence would be 'to loosen the bonds of society'. Religion was 'fundamental to morality' and even a key component of being a good citizen.[92] It was, in short, a component of the civilised society.

A second matter of contention before the Legislative Council was the matter of penalty for falsehood. Dr Martin was concerned that, as Māori would be subject to the same penalties as Europeans for swearing falsely, this might lead jurors to lend the same credit to their testimony as to evidence given on oath. Further, punishment 'would not make [Māori] moral characters; that they could not be compared with the Quakers, who gave their evidence on affirmation, it was not right to inflict the same punishment on the savage as the civilized Quaker'.[93] To the contrary, Charles Clifford thought Dr Samuel Martin's arguments to be reasons in favour of the bill: 'civilized men had a fear of society before their eyes, which could punish them in many ways; the savage had no such fear'. The governor agreed. Children found telling a falsehood could be corrected without regard to their weak intellect, and 'the uninformed savage was but a child of larger growth, but with more mature passions'. In any case, 'no definite punishment was mentioned'; it was to be left to the judge to determine the enormity of the offence if it could be proven that evidence had been given falsely and wilfully.[94] This was the more controversial matter. Allowing unsworn evidence by Māori excited no discernible opposition, but the matter of the ability of the 'uncivilized Māori' to recognise and attach importance to truth, and whether they should be punished in consequence, was doubted by several members of the council. Dr Martin insisted that the bill be altered and, while he might have argued out the matter, in the end the attorney-general's bill carried the day. All were in favour.[95] And with that New Zealand became the first colony to enact legislation to allow unsworn testimony before the courts.

91 *Evidence Further Amendment Act* 1869 (UK).
92 Allen, 179–81.
93 *The Southern Cross*, 13 July 1844, 3–4, reporting on the proceedings of the Legislative Council for Tuesday 9 July 1844.
94 ibid.
95 There was a third matter of contention, quickly dealt with. Was it possible to admit the evidence of natives of all countries, or just of those countries 'adjoining', as stated in the preamble? Based on the words of the preamble, this matter was settled in accordance with Swainson's interpretation that the scope be confined to those from adjoining colonies: ibid.

Conclusion

After the passing of the Ordinance, Māori continued to give evidence before all courts, but without the need to demonstrate a belief in future reward and punishment.[96] Unlike in New South Wales, where, despite the passing of the *Colonial Evidence Act*, Indigenous Australians remained unable to give evidence until 1876, the passage of the *Unsworn Testimony Ordinance* in New Zealand was not only without controversy, but welcomed in many quarters. This was not just because Māori had already been giving evidence before the Land Claims Court, but because of their place in settler society — many lived in towns, took part in commerce, were Christians and were literate. It would have been difficult to conduct day-to-day legal affairs in Auckland, Nelson or Wellington without involving Māori and impossible, in many cases, to secure conviction. In particular, of course, the very reason they could give evidence before the Land Claims Court was because without that evidence settlement simply could not have proceeded. The high level of interaction between Māori and pākehā in settlements like Wellington, so soon after Britain's acquisition of the colony, set New Zealand apart from the Australian colonies. The particular history of unsworn testimony in New Zealand serves to remind us that, beneath the broad legal frameworks of empire, the local micro-politics and the particular situation of the indigenous inhabitants led to very different and diverse outcomes.

Acknowledgments

My thanks to Megan Simpson, Damen Ward, Ned Fletcher, Brent Parker and Sam Ritchie. The usual disclaimer applies. Some of the materials in this article were recovered by the New Zealand Lost Cases Project. This project was funded by the New Zealand Law Foundation, and recovered Supreme Court cases, and contextual materials relating to those cases, from 1841–69. Source materials, cases and other general information are available at http://www.victoria.ac.nz/law/nzlostcases/

---

96   Before the Supreme Court see *R v William Johnson*, 1 March 1847, Martin CJ, reported in *New Zealander,* 6 March 1847, 3; Before the Resident Magistrate's Court (which replaced County Courts in 1846) see *R v Honeri, Rews and Ngatauhira*, 26 September 1949, Beckham JP, reported in *Daily Southern Cross*, 30 September 1859, 3.

II. Law in Community

Public Opinion, Private Remonstrance, and the Law: Protecting Animals in Australia, 1803–1914

Stefan Petrow

Introduction

Recent exposures of high rates of death aboard live animal export ships, and the 'abuse and torture' of animals in some Indonesian slaughterhouses have brought cruelty to animals to public prominence in modern Australia.[1] This mistreatment offends Australians' sense of what it means to be civilised, which is reflected in the fact that every Australian state and territory has passed complex and detailed laws declaring that the ill-treatment of animals is illegal.[2] These statutes affirm that 'humans have evolved to the point that they no longer regard animals as pure objects or things, able to be treated in any way they choose'.[3] As far as the statute law is concerned, society has expressed its 'collective choice' that anyone who subjects animals to pain, suffering or distress will be punished.[4] While these statutes are a necessary protection for animals, they are not sufficient to guarantee that animals are protected. Peter Sankoff has questioned whether the animal welfare paradigm can work effectively for other than 'extreme' cases of cruelty, which represent a small fraction of all the harm humans cause animals.[5] Much depends on the enforcement of the laws and, if a case makes it to court, on whether the pain or suffering is deemed reasonable and necessary. The courts rarely lay down in detail 'how the balancing test between necessity and animal harm should operate' and offenders often escape with lenient sentences.[6]

---

1   Malcolm Caulfield, 'Live Export of Animals', in *Animal Law in Australasia*, eds, Peter Sankoff and Steven White (Sydney: Federation Press, 2009), 153–73; Animals Australia, 'Cruel Cattle Exports to Indonesia Must Halt Immediately', press release 30 May 2011, http://www.animalsaustralia.org/media/press_releases. php?release=151 accessed 9 October 2011.
2   Deborah Cao, *Animal Law in Australia and New Zealand* (Sydney: Law Book Co., 2010).
3   Sankoff, 'The Welfare Paradigm: Making the World a Better Place for Animals?', in Sankoff and White, 14.
4   Mike Radford, *Animal Welfare Law in Britain: Regulation and Responsibility* (Oxford University Press, 2001), 11.
5   Sankoff, 16.
6   Sankoff, 18.

Mike Radford has argued that in Britain an understanding of the evolution of the legal protection of animals is 'essential for understanding the contemporary law'.[7] This assessment also rings true for Australia, where the continuities are more striking than the discontinuities. Despite nearly 200 years of animal protection laws in Australia, enforcement remains 'alarmingly inadequate' and the number of cases reaching the courts is small.[8] Only cases where the evidence is clear-cut are prosecuted and so most offenders plead guilty, leaving 'little case law ... to assist in future interpretation of the law'. Most of the small number of cases that are defended tend to involve factual and not legal issues. Commonly found terms in statutes such as 'unnecessary' or 'unreasonable' are applied on a case-by-case basis, depend on the interpretation of individual judges and magistrates, and give 'little idea of what actually constitutes permissible conduct'. Annabel Markham notes that, despite the trend of recent legislation to impose heavier penalties, increased severity did not result 'in any significant change in sentence levels' and 'moderate fines remain the norm'.[9] Researchers studying the operation of current statutes question 'whether the protections afforded by the legislation are more symbolic than real'.

The detection of animal cruelty is difficult and typically prosecutions depend, not on the police or other government agents, but on the work of the 84 Royal Society for the Prevention of Cruelty to Animal (RSPCA) inspectors Australia-wide, who investigated 53,544 complaints of cruelty and neglect involving 'farm animals, companion animals, pets and wildlife' in 2009–10.[10] The inspectors possess 'wide-ranging powers' and can enter and search premises, seize animals and relieve animal suffering.[11] Despite such powers, the RSPCA prosecuted only 247 cases, or about 0.46 per cent, of all the complaints its inspectors investigated and, of those cases, 185, or about 75 per cent, resulted in convictions, a high success rate due to 'a very high proportion of guilty pleas'.[12] Despite the high success rate, courts rarely impose custodial sentences even though only serious cases are prosecuted and usually in cases involving 'extreme violence', often verging on sadism.[13] Most offenders are fined 'modest' sums and thus receive 'the least severe sentencing option'. More severe non-custodial sentences such as community service or work orders are infrequently imposed. Orders prohibiting an offender from keeping an animal for a specified period or permanently, which are suitably punitive for repeat offenders, appear not to be used extensively,

---

7   Radford, 94.
8   Sankoff, 18–20.
9   Annabel Markham, 'Animal Cruelty Sentencing in Australia and New Zealand', in Sankoff and White, 290.
10   RSPCA web site at http://www.rspca.org.au/what-we-do/inspectorate.html and annual statistics at http://www.rspca.org.au/resources/ accessed 9 October 2011.
11   Cao, 172.
12   RSPCA, annual statistics; Cao, 174.
13   Markham, 294–96.

but more research is needed to verify that observation.[14] In short, inadequate sentencing practices undermine the power of statute law to protect animals and reinforce the traditional legal status of animals as 'property and not living, sentient beings'.[15] The history of animal protection law reveals this pattern.

Laws protecting animals were first passed in 1837 in Van Diemen's Land, gradually spread to the other colonies in the 1840s, were extended in the 1860s, early 1900s and 1920s, and were revised in the 1950s and the 1980s in all states.[16] While the level of research into historical cases of cruelty remains limited, it appears that relatively few cases of animal cruelty were prosecuted before the 1870s and, if they were, the courts held almost from their establishment that 'the protection of the animal was always legally invisible next to the primary issue of animal possession'.[17] No one took responsibility for prosecuting animal cruelty cases systematically until Societies for the Prevention of Cruelty to Animals (SPCA) were formed in Victoria, New South Wales and Tasmania in the 1870s. But as is the case with contemporary Australia, the percentage of complaints investigated by SPCA inspectors compared with the amount of cruelty practiced was small, the number of cases prosecuted in proportion to the cases investigated was also small, and the courts rarely imposed severe penalties on those offenders found guilty of cruelty. Circumscribed by limited resources, the SPCA also relied on educating public opinion to be kind to animals and remonstrating with individuals who mistreated animals to complement their prosecution of extreme cases of cruelty or recalcitrant owners. After 1900 the SPCA began to feel that the law was not effective in fundamentally changing human behaviour and turned more to education as their main weapon against cruelty. In this chapter, these generalisations will be supported by an examination of the operation of the law in Tasmania between 1803 and 1914, concentrating on the period from 1878 when the SPCA began its work of stamping out cruelty in Tasmania.

British developments influenced the reactions of the Australian colonies to animal cruelty and an overview of those developments follows. The law loomed large in efforts to stop brutality in Britain from the passing of the groundbreaking *Cruelty to Animals Act* in 1822 and the passing of many more laws thereafter expanding the definition of cruelty and making punishment more severe.[18] Although there was 'educational and symbolic value in getting kindness to animals incorporated into the law', animals did not gain 'more power' or 'more freedom', and much hinged on effective law enforcement to restrict

---

14   Cao, 176.

15   K. Sharman, 'Sentencing Under Our Anti-Cruelty Statutes: Why Our Leniency Will Come Back to Bite Us', *Current Issues in Criminal Justice* 13 (2002): 334.

16   Philip Jamieson, 'Animal Welfare: A Movement in Transition', in *Law and History: A Collection of Papers Presented at the 1989 Law and History Conference*, ed., Suzanne Corcoran (University of Adelaide, 1989): 24.

17   B. Salter, 'Possess or Protect? Exploring the Legal Status of Animals in Australia's First Colonial Courts: Part 1, The Unnatural Theft and Murder', *Australian Animal Protection Law Journal* 2 (2009): 40.

18   The various statutes passed in Britain are discussed in Radford, 33–89.

human misuse of their dominion over animals.[19] The SPCA was established in 1824 (becoming the Royal SPCA in 1840) to ensure that the law was rigorously enforced, especially against the 'visible ill-treatment' of horses on urban streets; the SPCA wanted to stop cruelty from being encouraged by bad example.[20] Michael Roberts is right to point out that initially the RSPCA was 'divided on the legitimacy and social effects of law enforcement as a policy' and sought to gain 'educational publicity via example-setting rather than tighter policing as an end in itself'.[21] After overcoming initial jealousy and suspicion, the RSPCA secured the co-operation of magistrates and the police, to support the work of its own paid inspectors and, by the 1840s, 'the principle of legislation to protect animals from cruelty had been firmly established'.[22] The RSPCA was one of the few important pressure groups that 'consistently collaborated with the authorities' and this resulted in increased convictions for cruelty by 1901.[23] Most RSPCA prosecutions were of working men because their cruelty was the most visible and its officers were prevented from entering 'private places' because of 'the sacredness of alleged rights of the citizen, the domicile and of private property'.[24]

In the second half of the nineteenth century, some animal protectionists again questioned whether using the law was the most effective way to change behaviour and warned against the dangers of infringing individual liberty by extreme legislation.[25] By the 1860s, education to reinforce prosecution had become an increasingly important part of the RSPCA's program.[26] It aimed to familiarise people with the nature of animal mistreatment and to engender kindness towards animals, but also to persuade onlookers to intervene and stop cruelty. Special efforts were made by the many female members of the RSPCA to educate children in schools and through the Band of Mercy movement.[27] From 1865 churches helped to educate their parishioners with sermons on Animal Sundays.[28] The RSPCA skilfully mobilised 'the general public's enthusiasm and even, on occasion, its sentimentality in defence of animals'.[29] Despite the perseverance and courage of animal protection enthusiasts, the struggle to

---

19   Brian Harrison, *Peaceable Kingdom: Stability and Change in Modern Britain* (Oxford: Clarendon Press, 1982), 121; John Passmore, 'The Treatment of Animals', *Journal of the History of Ideas* 36 (1975): 212.

20   Harriet Ritvo, *The Animal Estate: The English and Other Creatures in the Victorian Age* (Cambridge: Harvard University Press, 1987), 138, 146; Hilda Kean, *Animal Rights: Political and Social Change in Britain Since 1800* (London: Reaktion, 1998), 37, 50, 80.

21   M.J.D. Roberts, *Making English Morals: Voluntary Associations and Moral Reform in England, 1787–1886* (Cambridge University Press, 2004), 135.

22   Radford, 61.

23   Harrison, 83, 93, 111, 146–50.

24   Radford, 84.

25   Kean, 35.

26   Ritvo, 147; Harrison, 129.

27   Kean, 46; Arthur W. Moss, *Valiant Crusade: The History of the R.S.P.C.A.* (London: Cassell, 1961), 196–98.

28   Moss, 205–06.

29   Harrison, 108, 114, 117.

change cultural attitudes to animals never gained full acceptance and faced ridicule and resentment, evasion and resistance, especially amongst the poor whose recreations and livelihoods they attacked.[30]

The 'civilizing mission' of middle-class reformers in Britain was 'exported to the colonies' and found its 'most telling expression' in the formation of animal protection societies 'devoted to notions of progress towards a higher state of civilization'.[31] The key decade for the formation of animal protection societies in the Australian colonies was the 1870s, when four were formed.[32] By the 1870s tolerance of cruelty and immoral behaviour generally had greatly lessened in the Australian colonies and the debate over vivisection in Britain renewed interest in animal protection. The next section explores the changing attitudes to cruelty in Tasmania from the 1820s to the 1870s.

Changing attitudes to cruelty in Tasmania

Settled as Australia's second colony in 1803, Tasmania began life as the island penal colony of Van Diemen's Land and gained a reputation for brutality in the treatment of convicts and the Indigenous population.[33] British settlers to the island had been accustomed to be cruel to animals and 'the dominion of man' was reinforced by the freedom of all classes to hunt native animals for sport and food.[34] In 1826 the *Colonial Times* railed against the 'inhumanity' with which horses, oxen and other animals were treated in Van Diemen's Land.[35] Each day settlers saw 'the most brutal instances of ferocity' practised on public streets by both free arrivals and convicts. The *Colonial Times* advocated the enactment of legislation for the prevention of cruelty to animals. In 1832 this call was supported by the editor of *The Independent*, who, in Launceston, daily observed 'lamentable scenes of cruelty too shocking to relate'.[36]

No legislation was passed and cruelty continued to attract newspaper attention. In 1834 a man was seen hitting his horse's head repeatedly with the butt of his whip and, when passers-by remonstrated with him to stop, he replied that 'the

---

30   Ritvo, 166; Kathleen Kete, 'Animals and Ideology: The Politics of Animal Protection in Europe', in *Representing Animals*, ed., Nigel Rothfels (Bloomington: Indiana University Press, 2002), 27.

31   Dorothee Brantz, 'The Domestication of Empire: Human-Animal Relations at the Intersection of Civilization, Evolution, and Acclimatization', in *A Cultural History of Animals in an Age of Empire*, ed., Kathleen Kete (Oxford: Berg, 2007), 75, 79.

32   *Daily News*, 22 June 1878, 3; T. Bonyhady, *The Colonial Earth* (Melbourne: Miegunyah Press, 2000), 154.

33   Lloyd Robson, *A Short History of Tasmania*, updated by Michael Roe, 2nd ed. (Melbourne: Oxford University Press, 1997).

34   David Young, *Sporting Island: A History of Sport and Recreation in Tasmania* (Hobart: Sport and Recreation, Tasmania, 2005), 1–4.

35   *Colonial Times and Tasmanian Advertiser*, 24 March 1826, 3; 17 November 1826, 3.

36   *Independent* (Launceston), 11 February 1832, 2.

horse was his own, and he could do as he pleased with it'.[37] Such conduct 'can never be endured in a Christian country', where no man had 'a right to violate the laws of humanity by torturing any animal, because it is his property', declared the *Colonial Times*. While Lieutenant-Governor George Arthur showed no interest in dealing with animal cruelty, his successor Sir John Franklin was more temperamentally attuned to suffering of all kinds, whether human or animal. Soon after his arrival in Van Diemen's Land in 1837, Franklin travelled around the island and must have seen examples of mistreatment of animals.[38] He was also presumably aware of the enactment of new British legislation in 1835 against 'cruel and improper treatment'. Whatever his motives, Franklin passed the first legislation in Australian history to prevent cruelty to animals, The Prevention of Cruelty to Animals Act, in 1837, extending to Van Diemen's Land some of the provisions of the 1835 Act, known as Pease's Act.[39]

Philip Jamieson calls the 1837 Act 'a pale reflection' of Pease's British Act.[40] Few prosecutions were brought under the 1837 legislation possibly because, as the Chief Police Magistrate Matthew Forster suggested when the bill was debated, of 'the difficulty of determining what was cruelty'.[41] Moreover, the police were too preoccupied with other offences to pay much attention to animal cruelty.[42] Cock-fighting and, to some extent, dog-fighting remained popular pastimes for the convict classes at least.[43] In 1848 the *Britannia and Trades Advocate* thought that the prevention of cruelty legislation was not 'generally known' and noted 'the brutal indifference' with which men and some women treated their domestic animals.[44] To show kindness and consideration to animals was held to be 'a proof of weakness, and a fair subject of ridicule'. The newspaper declared that cruelty to animals was carried out to 'a greater extent' in Van Diemen's Land than 'we have witnessed in any other part of the *civilized* world'. It noted the absence of lectures, sermons or instructions to teach young boys and girls 'to feel kindly' towards animals.[45] The *Britannia and Trades Advocate* blamed women for allowing dogs to be deprived of water and food. It was 'unwomanly' to leave dogs 'pining with thirst, tied to a stake, with scarcely room to turn'. It urged teachers to educate their students to be kind to animals and the police

---

37 *Colonial Times*, 11 February 1834, 4.
38 Kathleen Fitzpatrick, *Sir John Franklin in Tasmania 1837–1843* (Melbourne University Press, 1949), 117–18.
39 Franklin to Glenelg, 4 December 1837, Colonial Office 280/81, 125, Despatch 128, Australian Joint Copying Project, National Library of Australia; Jamieson, 22.
40 Jamieson, 22.
41 *Hobart Town Courier*, 21 July 1837, 4; for examples of prosecutions see *Cornwall Chronicle*, 30 January 1841, 2; *Launceston Courier*, 15 March 1841, 2 and Jamieson, 22.
42 *Launceston Advertiser*, 26 October 1844, 3; Stefan Petrow, 'After Arthur: Policing in Van Diemen's Land 1837–1846', in *Policing the Lucky Country*, eds, M. Enders and B. Dupont (Sydney: Federation Press, 2001), 176–98.
43 Young, 17–18, 45.
44 *Britannia and Trades Advocate*, 24 August 1848, 4, emphasis in original.
45 *Britannia and Trades Advocate*, 15 November 1849, 4.

to enforce the 1837 Act. Individual citizens could also prosecute for cruelty, but this was even less common than police prosecutions.[46] As in contemporary Australia, much animal cruelty went uninvestigated and unpunished.

Further legislation had to wait until after self-government was introduced to Tasmania in 1856. Tasmania's leading animal protectionist, the writer Louisa Anne Meredith, was 'the prime mover in having Acts passed for the protection of wildlife'.[47] For example, she persuaded her politician husband Charles to introduce legislation protecting black swans and this was passed in 1860.[48] Other legislation was passed in the 1860s and 1870s to protect native game and birds either during the breeding season or at all times. Section 83 of the *Police Act 1865* imposed a £5 fine for anyone caught 'fighting, baiting or worrying' animals, but attracted no comment in the House of Assembly.[49] This was a common provision in police legislation and did not represent any particular concerns in the community.[50] It appears that this legislation was rarely enforced and dogfighting, dog worrying and cockfighting were 'passively suffered' by the police, especially on Sunday afternoons, until at least 1880.[51] In June 1886 a correspondent called 'Viator' told *Mercury* readers that 'insensibility to animal suffering in the Australian colonies' was worse than in 'more densely populated countries of the world'.[52] In Tasmania, with its experience of 'the awful cruelties of the convict era, it seems strange that cruelty to animals, tenfold more horrible and widespread, should be regarded with complacent apathy'.

Some Tasmanians found apathy increasingly intolerable and wanted to distance the colony from the cruelty and brutality of the penal past.[53] Kay Daniels has characterised the three decades from 1860 to 1890 as a 'period of transition in Tasmanian history from penal settlement to "civilized" society', by which she means a 'free community, increasingly dominated by the values of the middle class'.[54] These values included sexual purity and restraint, honesty, decency and respect for property and person. During this period, the middle class demanded an end to violence, idleness and criminality, the hallmarks of convictism, and

---

46   For a private prosecution that resulted in conviction see *Hobarton Guardian*, 7 December 1853, 3.

47   Vivienne Rae-Ellis, *Louisa Anne Meredith: A Tigress in Exile* (Hobart: St. David's Park Publishing, 1990), 184.

48   Louisa Anne Meredith, *Tasmanian Friends and Foes, Feathered, Furred, and Finned: A Family Chronicle of Country Life, Natural History and Veritable Adventure* (London: Marcus Ward, 1881), 158–59.

49   *Mercury*, 2 September 1865, 3.

50   Philip Jamieson, 'Duty and the Beast: The Movement in Reform of Animal Welfare Law', *University of Queensland Law Journal* 16 (1990–91): 241–42.

51   *Mercury*, 15 September 1880, 2.

52   Letter by 'Viator', *Mercury*, 23 June 1886, 3.

53   For a snapshot of the penal system see Robert Hughes, *The Fatal Shore: A History of the Transportation of Convicts to Australia 1787–1868* (London: Pan Books, 1988), 368–424.

54   Kay Daniels, 'Prostitution in Tasmania during the Transition from Penal Settlement to "Civilized" Society', in *So Much Hard Work: Women and Prostitution in Australian Society*, ed., Kay Daniels (Sydney: Fontana, 1984), 23, 49.

worked through many religious and benevolent institutions for the creation of a more respectable society.[55] This transition was especially obvious in Hobart where, in the 1870s, middle-class Protestant moral reformers demanded that the municipal police force (established in 1858) impose order on the streets by suppressing prostitution, ruffianism and juvenile delinquency and enforcing the liquor licensing laws.[56]

As part of their mission to transform Hobart into a civilised society, middle-class humanitarians also demanded in the 1870s that official action be taken to stop violence against animals. Criticism was directed at the municipal police for ignoring 'scenes of brutality' that regularly occurred on Hobart streets by licensed cabmen and owners of coaches who ill-treated their horses.[57] Animal protectionists thought that the modernisation of the law was urgently needed to stamp out such behaviour. They had an ally in the House of Assembly in the Fingal farmer William St Paul Gellibrand. Gellibrand's sister, Mary Selina Gellibrand, became a stalwart of the Tasmanian Society for the Protection of Cruelty to Animals (TSPCA) and no doubt urged her brother to introduce the Prevention of Cruelty to Animals Bill in October 1877, which extended 'the principles' of the *British Prevention of Cruelty to Animals Act 1849* to Tasmania.[58] William Gellibrand noted that similar legislation in Victoria, New Zealand and Queensland had worked 'remarkably well'.[59] The bill was well received in the assembly and passed without amendment. In the Legislative Council only one member opposed the bill and it was passed with minor amendments.[60]

The *Prevention of Cruelty to Animals Act 1877* repealed the 1837 Act. It sought to protect horses, cattle, donkeys, sheep, pigs, goats, cats, dogs and other domestic animals from being 'cruelly and unnecessarily' flogged, beaten, overdriven, overridden, overloaded, abused, tortured or otherwise ill-treated.[61] Offenders who were found guilty of such offences could be fined up to £10 in a court of summary jurisdiction. But enforcement remained lax and complaints of cruelty regularly appeared in the press.[62] It became clear that a SPCA was needed to give 'practical effect to the law'.[63] The cause was spurred on in July 1878 by an act of 'awful barbarity' when boys in Upper Goulburn Street exposed 'a helpless

55   Peter Bolger, *Hobart Town* (Canberra: Australian National University Press, 1973), 135–193.
56   Stefan Petrow, 'Arabs, Boys and Larrikins: Juvenile Delinquents and their Treatment in Hobart, 1860–1896', *Australian Journal of Legal History* 2 (1996): 37–59 and 'Creating an Orderly Society: The Hobart Municipal Police 1880–1898', *Labour History* no. 75 (1998): 175–94.
57   Letter by 'Nec Timeo Nec Sperno', *Mercury*, 18 February 1875, 2.
58   Weld to Carnarvon, 21 December 1877, Despatch 59, Colonial Office 280/384, 356, National Library of Australia, Australian Joint Copying Project.
59   *Mercury*, 31 October 1877, 3.
60   *Mercury*, 7 November 1877, 2; 9 November 1877, 3.
61   *Mercury*, 17 May 1878, 3.
62   Letter by 'Englishman', 24 May 1878, 3; Letter by 'Justice', *Mercury*, 3 June 1878, 3, 3.
63   Letter by 'Justice', *Mercury*, 3 June 1878, 3; *Mercury*, 15 July 1878, 2; *Third Annual Report of the TSPCA* (Hobart: TSPCA, 1881), 8.

cat to the worrying of dogs', and then slowly 'roasted the mutilated, suffering creature to death'.[64] Public pressure forced the police to prosecute one of the boys, Michael Maguire, for throwing the cat on the fire and he was fined £5. Cruelty would continue, asserted the *Mercury*, unless citizens joined together in 'a corporate body for the inculcation of the principles of humanity and the strongest punishment of all forms of barbarity'. This case was the motivation for 'a small band' of animal lovers to form a local SPCA, which became the most prominent and influential pressure group in late-nineteenth-century Tasmania and led the 'crusade against the vice and brutality of the oppression of animal life'.[65]

On 19 July 1878 a crowded public meeting, chaired by Governor Frederick Weld, formed the TSPCA.[66] Royal endorsement by Queen Victoria had strengthened support for the British SPCA and Weld's presence as the Queen's representative gave the local cause 'social standing and legitimacy'.[67] The leading speakers highlighted man's duty to 'brute creation'. Sir James Wilson, member for Hobart in the Legislative Council, thought that they should put down cruelty with 'the strong arm of the law as an example to all … evil doers'. The religious motivation behind the TSPCA's formation was illustrated by Dean H.B. Bromby, who stressed that prevention of cruelty was 'holy work' and constituted 'one of the foundations of Christianity'. Teaching the young to be kind to animals had social benefits: they would in later years 'possess many of the elements of nobility and betray a more considerate tenderness, more moral courage and a more chivalrous bearing towards others'.[68] The premier, W.R. Giblin, thought that the TSPCA was evidence of 'the growth of a vigorous and healthy sentiment in the colony'.[69] Cruelty stemmed from 'the assertion of a sense of dominion over the brute creation', but Giblin thought that few humans were 'fit to be entrusted with the absolute dominion of any living thing' and the TSPCA would check 'the abuse of this possession of powers to ill-treat'.

The new society had two main aims. The prime objective was to excite and sustain 'an intelligent public opinion regarding man's duty to animals'.[70] The other major aim was 'to prevent cruelty to animals by enforcing, where practicable, the existing laws' and to seek new legislation when 'expedient'. The TSPCA's first annual report clearly stated that 'prevention and not punishment

---

64   *Mercury*, 15 July 1878, 2; 19 July 1878, 2.
65   C.E. Walch, *The Story of the Life of Charles Edward Walch, with a Selection of His Writings* (Hobart: J. Walch and Sons, 1908), lxxii; *Mercury*, 2 August 1887, 3.
66   *Mercury*, 20 July 1878, 2.
67   Radford, 47.
68   Bromby's speech was printed in full from the reporter's notes, see *Mercury*, 30 July 1878, 3 and drew criticism for being 'a combination of fallacies' (Letter by J.L. Livingston, see *Mercury*, 2 August 1878, 3).
69   *Mercury*, 20 July 1878, 2.
70   ibid.

was the end to be attained'.[71] If remonstrance by 'word or by letter' did not work and the law was persistently broken, then the perpetrator was prosecuted. But the TSPCA strongly believed that, 'To educate to right thinking and right acting is a method more potent for good than to punish for wrong-doing'. After one year's work and 30 prosecutions, of which 25 resulted in convictions, the TSPCA thought it had demonstrated the need for active supervision of animals and that its aims were not 'Quixotic, wasting its resources and energies upon the impracticable'.[72] The TSPCA described its work as 'coercive persuasion'.[73] No prosecution was undertaken without seeking the opinion of leading lawyer John Mitchell, who was the society's honorary legal adviser.[74] In subsequent annual reports, the TSPCA continued to remind fellow colonists of its guiding principles that 'kindness of rebuke and remonstrance' was appropriate for offenders who were 'young and thoughtless, or poor and struggling', but warned that 'strict justice' would be applied to 'the wilfully cruel and cowardly'.[75]

Inspired by Meredith's move to that city, a branch of the SPCA was founded in Launceston in August 1879.[76] One of the founders, Anglican archdeacon Francis Hales, declared that they had not formed 'a prosecuting society' but 'an educating society'.[77] Their aim should be to teach labourers and children that they had a 'duty' to treat animals 'kindly' from 'a sense of their responsibility to their Creator who formed them both'. Most cruelty arose from 'thoughtlessness' and, by helping people 'to understand the sufferings they thus inflict', the society 'might rank next to Christianity as a means of developing the highest moral instincts'. Betraying a dislike for the increasingly inquisitorial actions of the Hobart-based society, the *Launceston Examiner* hoped that the Launceston branch would seek rather 'to persuade than to coerce' and warned that the community 'will not tolerate a system of espionage that may become an engine of persecution'.[78] The branch should 'foster habits of gentleness and consideration among all social classes of the community and especially to encourage them amongst the young'.[79] The branch must not infringe 'individual liberty' when doing its legitimate work.

The Launceston branch, having absorbed the message, stressed in its first annual report that it had avoided exercising 'over much zeal at the outset' lest it antagonise the community and not gain public support.[80] Indeed, its proceedings

---

71 *Mercury*, 19 July 1879, 2.
72 ibid.
73 *Mercury*, 8 August 1879, 2.
74 *Mercury*, 3 September 1878, 2.
75 *Second Annual Report of the TSPCA* (Hobart: TSPCA, 1880), 7.
76 Rae-Ellis, 216.
77 *Launceston Examiner*, 21 August 1879, 3.
78 *Launceston Examiner*, 11 September 1879, 2.
79 *Launceston Examiner*, 16 September 1879, 2.
80 *Launceston Examiner*, 22 September 1880, supplement, 1.

were characterised by 'such cautious discretion' that many supporters thought it was 'somewhat too conciliatory'. In most cases 'careful enquiry' was followed by 'an earnest remonstrance' to an offender and, as many cruelties arose from 'thoughtlessness, custom or gross ignorance', this was sufficient to stop cruelty. But some members thought that punishment was necessary in 'extreme or obstinate cases'.[81] For example a 'thoroughly brutal' master who overloaded, flogged or starved his horse would not be 'converted to humanity by soft words only'. The branch willingly sought to punish anyone who 'persistently' disregarded 'the voice of mercy'.[82] But the Launceston branch operated intermittently. In about 1885 it virtually disappeared from public view until it was reorganised in 1892, and then disappeared again around 1906 and was not reorganised until 1923.[83] The lack of continuity weakened its effectiveness and the law was a dead letter when the society lapsed. The next section will examine how the SPCA went about its work in Tasmania, with special emphasis on the more active Hobart branch.

Public opinion, private remonstrance and prosecution 1878–1904

Immediately after its formation, the TSPCA set about making the Tasmanian public aware of the reason for its existence. The society realised that many people, and even the police, were unaware of the new Act and printed placards and posters outlining the society's aims and sections of the Act, which were circulated in town and country.[84] The press, especially the *Mercury*, was a useful ally in spreading the aims of the TSPCA and denouncing cruelty to animals.[85] The *Mercury* supported the TSPCA because it brought Tasmania 'into the fold of European humanity'.[86]

A crucial step in building caring public attitudes towards animals was to exert influence in day and Sunday schools.[87] The TSPCA believed that 'among the young — the coming men and women of our community — rests the most hopeful part of the society's operations'.[88] The TSPCA sought to bring into action 'the divinely implanted instincts of tenderness and love, and pity which are latent

---

81   Letter by 'M', *Launceston Examiner*, 30 October 1880, 3.
82   *Examiner*, 9 October 1900, 7.
83   *Launceston Examiner*, 20 August 1892, 4; Minute book, SPCA, Launceston, 21 June 1923, NS870/1/1, Tasmanian Archives and Heritage Office (TAHO), Hobart.
84   *Mercury*, 24 July 1878, 3.
85   *Mercury*, 27 August 1878, 2.
86   *Mercury*, 21 October 1878, 2.
87   *Mercury*, 27 August 1878, 2.
88   *Mercury*, 19 July 1881, 3.

in every child'.[89] Following the Victorian system, the society invited the public schools in Hobart and some schools in the country to join its Scholar's Branch and pay a fee of one penny per year per child.[90] Essay competitions were held yearly on the subject of 'man's duty to animals'. Meredith hoped that writing essays on such topics would help develop in students 'a keener perception of what is beautiful and lovable in animal nature' and that the children would note 'with gentler sympathy and sharper censure any act of cruelty they may encounter'.[91] In addition to the Scholar's Branch in the schools, the TSPCA encouraged the formation of Bands of Mercy, comprised of children living in a particular district.[92] The wife of the governor, Lady Teresa Hamilton called the members of bands 'soldiers, bound to stand shoulder to shoulder in the cause of mercy'.[93]

By August 1887, 24 schools and Bands of Mercy had affiliated with the TSPCA and over 2000 children had become members, pledging themselves to prevent 'suffering or oppression'.[94] The Board of Education agreed to tell teachers about the aims of the TSPCA.[95] Sunday Schools were asked to urge 'kindness to animals upon the attention of their scholars' and four had joined by July 1882.[96] Following the 'exact discipline' of the RSPCA, funds obtained from fines were not used for general running expenses or the inspector's salary, but were used to pay for literature for the Scholar's Branch.[97] A legacy of £100 was devoted to pay for awards for essay prizewinners.[98] Numbers for the Launceston branch are harder to divine but, by September 1880, over 700 children had enrolled in the Scholar's Branch.[99] Complementing the work of the Launceston SPCA was the branch of the English Dicky Bird Society, which urged children through the columns of the *Tasmanian* to protect native birds and had 1680 members throughout Tasmania by 1892.[100]

Another crucial way in which SPCA branches spread their message was through the work of the key officer, the inspector. In Hobart, the first inspector was George Stuart, the visiting officer of the Board of Education, who was employed

89   *Mercury*, 2 December 1885, 3.
90   *Mercury*, 19 October 1878, 2; *Mercury*, 19 July 1879, 2.
91   *Launceston Examiner*, 9 June 1880, 2.
92   *Mercury*, 2 December 1885, 3.
93   *Mercury*, 6 October 1890, 4.
94   *Mercury*, 2 August 1882, supplement, 1; *Mercury*, 2 August 1887, 3.
95   Press reports of meetings, March 1880, NS 647/1/4, TAHO.
96   *Mercury*, 11 October 1879, 3; *Fourth Annual Report of the TSPCA* (Hobart: TSPCA, 1882), 11.
97   *Mercury*, 15 July 1880, 3; Letter by M.S. Gellibrand, *Mercury*, 2 April 1891, 3.
98   *Second Annual Report of the TSPCA*, 8.
99   *Launceston Examiner*, 22 September 1880, supplement, 1.
100   Will Mooney, 'Farmers' Foes or "Feathered Police"? Native Birds, Agriculture and the "Balance of Nature": Tasmania and Australia c. 1860 to 1920', *Tasmanian Historical Research Association Papers and Proceedings* 58, no. 2 (2011): 166; *Tasmanian*, 11 October 1890, 4.

until July 1880 when retired police sergeant Patrick Duggan was appointed.[101] Duggan was 'an esteemed ex-member of the force' and his appointment was expected to improve co-operation with the police. Duggan remained the society's inspector until his death in September 1895 when another ex-policeman, Robert Large, was appointed to the position. The inspectors visited various workplaces where livestock were used or housed, such as the wharves, stables, quarries, the railway station, cabstands, public pounds and sale yards. Duggan gave much attention to the municipal slaughter yards and ensured that sheep had not been deprived of food and water.[102] The TSPCA also warned against 'the scalding of pigs before quite lifeless' and strove to exercise its powers 'to secure the merciful slaying of stock'.[103] The inspectors traversed Hobart and surrounding suburbs and districts warning citizens to treat their animals kindly. Duggan extended his supervision beyond the suburbs of Hobart to Glenorchy, Brighton and Bridgewater to the north, Bellerive and Sorell to the east, and Huonville to the south.[104] To Duggan's 'unwearied industry, discretion and courtesy, the cause of humanity owes its strongest support', asserted the TSPCA annual report of 1884.[105] Large was equally conscientious in his work and remained the inspector until his death in 1930.[106]

In Launceston, Meredith was disappointed at the lack of action by the municipal police and advocated appointing an inspector to enquire into and report on cases of cruelty.[107] In November 1880 ex-soldier and policeman William Sessions was appointed and was sent to Hobart for a week to be tutored in his duties by Duggan.[108] Sessions proved his worth after one year. In his supervision of the streets, wharves, railway stations and sale yards he detected cases of mistreatment and his work had 'a preventive influence'.[109] When Sessions retired due to ill health in August 1883, the TSPCA chose another ex-soldier and former Corporation of Glasgow employee Alexander Kirkland to be its inspector.[110] From about 1893 a series of short-term and part-time appointments filled the position of inspector with the help of some members who acted as honorary inspectors.[111] Declining support left the branch without an inspector from about 1900 to 1914, but its work was carried on by developing closer

---

101 *Mercury*, 8 August 1878, 2; 15 August 1878, 2; 15 July 1880, 3; *Second Annual Report of the TSPCA*, 7; *Mercury*, 11 November 1880, 3; 14 September 1895, 4; 24 September 1895, 2.
102 *Mercury*, 5 February 1881, 3; 13 June 1882, 3; 2 December 1885, 3.
103 *Mercury*, 9 December 1884, 3.
104 Press reports of meetings, 10 August 1881, NS 647/1/4, TAHO.
105 *Sixth Annual Report of the TSPCA* (Hobart: TSPCA, 1884), 6.
106 *Mercury*, 25 November 1930, 6.
107 *Launceston Examiner*, 30 September 1880, 2; 3 November 1880, 3.
108 *Mercury*, 29 December 1880, 3.
109 *Launceston Examiner*, 14 December 1881, 3.
110 *Launceston Examiner*, 7 September 1883, 2.
111 *Launceston Examiner*, 22 August 1894, 7; 1 October 1895, 7; 1 October 1897, 5.

relations with the police and state schools.[112] The police prosecuted those who disregarded 'the voice of mercy', but they too put more effort into spreading 'a more intelligent conception of man's responsibilities' to animals.

The inspectors registered the names of anyone found guilty of cruelty and kept a record of cautions and remonstrances.[113] They initially tried 'every power of private remonstrance before resorting to publicity and punishment'.[114] This was shown in the way in which inspectors dealt with the treatment of horses, to which most of their efforts were directed. At first, Stuart tried to persuade individual owners to rest injured or tired horses. He advised owners not to turn the hose on horses 'heated and exhausted by fatiguing work', which damaged their health.[115] He advised cab owners that clipping horses in cold weather deprived them of 'the protection of their winter coats'. Some owners reprimanded their workers for mistreating horses and thanked Stuart for his information.[116] In June 1879 Gellibrand reported that the society investigated every allegation of 'ill-usage' and received 'the willing co-operation of all those with whom it became their duty to remonstrate'.[117] This proved that cruelty was due to 'ignorance or thoughtlessness' and not 'wilful barbarity' and that the work of the society was 'understood'. Inspectors such as Duggan could only deal with 'open, flagrant cases', and 'much cruelty, practised in private', was 'beyond his power to prevent or to bring forward for punishment'.[118]

In Launceston, Sessions issued cautions to owners not to work horses with swollen or sore collars and invariably found 'the amelioration had been promptly attended to'.[119] In 1892 a senior member of the Launceston branch, Henry Button, claimed that the greater 'tenderness' with which horses were treated was due to 'a great extent' to the efforts and influence of the TSPCA.[120] In 1894 the Launceston branch offered prizes at the agricultural show for horses that were judged to have been kept in the best condition.[121] Prizes were offered to cab, racing, delivery and wood carthorses.

In addition to its efforts to educate the public and remonstrate with offenders, the TSPCA did prosecute extreme cases of cruelty. Between 1878 and 1890 the average annual number of prosecutions was 67, while between 1891 and June

---

112 *Examiner*, 9 October 1900, 7; Letter by J.E. Clarke, 6 October 1903, 6; Letter by J.M. Fysh, 1 September 1906, 10.
113 *Mercury*, 3 September 1878, 2.
114 *Mercury*, 10 September 1878, 2.
115 *Mercury*, 1 October 1878, 3.
116 *Mercury*, 19 October 1878, 2.
117 *Mercury*, 20 June 1879, 3.
118 *Mercury*, 11 August 1884, 2.
119 *Launceston Examiner*, 13 May 1881, 3.
120 ibid., 20 August 1892, 4.
121 ibid., 27 September 1894, 7.

1904, when the society's public presence lessened, the annual average was 22.[122] Most of those prosecutions involved cruelty to horses, which were numerous, for they were used in many different occupations and for transport for residents and tourists.[123] As Hilda Kean has argued for Britain, their mistreatment was clearly visible on city streets and showed that the society's intervention was based on real evils not emotional overreaction.[124] In Launceston details of prosecutions are patchy, with 51 prosecutions being positively recorded between 1882 and 1894.[125] Presumably most prosecutions also involved horses, because Sessions found 'many' examples of horses in 'a poor and emaciated condition, underfed, badly housed, and hardly fit for work'.[126]

Cab owners were a particular target of the TSPCA as many knowingly overused and neglected the horses in their care. In February 1879 the TSPCA tried to awaken them to their responsibilities by issuing copies of the Cruelty Act, the society's handbills and the Victorian Society for the Protection of Cruelty to Animals (VSPCA) pamphlet 'Claims of Animals'.[127] Overloading of cabs continued, but the TSPCA felt powerless to stop it. The power to prevent overloading of public conveyances fell within the jurisdiction of the police by s. 153 of the *Police Act 1865*.[128] In one case, two omnibus horses were worked so hard that at the end of the day they could barely 'crawl along'.[129] After the society asked the Hobart City Council to stop 'this very cruel custom', the newly-appointed Superintendent of Police Frederick Pedder ordered his men to prevent overloading of omnibuses and night cars.[130]

Harder to deal with was the persistent working of horses that were lame or 'weakened by age and insufficient food'.[131] The society regularly noted examples of feeble and thin horses on cabstands caused by 'scanty feeding and general inattention'.[132] It was difficult to prove 'actual cruelty' under the Prevention of Cruelty Act because of 'technical difficulties' and it would take a long time to eradicate the mistreatment by 'isolated punishments'. Mistreatment could be stopped in a day if the mayor used his powers under ss. 136 and 137 of the Police Act and ordered monthly inspections of horses on cabstands. The TSPCA received support from the recently formed Hobart Town Cabmen's

---

122   These averages are drawn from the incomplete statistics found in annual reports of the TSPCA.

123   The economic importance of horses in Tasmania has been shown in K.M. Dallas, *Horse Power* (Hobart: Fullers Bookshop, 1968).

124   Kean, 39–69.

125   *Launceston Examiner*, 20 December 1882, 3; 29 December 1883, 3; 9 May 1885, 3; 18 August 1893, 3; 22 August 1894, 7.

126   *Launceston Examiner*, 9 May 1885, 3.

127   *Mercury*, 7 February 1879, supplement, 1.

128   Press reports of meetings, January 1880, NS 647/1/4, TAHO.

129   Press reports of meetings, February 1880, NS 647/1/4, TAHO.

130   Press reports of meetings, February and March 1880, NS 647/1/4, TAHO.

131   *Mercury*, 8 August 1879, 2.

132   *Mercury*, 15 July 1880, 3; *Second Annual Report of the TSPCA*, 7.

Protective Union, who wanted to raise their status 'socially and morally' and stop mistreatment of horses. This is an example of how the society's publicity and teachings in how best to treat animals could gradually change working-class attitudes, but it also showed that the success of its message depended on individuals wanting to change that behaviour. Six members of the cabmen's union were appointed honorary members of the TSPCA. After the mayor W.H. Burgess visited the cab and car horses, he ordered that horses whose condition 'evidenced wilful neglect and under-feeding' should be withdrawn from service.[133]

Burgess's successor as mayor, James Harcourt, was also sympathetic to the society and in 1882 appointed Acting-Sergeant Franklin to accompany Duggan in regularly inspecting all horses used by licensed vehicles and relieve unfit horses from work.[134] Cab drivers tried to evade this inspection in ingenious ways. They tried to conceal wounds by using acid and plugs of grease and hair.[135] The acid was 'the most cruel agent' because it scorched the skin, caused great pain and left a suppurating sore even larger and more painful than the original injury. Horses with injured or broken knees, caused by poorly made roads, were still used by cab owners, who covered up the injuries using black ointment on kneecaps.[136] Even when guilt was proved, magistrates inflicted 'trifling punishments' because of the poverty of offenders.[137] The society believed that it was an 'error of justice' to award small fines for 'deliberate and repeated offences', weakening 'the vigour and discipline' of the law and the effect of the society's 'teaching of humanity'. With time, the society found that cautioning offenders did not work effectively because 'the wilfully cruel man' took advantage of 'mistaken leniency' to continue to work unfit animals many times until he was prosecuted.[138] Light fines were 'a parody upon the laws' designed to stop cruelty and presaged the leniency shown by courts in the twenty-first century.[139]

Members of the TSPCA responded to needy offenders by giving some poor families sustenance from their own pockets while they rested an injured or tired horse, buying a new collar, lending others money to buy 'a fresh horse', or buying a 'wretched worn-out animal' so it could be destroyed.[140] Cab and cart horses felt the extremes of winter and members of the society distributed 72 rugs to keep them warm while standing still. But the society found that such kindnesses 'induced fresh infractions of the law' and Duggan had to prosecute

---

133 Town Clerk, to Secretary TSPCA, 27 July 1880, MCC 16/7/7, 608, TAHO; *Mercury*, 14 August 1880, 3.
134 *Mercury*, 25 October 1882, supplement, 1.
135 *Mercury*, 18 June 1883, 3.
136 *Mercury*, 24 February 1879, 2; 21 March 1879, 2; 4 April 1879, 2.
137 *Seventh Annual Report of the TSPCA* (Hobart: TSPCA, 1885), 6.
138 *Mercury*, 2 August 1887, 3.
139 Minute book of the SPCA, Launceston, 14 October 1902, NS870/1/1, TAHO.
140 *Mercury*, 21 October 1878, 2; *Seventh Annual Report of the TSPCA*, 7; *Mercury*, 2 December 1885, 3.

again.[141] Or, the kindness resulted in the increased trafficking of 'poor worn-out suffering horses, cruelty thereby assuming a given money value'. Weak enforcement of the law and actions of generosity combined 'to crush down the fear of punishment, and … to strengthen the power of lawlessness'. The non-enforcement of the Police Act against omnibuses, cabs and cars allowed horses with 'tottering' gaits and 'emaciated frames' to endanger the 'public safety' and defy 'humanity'. In 1885 two horses fell exhausted on to the streets, 'the last compulsory effort proving too much for aged frames weakened by semi-starvation'.[142]

The City Council finally acted decisively in 1890 when Mayor John Watchorn ensured greater attention was paid to supervising cab horses and dealt with 'some abuses' that had previously been ignored.[143] This greatly improved the way that cab horses were treated, but 'the poor omnibus horses' were licensed and supervised at the police office and only the police magistrate had the power to stop the overloading of passengers. Mary Gellibrand called this 'licensed cruelty' because those in authority did not enforce 'proper restrictions'.

The overworking of coach horses worsened to the extent that tourists from an unnamed 'neighbouring colony' described their condition in 1899 as 'a disgrace to Tasmania and a blot on civilisation'.[144] The TSPCA investigation revealed some improvements. Horses were no longer driven with sores or 'cruelly flogged' and were mostly 'well fed and fairly tended'.[145] But profit-hungry coach owners still used too few horses for too many passengers with heavy luggage and used weakened and small horses too often on long stages without adequate rest. In many cases of cruelty the offenders pleaded guilty and escaped with a small fine but, if evidence had been presented and witnesses examined, 'a much heavier penalty' might have been inflicted.[146] This too parallels the tactics of modern-day offenders who seek to escape heavy punishment as discussed in the introduction.

Duggan was mostly judicious in the cases he brought to court and often gained a conviction, failing, thought the *Mercury*, only where an 'unscrupulous line of defence' was adopted.[147] Police Magistrate Tarleton thought the Cruelty to Animals Prevention Act was 'a very proper Act', but 'such a highly penal statute' demanded that knowledge of guilt had to be clearly proved.[148] Sometimes

---

141   *Seventh Annual Report of the TSPCA*, 7.
142   ibid.
143   Letter by M.S. Gellibrand, *Mercury*, 14 March 1890, 3.
144   *Mercury*, 31 March 1899, 2.
145   Letter by M.S. Gellibrand, *Mercury*, 11 April 1899, 3.
146   *Mercury*, 1 October 1904, 6.
147   *Mercury*, 3 January 1882, 2.
148   *Mercury*, 29 March 1879, 2; 30 April 1879, 2.

Tarleton censured Duggan's 'somewhat exaggerated tone and style'.[149] In February 1880 Tarleton dismissed two cases against James Hogan for using unfit horses in his carting business and accused Duggan of persecuting him.[150]

The acting chairman of the TSPCA James Macfarlane defended Duggan's 'cautious, considerate and yet energetic' methods.[151] He reiterated that they used the law only against 'very flagrant cases' after an information had been sworn first, but for every prosecution at the police office, at least 20 cases of cruelty escaped punishment because of the 'difficulty of legal proof and non-willingness of witnesses'. As the 'influence of kindness' had 'never been forgotten', the committee felt 'surprise and pain' when reading Tarleton's remarks and denied abusing their power. Macfarlane pointed out that Tarleton had seen Hogan's horse 19 days after the cruelty had been first discovered and the wound had healed. As to the accusation of persecution, Macfarlane pointed out that Hogan and his employees had been previously convicted six times for cruelty before Tarleton himself, three times by the police and three times by the society.

The *Mercury* agreed that the evidence presented in the Hogan case did not justify Tarleton's 'hostility' and 'false aspersions'.[152] After all, Hogan had consistently broken the law and tricked Tarleton into questioning the 'steadfast impartiality' of the TSPCA's work. Hogan was typical of those owners who saw their horses 'simply as beasts of burden, or articles of merchandise' and asserted 'a right' to treat horses as they liked.[153] Despite opposition and misrepresentation, the TSPCA did its work with 'discrimination, judgment and forbearance'. But the society's morale was dented by the difficulties of finding enough legal evidence to support their 'moral evidence' of cruelty.[154] Cases of brutal flogging, kicking and mouth wrenching were especially difficult because Duggan was defeated by the 'technicality of evidence' and failed to secure 'the rights of justice', not least when seeking to punish the owners as well as the drivers of horses. Tarleton demanded proof in criminal cases that the owner knew that his horse was in an unfit condition to be worked, and that evidence was difficult to obtain.[155] Typically in cruelty cases it was not, and is not today, always easy to determine whether suffering was 'unreasonable or unnecessary' and much depended on the circumstances of a particular case.[156]

---

149 *Mercury*, 15 September 1880, 3.
150 *Mercury*, 24 February 1882, 2; 6 March 1882, 2.
151 Letter by James Macfarlane, *Mercury*, 25 March 1882, 3.
152 *Mercury*, 28 February 1882, 2; 27 March 1882, 2.
153 *Mercury*, 14 November 1882, 2.
154 *Seventh Annual Report of the TSPCA*, 8.
155 *Mercury*, 1 April 1891, 2.
156 Sankoff, 14, 20.

After Tarleton retired to official acclaim in 1894, his successor as police magistrate, Bernard Shaw, continued his policy.[157] Shaw exercised his power feebly and Mary Gellibrand alleged that his 'sympathy actively works for the offenders'.[158] Statistics drawn from the annual reports of other colonial societies received by the TSPCA supported her case. In 1895–96 the average penalty imposed in Hobart was 6s 1/2d, whereas in Victoria it was £2 and in Otago £2 6d.[159] One specific example occurred in September 1896 when the society prosecuted the notoriously brutal municipal dog-catcher Samuel Dunbabin for ill-treating a spaniel by tightening a wire noose around the dog's neck so hard that 'its eyes and tongue protruded'.[160] Shaw agreed that the action caused the spaniel 'unnecessary pain', but it was not an 'aggravated case' and he fined Dunbabin a mere 5s and 12s costs. But the example of West Coast magistrates belied any idea that the law was weak. They 'constantly imposed heavy fines for all cruel offences' and greatly reduced 'that brutality which disgraced earlier days' and taught offenders 'understanding and respect for the law'.[161] Their 'courage and justice' were 'an object-lesson on the improvement which follows the firm administration' of the law.[162]

The brief of the TSPCA included amending the law when required and this occurred in the carrying of poultry. In October 1878 the society learnt that the legs of poultry carried to market were tied so tightly that, when they tried to struggle free, their legs fractured.[163] The committee persuaded the attorney-general to introduce an amendment to the *Police Act Amendment Act*, based on Victorian legislation, to require the carrying of poultry in crates and baskets and making tying legs together an offence.[164] The House of Assembly ridiculed the idea and the amendment was lost. The colonial treasurer W.R. Giblin described the suggestion as 'over-legislation', which would create 'hardship' for the poor who could not afford crates and baskets. In May 1879 Charles Meredith for the TSPCA guided through the assembly an amendment to the Cruelty to Animals Act to punish persons who caused an animal to suffer when conveying it in vehicles.[165] According to British law, this included the carrying of poultry.[166] By

157 *Mercury*, 22 September 1894, supplement, 1; Letter by 'Humanitas', *Mercury*, 29 September 1894, 3.
158 Letter by M.S. Gellibrand, *Mercury*, 12 January 1897, 4.
159 Letter by M.S. Gellibrand, *Mercury*, 27 November 1896, 3.
160 *Mercury*, 10 September 1896, 2.
161 Letter by M.S. Gellibrand, *Mercury*, 2 September 1902, 2,.
162 Minute book of the SPCA, Launceston, 14 October 1902, NS870/1/1, TAHO.
163 *Mercury*, 4 October 1878, 2.
164 *Mercury*, 16 October 1878, 3.
165 *Mercury*, 23 May 1879, 3.
166 *Mercury*, 19 July 1879, 2.

1881, Duggan reported that the amendment had been 'effectual'.[167] He waged 'a constant warfare' against the 'improper' carrying of poultry and also dealt quickly with overcrowding in boxes and baskets.[168]

Another amendment to the law was introduced independently of the TSPCA. In November 1887 Dr Arthur Young, Member for East Devon, urged the House of Assembly to stop the 'cruel way' in which sheep were imported from Melbourne to Tasmania.[169] They were 'driven long distances' to Melbourne and then 'closely packed' in a ship without food or water. When they arrived at Torquay in Young's electorate, they were dipped and once again packed tightly in a train at Latrobe before being sent to different areas of Tasmania. With the support of the assembly, the minister for lands, Edward Braddon, quickly introduced the Cruelty to Animals Amendment bill to ensure that sheep were not mistreated on Tasmanian trains and it passed both houses without dissent.[170] The TSPCA praised the measure and hoped that, 'as occasion may show the necessity and virtue of interference, the Executive will promptly take its stand against every form of cruelty'.[171]

In November 1890 the society became agitated when it heard that 700 sheep had been stowed in the holds of the steamer *Wendouree* on top of a coal cargo and not been fed for seven days because it would 'injure the coal'.[172] The society failed to prosecute the captain and chief officer because the law officers of the Crown asserted that the offence had occurred on 'the High Sea' and the 1887 legislation did not apply there. The TSPCA tried hard to enforce the law so that animals carried in ships were 'properly treated' but, by 1901, had 'not succeeded to any great extent'.[173] From 1891 lack of funds meant the work of the TSPCA devolved to the inspectors and Mary Gellibrand until her death in 1903, but the revival of its public activity in 1904 was accompanied by the enactment of more vigorous legislation.[174]

The *Prevention of Cruelty to Animals Act 1904* and its aftermath

Cruelty to animals legislation had been strengthened in Britain and other Australian jurisdictions by the early twentieth century and Tasmania lagged

---

167   *Mercury*, 6 July 1881, 3.
168   *Sixth Annual Report of the TSPCA*, 6; *Mercury*, 7 December 1888, 3.
169   *Mercury*, 4 November 1887, 3.
170   *Mercury*, 8 December 1887, 4; 16 December 1887, 3.
171   *Mercury*, 7 December 1888, 3.
172   TSPCA committee meeting, 27 November 1890, NS647/1/1, TAHO.
173   *Mercury*, 16 October 1901, 2, the view of J.W. Evans.
174   *Examiner*, 14 December 1903, 6.

behind.[175] In October 1904 member of parliament for Cumberland, lawyer and farmer John Dennistoun Wood, arguing that every animal was 'susceptible of enduring great pain', consulted the TSPCA before introducing a new bill based on British legislation and similar to a recent Queensland statute. It extended the law's protection from domestic animals to any animal or bird, whether free or in confinement.[176] Wood's bill followed British law in empowering justices to impose imprisonment of one month instead of a fine for a range of offences including 'overworking' and 'causing unnecessary suffering'. Another amendment 'authorised the destruction of any animal so diseased or injured that its existence would be a cause of misery to it'.[177]

Despite increasing the severity and scope of cruelty to animal provisions, the new Act did not greatly change the society's focus, but did help with prosecutions for overloading and over-driving of horses.[178] After Shaw's retirement in March 1904, the new police magistrate for Hobart, W.O. Wise, interpreting the law more sympathetically, showed a greater willingness to impose 'deterrent fines' for 'wilful or thoughtless' cruelty to animals.[179] The clearest example occurred in February 1905 when Thomas Johnson, alias George Birchall, felled his horse with a stone, hit it repeatedly on the head and left it lying in a drain until the next day before killing the animal and removing it on the order of the Sandfly road trust.[180] Wise called this 'the grossest case of cruelty that had ever come before the court'. As Johnson had not paid two previous fines for other offences, Wise sentenced him to one month's imprisonment. This was the first imprisonment for cruelty under the new Act and, much to the society's satisfaction, Wise continued to impose severer sentences than his predecessors.[181] Cases that were prosecuted by the society were still dismissed on occasion, mainly because perjury was a common practice, witnesses were reluctant to attend court and 'uncertainty' remained over the definition of overdriving, overloading and starving.[182] These difficulties, and the gradual transition from the horse to the motor car, resulted in a drop in the number of prosecutions: between July 1904 and 1913 the annual average was 19.[183] In Launceston, the failure of witnesses to give evidence in court was attributed by the society to a lack of 'moral courage' or a 'fear of giving offence, either for business or other reasons'.[184]

---

175   Jamieson, 'Animal Welfare', 23–28.

176   *Mercury*, 1 October 1904, 6; 22 October 1904, 6.

177   *Mercury*, 17 October 1904, 7.

178   Minutes of TSPCA, 3 February 1905, NS 647/1/1, TAHO. Native fauna and birds were regarded as outside the purview of the society before 1914.

179   *Mercury*, 27 August 1904, 7.

180   *Mercury*, 15 February 1905, 4, 6.

181   Minutes of the TSPCA, 23 June 1905, NS 647/1/1, TAHO; *Tasmanian News*, 16 November 1905, 2.

182   *Mercury*, 14 March 1906, 5.

183   These figures are compiled from statistics given in annual reports.

184   *Examiner*, 22 February 1906, 7.

From 1904, until it suspended public meetings with the onset of war in 1914, the TSPCA continued its work of inspection and prosecution where cautions were disregarded.[185] But, active members remained in short supply (membership was a low 137 in 1913), and much of the burden fell on Large and the new secretary, educationalist Miss Fanny Garrett, who made animal protection work 'the main object of her life' until her death in 1926.[186] Garrett was more circumspect than Mary Gellibrand and, with her quiet guidance, the society generally remained moderate in outlook, avoiding 'the realm of public spectacle'.[187] While the focus of animal protectionists was on domestic animals, visiting German anthropologist and anatomist, Hermann Klaatsch noted that native animals 'were being totally exterminated, with no understanding and with no pity, the hard-hearted and ignorant colonists shooting everything on sight'.[188] The protection of native animals and birds was taken up by new organisations, such as the Field Naturalists Club, the Gould League of Bird Lovers and the Anti-Plumage League, which complemented the work of the TSPCA branches.[189]

After nearly 30 years of operations, the TSPCA came to realise that laws, though still necessary to punish vicious offenders, 'will not make men and women humane, any more than it will make them moral'.[190] As the *Mercury* put it, dependence on 'prohibitory legislation and the power of punishment' would not result in 'radical improvement' in 'the habit of mind' that perpetrated 'barbarous conduct'. This view might have been related to the difficulties of securing new legislation to stop sports that resulted in the killing of animals such as pigeon-shooting matches and rabbit and hare coursing.[191] The society thus renewed its efforts to form Bands of Mercy, mostly dormant since 1890. In 1907 parents and teachers were urged to inculcate in children 'the duty of being kind and considerate to all dumb creatures', especially domestic animals.[192] By 1909, 18 Bands of Mercy had been affiliated with the TSPCA.[193] Many of the essays written by children for the prizes offered by the society showed 'great love for animals, close observation, and great kindliness of heart'.[194] Another educational initiative was the Society's appeal to the clergy to preach on 'Man's

185 *Mercury*, 18 June 1919, 8.
186 Letter by H.T. Gould, *Mercury*, 27 March 1908, 2; *Thirty-Second Annual Report of the TSPCA* (Hobart: TSPCA, 1910), 7; *Thirty-Sixth Annual Report of the TSPCA* (Hobart: TSPCA, 1914), 16–18.
187 Kean, 145.
188 Robert Paddle, *The Last Tasmanian Tiger: The History and Extinction of the Thylacine* (Cambridge University Press, 2000), 168.
189 *Thirty-Fourth Annual Report of the TSPCA* (Hobart: TSPCA, 1912), 11.
190 *Mercury*, 15 March 1906, 4.
191 For example, the TSPCA-sponsored Cruelty to Animals Bill, designed to stop such practices, did not pass the second reading, *Mercury*, 7 November 1906, 6.
192 *Mercury*, 13 July 1907, 7.
193 *Mercury*, 17 March 1909, 6.
194 *Thirty-Fourth Annual Report of the TSPCA*, 13.

Duty to Animals' as was done regularly in England.[195] Animal Sunday sermons were first given on 12 July 1908 and became an annual event in some churches, but reached only small numbers of people.[196]

Conclusion

After over three decades of activity, the branches of the SPCA in Tasmania offered divergent accounts of their impact. By 1910 the secretary of the Launceston SPCA, Mrs J.M. Fysh, pointed out weaknesses that limited the branch's effectiveness. Fysh noted that the branch was dominated by women and, apart from a male chairman, men did not participate in the cruelty prevention work.[197] While the police usually investigated complaints of cruelty, 'indifference and apathy' were widespread in Launceston. Men preferred to spend their spare time in pleasurable activities and not 'laying a hand on sundry slavers in horseflesh'.[198] Fysh later reflected that 'individual selfishness, want of thought, want of proper knowledge how to treat animals, dislike to interfere with the much-abused "liberty of the subject"' and the failure of mothers to teach children 'the principles of kindness' all worked against the society's efforts.[199]

The TSPCA struck a more positive note. By May 1912 it had noted significant changes in public attitudes, helped greatly by its enforcement of the law and educational initiatives. It found evidence of 'greater sensitiveness of public conscience and opinion, with acceptance of the rights of animals, and of man's duty towards them'.[200] In Hobart, 'cases of neglect and abuse, that formerly passed unheeded', were immediately 'noted and disapproved' and the society or the police were informed. Drivers of horses 'readily invited and acted on advice for sick animals' and accepted offers of literature on the subject. Hobart had certainly not been purged of cruelty to animals, the killing of animals for sport remained 'a relic of barbarism and savagery', and the lone inspector could not respond to the constant appeals from rural areas, but we should acknowledge what had been achieved.[201] The 'moral influence' of the TSPCA had helped to change long entrenched practices and contributed to the 'uplifting and ennobling' of city life.[202]

---

195   Minutes of the TSPCA, 13 July 1908, NS 647/1/1, TAHO; *Mercury*, 17 March 1909, 6.
196   *Thirty-Second Annual Report of the TSPCA*, 5.
197   Letter by J.M. Fysh, *Examiner*, 23 September 1910, 3.
198   Letter by G. Garet, *Examiner*, 28 September 1910, 3.
199   *Examiner*, 9 April 1919, 6.
200   *Mercury*, 24 May 1912, 6.
201   The quote comes from Bishop John Mercer, *Mercury*, 24 May 1912, 6. See also his lecture 'Have animals souls?', *Mercury*, 28 June 1912, 8; *Thirty-Sixth Annual Report of the TSPCA*, 4.
202   *Thirty-Sixth Annual Report of the TSPCA*, 11.

Moreover, while the two SPCA branches in Tasmania took great efforts to ensure that the law was of more than symbolic protection to animals, both faced a number of obstacles that limited their effectiveness and mirrored the experience of their counterparts throughout Australia in the twenty-first century. First, they relied on their own inspectors to prosecute cases and could not rely on the police or private individuals to initiate prosecution, leaving much cruelty untouched by the law. Second, the failure of witnesses to attend court or the use of a guilty plea by offenders obviated the need for witnesses or the presentation of evidence and contributed to the imposition of lesser penalties. Third, the number of cases reaching court was small because magistrates insisted on high evidentiary standards and dismissed cases on technical grounds relating to the extent and nature of the cruelty. Finally, magistrates were generally reluctant to impose heavy fines, even on repeat offenders, especially if they were poor and relied on animals for their livelihood. In short, the continuities between past and present in the enforcement of anti-cruelty laws are remarkably strong. They demonstrate that the weak enforcement of the law and lenient decisions of today have a long lineage and the time has come to take a completely different approach to law enforcement against animal cruelty. Unless the police are empowered to treat any harm to animals as an illegal abuse of responsibility worthy of prosecution, and unless courts are directed to impose mandatory heavier sentences for such harm, including heavy fines, custodial sentences and prohibition on keeping animals for serious cases of abuse, then animals will continue to experience pain and suffering of the kind endured over 200 years of white settlement.

Using the Law: Working-Class Communities and Carnal Knowledge Cases in Victoria, 1900–06

Jennifer Anderson

The case, *R v Gravino*, which came before the Supreme Court of Victoria in 1905, illustrates well the complex debates which often preceded state involvement in sexual assault cases and are revealing about community decisions to engage with the legal system. On 7 March 1905, 14-year-old Elsie Griffiths disclosed to her mother that their neighbour, 17-year-old Charlie Gravino, had sexually assaulted her or, in her words, 'had me down at his place doing rude things'. Elsie's father was dead, and her mother, Catherine Griffiths, kept a laundry in the Melbourne suburb of Brunswick, behind which Elsie lived with her mother, her 11-year-old brother Albert and her adult sister, Kate. The previous evening, Elsie had been sent out to look for her brother, when she met Charlie at the end of the lane. The two went into Charlie's house, calling out for Albert. There, apparently taking advantage of no one being home, Charlie pushed Elsie down onto the ground and attempted to rape her.[1] On the evening of 7 March, Catherine took Elsie to Charlie's house, where they spoke to Charlie in front of his mother and stepfather. Catherine asked Charlie whether he had assaulted Elsie and he eventually admitted that 'he might have done'. At that point, according to Catherine, Charlie's mother 'asked me to forgive the boy' and she and Charlie shook hands. Catherine was prepared to forgive Charlie, she told the court, because 'no harm ha[d] been done to her [Elsie]. I said this because she wasn't monthly, she was too young'.[2] This outcome, however, did not satisfy Elsie's elder sister Kate, who evidently held a different opinion as to what constituted 'harm'. The next day, Kate took matters into her own hands and demanded a written apology from Charlie, 'for satisfaction for my sister's character'. When no letter was forthcoming, Kate took Elsie to the police and then the hospital. After the medical examination, Charlie was charged with the attempted carnal knowledge of Elsie Griffiths.[3]

---

1   Statement of Elsie Griffiths, *R v Charles Gravino*, Melbourne Supreme Court, 23 May 1905, Public Record Office Victoria (PROV), VA 667 Office of the Crown Solicitor, VPRS 30/P/0000 Criminal Trial Briefs, Unit 1385, Item 163. Charles was charged with attempted carnal knowledge because there was no medical evidence of actual penetration. He was convicted of indecent assault, see commentary in 'Criminal Court', *Age* (Melbourne), 26 May 1905, 10.
2   By which she meant that Elsie had not yet started menstruating, statement of Catherine Griffiths, ibid.
3   Statement of Kate Griffiths, ibid.

In some ways, *Gravino* was an atypical carnal knowledge case to come to the attention of the Melbourne police in 1905. Siblings rarely intervened to the extent that Kate Griffiths did and, without her involvement, the matter probably would have gone no further. Like the families in *Gravino*, many parties in such cases were working class and, while these discussions were critical to the participants, they have attracted little academic attention. Since the 1980s, there has been a significant amount of feminist historical and legal scholarship on sexual crimes, with two main areas of interest. One strand of inquiry has examined the development and enforcement of legislation prohibiting under-age sexual activity. Scholars have argued that middle-class reformers, including feminists, child rescue workers and social purists, advocated more stringent definitions of permissible sexual conduct from the 1870s and 1880s, as part of a drive both to delineate childhood and to control adult male sexuality.[4] The same literature has suggested that the regulatory attempt was thwarted, at least in part, by ambivalent attitudes towards female sexuality in law.[5] A second, albeit overlapping, strand has focused on court proceedings, exploring the influence of contemporary attitudes to gender, morality, class and race on the outcomes of prosecutions and on legal rules and practice.[6] Such scholarship has often been overtly present centred, tracking historical precedents for the continuing problems women face in prosecuting sexual offences, and lending support to campaigns to alter rules of evidence and court practice.[7] It has also offered explanations for why so few matters progressed to trial and for low conviction rates.[8]

Yet, before the legal process was engaged, offending behaviour had first to come to the attention of the authorities. If we assume, then as now, that most young women, or their families, did not make their experiences of sexual offences against them public,[9] studying the circumstances of those who did opens up

---

4   In Australia see Jill Bavin-Mizzi, *Ravished: Sexual Violence in Victorian Australia* (Sydney: University of New South Wales Press, 1995), 14; Bavin-Mizzi, 'Understandings of Justice: Australian Rape and Carnal Knowledge Cases, 1876–1924', in *Sex, Power and Justice: Historical Perspectives of Law in Australia*, ed., Diane Kirkby (Melbourne: Oxford University Press, 1995), 19–20. In the United Kingdom see Lucy Bland, *Banishing the Beast: English Feminism and Sexual Morality, 1885–1914* (Harmondsworth: Penguin, 1995), xiii–xvii, 97, 110–12, 122–23; Louise A. Jackson, *Child Sexual Abuse in Victorian England* (London and New York: Routledge, 2000), 1–6, 12–17. In the United States, see Mary E. Odem, *Delinquent Daughters: Protecting and Policing Adolescent Female Sexuality in the United States, 1885–1920* (Chapel Hill and London: University of North Carolina Press, 1995), 1–7, 9–10.

5   Jackson, 3–4; Odem, 64, 71–72; Bavin-Mizzi, *Ravished*, 42, 83–84; Constance Backhouse, 'Skewing the Credibility of Women: A Reappraisal of Corroboration in Australian Legal History', *Western Australian Law Review* 29 (2000): 29, 79–107.

6   Odem, 64–81; Bavin-Mizzi, *Ravished*, 10–13, 42–67, 83–87. See also Judith Allen's classic *Sex and Secrets: Crimes Involving Australian Women Since 1880* (Melbourne: Oxford University Press, 1990), 57–62, which outlined the difficulties facing both rape and carnal knowledge victims in prosecuting cases successfully.

7   Allen, 2, 14, 252, 255; Backhouse, 80–81.

8   Bavin-Mizzi, *Ravished*, 197–203.

9   The general belief is that sexual offending against women and children, in Australia and elsewhere, has always been significantly under-reported. See Allen, 9–10; Jackson, 25–26.

alternative, and equally interesting, lines of inquiry. Which groups tended to appear before the courts and what triggered the decision to notify the police? What did parties feel they had to gain, or lose, by legal involvement? Did they have any preliminary understanding of the legal process, which might affect their decision to make a complaint or to stay silent? Given the strong working-class presence in this jurisdiction, such questions also invite us to consider the extent to which such communities were agents in these proceedings, or whether they were more often the subjects of state intervention. To date there have been no Australian studies on this point, although scholars in the United Kingdom and United States have considered similar questions. Louise Jackson's study of child sexual abuse in Victorian England argued that working-class populations had informal as well as formal methods of dealing with sexual offending, with cases more likely to be reported if they involved non-family members. Incest in particular was likely to be hidden.[10] She suggested that the police were not the automatic resort for such communities as relationships with authority were often fractured, although she also contended that they still viewed the law as the 'appropriate final resolution'.[11] By contrast, Mary Odem's work on statutory rape cases in the Californian courts in the 1910s indicated that working-class, and particularly immigrant parents, used age of consent legislation to try and control daughters whose sexual relationships flouted familial and community expectations.[12]

The varying conclusions in these works can be explained in part by the different subjects of the studies, as well as the differences of time and place. Jackson was examining non-consensual sexual activity, or the rape of (mostly) young children. Odem focused on older girls who were more likely to be engaging in consensual sexual relationships. 'Carnal knowledge' cases, of course, covered the spectrum, from the forcible abuse of small girls to adolescent relationships. Nevertheless, given the lack of Australian research on this point, it is worthwhile to start by examining the available cases more generally, to see whether patterns that have been identified in British and American sources also held here. My primary source was the records of carnal knowledge proceedings listed in the Melbourne Supreme Court between 1900 and 1906. The majority of the matters came from the city of Melbourne, but the jurisdiction of the court also encompassed country areas where the court did not travel on circuit, so allowing for exploration of a mix of urban and rural cases. Most of the transcripts for these cases have survived and offer a rich source for the views of the witnesses who appeared before the courts. My approach was strongly influenced by the work of historians like Mark Peel, who have argued that we should heed the 'real voices' of working-class communities, the subjects of intervention, as

---

10   Jackson, 31, 47–48.
11   ibid., 36–40.
12   Odem, 40–47.

much as the regulators whose views have so often dominated.[13] Documenting 'in their own words' why people chose to use the law, in this particularly emotive and difficult area, throws important illuminations on attitudes towards sexual offending, the law and the reach of the regulatory state in Australia in our period.

The first part of the chapter outlines the legislative background and the sources used in the study. The second and third parts explore who reported sexual offending to the police, beginning with the circumstances in which state agents were involved from the outset, before turning to the more common scenarios in which family members made the decision to engage with the legal system. The fourth considers the expectations that families seem to have brought to court and, by outlining the outcomes in these cases, suggests that expectation and reality were often sharply divergent. I conclude by summarising the circumstances in which working-class communities in Victoria at this time used the law to regulate sexual conduct and what was distinctive about their choices.

Jurisdiction and sources

The offence of carnal knowledge of a girl under the age of 16 was created in the colony of Victoria by the *Crimes Act 1891*, which raised the age of consent from 12 to 16. This Act replaced in part the *Crimes Act 1890*, itself simply a restatement of earlier legislation. The 1890 Act had contained two such offences. Carnal knowledge of a girl under 10 was a capital offence. Carnal knowledge of a girl between 10 and 12 was a misdemeanour, punishable by a term of imprisonment.[14] The new Act left the capital offence alone, but established an overarching felony of 'carnal knowledge of a girl between 10 and 16', punishable by a maximum of 10-years imprisonment. If the defendant was the girl's teacher, the maximum sentence was 15-years imprisonment.[15] The Act also created associated charges of attempted carnal knowledge and assault with intent to carnally know, misdemeanours punishable by three years imprisonment (five if the defendant was the girl's teacher).[16] Consent was no defence to either charge unless the girl was the same age or older than the defendant, a requirement the Victorian Supreme Court interpreted very strictly.[17] The 1891 Act was modelled closely on the 1885 English *Criminal Law Amendment Act* and, like that Act, was the result of extensive campaigning by women's groups, social purists,

---

13   Mark Peel, *The Lowest Rung: Voices of Australian Poverty* (Cambridge University Press, 2003), 11–15.
14   *Crimes Act 1890* (Vic), ss. 45 and 47.
15   *Crimes Act 1891* (Vic), s. 5(1).
16   ibid., s. 5(2).
17   ibid., s. 6. In *R v Hibbert* 1906 *Victorian Law Reports* at 198 Hodges J held that 'the same age or younger' should be interpreted as 'born on the same day or younger'.

clergy and charitable organisations, who had argued that the existing legal framework left young girls vulnerable to sexual exploitation.[18] Nevertheless, there were also significant differences. Unlike the English Act, the Victorian version contained no defence of reasonable belief that the girl was over 16,[19] and allowed a more generous time frame for prosecution.[20] The 1891 Act also created a new offence of incest, or carnal knowledge of a daughter, lineal female descendant or stepdaughter, an offence not limited by the girl's age.[21]

Carnal knowledge charges were heard before judge and jury in the Supreme Court. The trial was preceded by a committal, or preliminary, proceeding in the local police court, presided over by a bench of magistrates. Between 1900 and 1906, 70 carnal knowledge and related cases were listed for hearing in the Melbourne Supreme Court: of these, 69 actually proceeded to trial. These cases were a small number of the total listings — there were between seven and 14 each year, out of a total of between 500–600 cases overall. In the absence of exact records we can only speculate as to how many matters did not make it past committal although, from newspaper reports and contemporary commentaries, it would seem that there was a fair rate of attrition at the police court stage.[22] Of those that did advance to the higher court, 30, or 43 per cent, ended in acquittal. In 26 cases (37 per cent) defendants were convicted of the principal charge in the Crown indictment and, in 4 matters (6 per cent), the defendant was convicted of a lesser charge. Seven defendants (10 per cent) pleaded guilty, and one pleaded guilty to a lesser charge. In two cases the prosecution ultimately entered a *nolle prosequi*, in one case before trial because the defendant had died and in the other after two trials where the jury disagreed. Rates of conviction, however, varied significantly from year to year, from a low of 25 per cent in 1906, to a high of 71 per cent in 1903, with no definitive pattern except that the acquittal rate increased slightly in years with higher numbers of cases.

Where a carnal knowledge case was listed for hearing in the Melbourne Supreme Court, the Victorian Crown Prosecution Office prepared a brief of evidence

---

18   Women's Christian Temperance Union of Victoria, *Fourth Annual Report during the Year 1891* (Melbourne: Peacock Bros. Printers, 1892), 4–5; 'The Protection of Girls — Deputation of Clergymen to the Premier', *Age* (Melbourne), 19 August 1891, 5; 'Protection of Young Girls', *Age* (Melbourne), 14 November 1891, 4.

19   *Criminal Law Amendment Act 1885*, 48 & 49 Vict c. 69, s. 5.

20   The *Criminal Law Amendment Act 1885* initially limited prosecution to within three months of the commission of the offence, see s, 5. The 1891 Victorian Act (s, 7) allowed 12 months.

21   *Crimes Act 1891* (Vic) s. 8.

22   In the 1890s the Victorian Women's Christian Temperance Union had launched a high-profile campaign to increase the numbers of defendants who were committed for trial, see Women's Christian Temperance Union, *Eighth Annual Report during the Year 1895* (Melbourne: Spectator Publishing Co, 1896), 12, 46–47. Feminist commentators continued to criticise the operation of the committal system into the twentieth century, see, for example, the remarks in the journal *Woman's Sphere* (edited by the prominent feminist and suffrage campaigner Vida Goldstein), 'General Comments', vol. I, no. 9, May 1901, 73–74; 'Letter to the Editor', vol. I, no. 12, August 1901, 99; 'Children's Courts and Police Matrons', vol. II, no. 18, 10 February 1902, 145; 'Comments', vol. III, no. 34, 10 June 1903, 306.

which contained typed transcripts of the evidence given by the witnesses at the committal hearing and the other documents on which the Crown relied to make out its case. These generally included the girl's birth certificate, the complaint and warrant, statements from expert witnesses, subpoenas and bail documents, and occasionally other legal correspondence. The brief sometimes also included letters between a girl or her family members and the defendant, if this material was seen to assist the case. The transcripts were evidently mediated by the questions asked and, to some extent, they were overlaid with legal language.[23] When combined with these additional records, however, they allow us to piece together a reasonably accurate picture of the relationship between complainants and defendants, the social standing of the parties and how the matter came to the attention of the police.

In the overwhelming majority of carnal knowledge cases the parties knew each other, often well. I accessed the prosecution briefs for 68 of the 70 cases listed for trial between 1900 and 1906,[24] and divided the relationships in these cases into five broad categories. The first was members of the same household, which included both family members and non-relatives, such as fellow employees (20 cases, or 28 per cent). The second (also 20 cases) included non-resident family members, friends and neighbours. In nine cases (12.6 per cent) complainant and defendant identified themselves as boyfriend and girlfriend. The fourth category I called 'acquaintances', which I used to describe situations in which the parties knew each other slightly, even if they had only met on the day of the incident (12, or 17.6 per cent). In only six cases were the defendants total strangers (9 per cent). One matter fell outside these categories, where the defendant was the girl's former teacher.

The ages of the girls involved varied from 16 months to 21 years, although there was a significantly larger number of older complainants, or girls who had passed through puberty. Specifically, there were six children under 10 at the time of the offence (8.4 per cent) and 10 (14 per cent) aged between 10 and 12. Thirteen girls were 13 years old (18 per cent), 17 girls were 14 (24 per cent), 21 were 15 (29.5 per cent), 2 were 16 (3 per cent), one was 17 and one 21.[25] Three of the four girls over 16 were complainants in incest charges and the 17-year-old the (reluctant) complainant in a charge of abduction with intent to carnally know, where the age of consent under the 1891 Act was 18.[26] Most of the younger children were old enough to be deemed capable of giving sworn evidence, a factor important to magistrates when they decided to allow a case to proceed to trial.

---

23   The witnesses, for example, invariably refer to the defendant as 'the accused', 'the defendant' or 'prisoner' and, in some cases, it is clear that a child's evidence has been doctored to make it flow more logically. In other circumstances, however, the transcript is apparently very literal, including witnesses' grammatical errors, contemporary turns of phrase and slang.

24   One brief was missing and one was unable to be ordered.

25   There were in total 72 complainants, as three cases involved two complainants each.

26   *Crimes Act 1891* (Vic), s. 17 (1).

Of the 68 cases, 44 (64.7 per cent) came from the city of Melbourne, with the remaining 24 from a variety of country areas. The numbers reflected the court's jurisdiction as well as the greater population concentration in Melbourne. The Victorian Supreme Court travelled on circuit to larger country towns, so the rural cases which made their way to Melbourne were usually from areas closer to Melbourne than other regional centres. A number of matters, for example, came from the foothills of the Dandenongs and four cases were from the seaside town of Sorrento, 112 kilometres south of Melbourne. The overwhelming majority of complainants and defendants, from both urban and rural areas, were working class. I assessed the parties' class on the basis of where they lived, how they described their living arrangements, their occupation if they had one, and their parents' occupations. Of the 44 cases from Melbourne city, in all but five cases, the parties lived in extensively working-class areas, from the southern suburbs of South and Port Melbourne to Footscray in the west and North Melbourne, Carlton, Collingwood, and Fitzroy in the inner north and east. The only complainant who resided in a definitely middle-class area (Armadale in the southeast) was a domestic servant living in her employer's house. Where complainants worked, they were employed mostly as domestic servants or in factories. Defendants recorded a variety of occupations, both skilled and unskilled. Most of the girls, though, did come from fairly solid middle or upper working-class backgrounds. Only eight of the 68 cases involved girls from very impoverished, or fringe-dwelling families, including one current and one former state ward.

Case studies (1): State agents and professionals

Proceedings in the carnal knowledge jurisdiction began with the signing of a formal complaint before a police officer or magistrate. Signing the complaint was usually the responsibility of a family member. Police prosecuted on their own initiative in only four of these cases. Where police were involved from the outset, there was invariably an additional public order issue, often of suspected juvenile prostitution. In *R v Kelly*,[27] for example, Constable Edward Monkivitch was on duty outside the Exhibition Gardens in Carlton in May 1906, when he observed John Kelly behaving suspiciously towards 13-year-old Elsie Lawson. He followed the two and caught Kelly about to have intercourse with Elsie under a tree. At the police station, Elsie disclosed that Kelly had said he would give her sixpence if she went with him and that she had met him the Saturday before,

---

27   Melbourne Supreme Court, 15 May 1906, PROV, VPRS 30/P/0000, Unit 1421, Item 214.

when he had given her a shilling.[28] Police members who intervened in such situations seem to have been both particularly observant and committed to the cause. In *R v Martin*,[29] Constable Henry Grisfield apprehended 11-year-old Sarah Lawton and 12-year-old Gertrude Bigwood in Bourke Street, Melbourne, as they were being led away by a man. He took the girls to the station and obtained statements that also implicated Edward Martin, a Collingwood bootmaker. Grisfield then undertook an extensive investigation into Martin's behaviour, which ended in a successful prosecution for carnal knowledge of Sarah. Grisfield simultaneously charged both girls with neglect and asked that they be committed to the Industrial Schools. The jury in Martin's trial commended Grisfield for 'taking young girls off the streets'.[30]

Active police members were also sometimes instrumental in persuading family members to make a complaint against a defendant, particularly when they viewed conduct as infringing public order as well as private morality. Constable John Brophy had been keeping an eye on 15-year-old Alice Saunders, an orphan in service at Moonee Ponds, for some time, as he had 'heard that it was common talk amongst the boys that this girl was "good enough"'.[31] When he discovered that she had become intimate with 17-year-old Charles Wilson, he interviewed her and accused her of the affair, which she denied. Brophy then wrote to her older brother, Herbert Saunders, who was living on Phillip Island, outlining the situation and advising him to come to Melbourne at once. Herbert came to town and, between them, they managed to get Alice to make a statement against Charles. Brophy then took Herbert Saunders before the city magistrate to obtain a warrant for Charles's arrest in October 1906.[32] Police were also closely involved in the investigation of a sailor, William Doyle, for the carnal knowledge of 13-year-old Daisy Hamilton in January 1902. Daisy, also an orphan, lived with her older brother and sister in the port suburb of Williamstown. When she did not return home on the night of 18 January, her brother Walter reported her missing. Senior Constable Norgate saw her the next morning and asked her where she had been. She told him she had slept in a paddock, but he threatened her with the reformatory if she did not tell the truth. The next day he went to the pier and, seeing Daisy with Doyle, launched an inquiry that ended in Doyle's conviction for carnal knowledge.[33]

---

28   Statement of Elsie Lawson, ibid.

29   Melbourne Supreme Court, 15 February 1904, PROV, VPRS 30/P/0000, Unit 1348, Item 68.

30   'Criminal Court', *Age* (Melbourne), 29 February 1904, 9, and 'Police Intelligence', 3 March 1904, 9.

31   Statement of John O'Connell Brophy, *R v Charles Wilson*, Melbourne Supreme Court, 15 November 1906, PROV, VPRS 30/P/0000, Unit 1434, Item 442.

32   Statements of Herbert Saunders and John O'Connell Brophy, ibid. Charles was convicted of attempted carnal knowledge, although the court remarked that the evidence showed 'evidence of revolting immorality amongst a number of boys and girls', see 'Criminal Court', *Age* (Melbourne), 22 November 1906, 10.

33   Statements of Daisy Hamilton and Henry Norgate, *R v William Doyle*, Melbourne Supreme Court, 17 February 1902, PROV, VPRS 30/P/0000, Unit 1280, Item 122.

Other state agents and professionals occasionally reported carnal knowledge cases to the police. When they acted, the girl had invariably been committed to their care and they were standing permanently or temporarily in place of her family. The Victorian Department of Neglected Children had the formal guardianship of all state wards until they turned 18, and sometimes beyond,[34] but a departmental officer instigated the complaints system in only two of these matters. William Buswell notified the police in March 1901 after 15-year-old Margaret Green became pregnant, apparently to her employer's son, William Orr. Margaret had been a state ward since infancy and was licensed to Mrs Orr under an agreement with the department.[35] In *R v O'Gallaghan* a nurse at the Industrial Schools depot alerted the authorities after nine-year-old Sylvia Derrick disclosed a sexual assault by her mother's de facto husband, Eugene O'Gallaghan, from whom she had contracted syphilis. Sylvia had recently been removed from her mother's care following allegations of neglect.[36] In two other cases, refuge workers apparently persuaded girls to make formal statements about sexual misconduct. In 1902, Louisa and Lydia Ward, aged 21 and 17 respectively, disclosed to Mrs Pittman, manager of the Girls' Rescue Home in Armadale, that their father had sexually abused them for many years, resulting in Louisa's pregnancy.[37] In 1906, 16-year-old Bessie Martin made a statement to the Carlton Refuge Committee that a family friend, Francis Hendry, had assaulted her earlier that year. Bessie came to live in the refuge six months later and only then made a complaint.[38]

As the intervention of the refuge workers suggests, professionals, like the police, might also influence complainants or their family to report sexual offending, even if they did not personally notify the authorities. No doctor, for example, actually reported a suspected carnal knowledge offence, at least amongst these cases. In several incidents, however, their recommendations assisted family members to make an obviously difficult decision. In one particularly serious case, *R v Thomas Brown*,[39] from August 1900, Alice Anderson knew that her 16-month-old baby girl Etta had been sexually assaulted and suspected their neighbour, Thomas Brown, who had been in the shed with Etta just before she returned to the house bruised and bleeding. Despite Etta's age, Alice revealed the assault to no one except her husband Albert for two weeks, explaining that she 'did not want to make it public for the child's sake'.[40] Two weeks later,

---

34   *Neglected Children's Act 1890* (Vic) s. 25.
35   Statements of William Buswell and Margaret Green, *R v William Orr*, Melbourne Supreme Court, 15 April 1901, PROV, VPRS 30/P/0000, Unit 1238, Item 18.
36   *R v Eugene O'Gallaghan*, Melbourne Supreme Court, 15 November 1901, PROV VPRS 30/P/0000, Unit 1268, Item 489.
37   *R v John Ward*, Melbourne Supreme Court, 15 April 1902, PROV, VPRS 30/P/0000, Unit 1287, Item 223.
38   *R v Francis Hendry*, Melbourne Supreme Court, 12 December 1906, PROV, VPRS 30/P/0000, Unit 1438, Item 495.
39   Melbourne Supreme Court, 15 August 1900, PROV, VPRS 30/P/0000, Unit 1223, Item 335.
40   Statement of Alice Anderson, ibid.

when Etta still had a discharge, which did not seem to be improving, Alice took her to Dr Strahan who found that the baby had definitely been assaulted and 'told the mother to inform the police'.[41] Alice and Albert still prevaricated for a time, Albert telling the court that 'I had no money and … I was afraid that the man might injure me'.[42] Eventually, though, they did go to the police. Similarly, Victoria Ginn gave birth to a baby boy in July 1900, when she was 17. The child was her father's, although Victoria told her family at the time that she had had a liaison with a married man. In late 1901 she took the baby to the Children's Hospital where the doctor apparently diagnosed congenital syphilis and told Victoria that the child's father should be publicly exposed and punished.[43] Victoria then made a complaint against her father.

Case studies (2): Family, friends and complainants

By far the more usual scenario, though, was that in which a member of the girl's family notified the police. In 50 out of 68 cases (73.5 per cent) a relative, mostly a parent, reported the offence. This decision was rarely an easy one. It often occurred only after extensive efforts to negotiate a settlement, financial or otherwise, out of court. Patterns of negotiations reflected power relations within families and communities. If available, and not the defendant, fathers usually filed the complaint, and they were also expected to take a leading role in negotiations. In *R v Leftley*,[44] a typical example, 15-year-old Blanche Howes had been in a sexual relationship with, and became pregnant to, 19-year-old Harry Leftley. After Blanche sought medical advice about the pregnancy, the doctor told her mother, Mary. Mary informed her husband, Frederick, who, unusually, sought legal advice. The solicitor presumably advised him to try and negotiate. On 7 July 1904, Mary Howes and Blanche spoke to Mrs Leftley. Mary advised that the pregnancy had already proved costly and asked 'what they were going to do for me'. Mrs Leftley advised her that 'she would leave it to her husband'.[45] Shortly afterwards, Frederick Howes arranged a meeting with Harry and his father. Harry denied responsibility and Mr Leftley offered no financial recompense. In August 1904, Blanche herself confronted Harry and told him that if he did not do anything 'father is going to take it to Court'. Harry retorted that his father would spend 'every cent he had' defending the case.[46]

---

41 Statement of Edward Alfred Strahan, ibid.
42 Statement of Albert Anderson, ibid.
43 Statement of Victoria Ginn, *R v William Ginn*, Melbourne Supreme Court, 10 December 1901, PROV, VPRS 30/P/0000, Unit 1274, Item 596.
44 Melbourne Supreme Court, 22 May 1905, PROV, VPRS 30/P/0000, Unit 1384, Item 135.
45 Statement of Mary Howes, ibid.
46 Statement of Blanche Howes, ibid.

Despite this, the Howes family still apparently hoped for recompense even after the baby's birth in December 1904, for Frederick did not make a complaint to the police until April 1905.[47]

When a girl's father was dead, or he or a stepfather was the defendant, mothers usually stepped in, although a male family member or friend sometimes assisted them. In *R v Saddington*,[48] 15-year-old Florence Grumont and 18-year-old Hedley Saddington were fellow servants at a property near Mt Macedon. In January 1906, Florence complained to her widowed mother, Mary Grumont, that Hedley had sexually assaulted her four times between November and December 1905. Mary consulted William Donald, senior gardener at the house, for his views on the situation. Donald told her that 'if it was my child I would send for the police', but Mary was reluctant to do this, declaring that she '[didn't] want this thing made public' for the sake of Florence's reputation. Donald then arranged a meeting between himself, Hedley and Mary. Mary told Hedley she would not take the matter further if he '[w]ould keep his mouth closed in regard to the affair'. A few days later she reported the matter to the police because 'Saddington had been up reading reports about me and my daughter — I thought he ought to have kept silence [sic]'.[49] In a rather different scenario, in *R v Upton*[50] 14-year-old Gertrude Furzer was living with her widowed mother in a hotel in South Melbourne when she became involved with Herbert Upton, a married man with whom her brother was boarding. Their increasingly futile attempts to conceal the relationship finally ended when Gertrude became pregnant and her mother notified the police. Before that, Richard Alexander, barman at the hotel, had attempted to intervene with Herbert, telling him that 'he was a married man and should be ashamed of himself'.[51] Richard and several other neighbours gave evidence at the trial against Herbert.

Alexander might have assisted Mrs Furzer in remonstrating with Herbert and supporting her at trial, but it never seems to have occurred to him to go to the authorities himself. Such was the general respect for parental authority that other family members and friends rarely reported a suspected carnal knowledge case to the police except, again, where they stood in a parental capacity to the girls or, occasionally, when a mother failed to make a complaint against an offending father. *Gravino*, with the older sister's decisive intervention, was unusual. In *R v Mitchell*,[52] Grace Frith, aged 12, was an orphan living with a foster family, who were effectively her employers, when she complained that the father of

---

47   Statement of Frederick Howes, ibid.
48   Melbourne Supreme Court, 15 February 1906, PROV, VPRS 30/P/0000, Unit 1414, Item 82.
49   Statements of Mary Grumont and William Donald, ibid. Hedley Saddington was acquitted, the *Age* noting that Florence was 'a hysterical character' whose 'evidence could not be relied upon', see 'Criminal Court', *Age* (Melbourne), 23 February 1906, 8.
50   Melbourne Supreme Court, 26 May 1905, PROV, VPRS 30/P/0000, Unit 1386, Item 178.
51   Statement of Richard Alexander, ibid.
52   Melbourne Supreme Court, 25 May 1903, PROV, VPRS 30/P/0000, Unit 1324, Item 217.

the household had raped her. Her aunts reported the case to the police.[53] In *R v Bower*,[54] Myrtle Bower, also 12, was living with her father and younger siblings in Footscray when her father sexually assaulted her. Myrtle's mother was dead, and she eventually told Alice Tischler, who had been employed for a time by her father to look after the children, that she had an unusual discharge. Having also seen Frank Bower behave suspiciously towards Myrtle one night when he came home drunk, Alice notified the police.[55] Mothers who suspected their husbands of assaulting their daughters could find the decision to involve the authorities a very difficult one. Court transcripts indicated that they were often the victims of brutality themselves, as well as being financially dependent. In *R v Plozza*,[56] Giacomo Bombardieri, uncle of 12-year-old Catterina Plozza, stepped in after his sister, Catterina's mother, refused to make a complaint against her husband, Giovanni Plozza. Catterina had told Giacomo that she had been assaulted, and Giacomo had himself tried to warn Giovanni off, without success.[57]

The same deference to parental prerogative also militated against girls making complaints personally. Once a girl involved her family members, her own decision-making power was severely restricted, as the family subsequently decided on the course of negotiations and if the offending would be reported to the police. This meant that some girls gave their evidence reluctantly and defiantly, emphasising the consensual nature of their relationships with the defendants. Kate Flynn, aged 17, had become involved with Edward Mackney, a married man and a family friend. On 12 October 1902 she ran away with him to Geelong, where they remained living together for a month until the police arrested her on a charge of vagrancy. Kate gave evidence of some pressure from Mackney to come away with him, but the escape itself was carefully planned — he paid for a new dress and gave her a wedding ring to wear — and she agreed to live with him in Geelong 'as his wife'.[58] On the few occasions when girls did notify the police themselves they either lacked this close network of relations and friends or had moved beyond the reach of parental control. In *R v Waterhouse*,[59] 13-year-old twins Hilda and Winifred Waterhouse complained to the police that their father, Henry, had raped them and made them perform oral sex on him, sometimes in front of each other, on multiple occasions over a three

53 Statement of Grace Frith, ibid.
54 Melbourne Supreme Court, 15 June 1903, PROV, VPRS 30/P/0000, Unit 1327, Item 287.
55 Statement of Alice Tischler, ibid.
56 Melbourne Supreme Court, 15 October 1901, PROV, VPRS 30/P/0000, Unit 1261, Item 400.
57 Statement of Giacomo Bombardieri, ibid.
58 *R v Mackney*, Melbourne Supreme Court, 17 December 1902, PROV, VPRS 30/P/0000, Unit 1309, Item 563. As Kate was over 16, Mackney was charged with abduction of a girl under 18 from her parent with intent to carnally know. At the first trial he was convicted, but appealed. The issue at appeal was the relevance of Kate's consent, as the trial judge had directed that this was irrelevant. The appeal court held by majority that her 'willing participation' could be a defence to this charge, although not the ordinary carnal knowledge charge, and Mackney was subsequently acquitted by direction at a retrial. For the appeal decision, see *R v Mackney* 19 *Victorian Law Reports* 1903, 22–28.
59 Melbourne Supreme Court, 15 July 1905, PROV, VPRS 30/P/0000, Unit 1393, Item 275.

or four month period. The girls' mother had left the household for England in April 1904, and they lived with their father and older sister above their father's shop in Lonsdale Street, Melbourne. The girls reported the offending to police after they had been in service for several months, presumably gaining confidence from distance.[60]

Given this complex of family and community relationships that complainants and their families had to negotiate in the course of taking a matter to court, it was hardly surprising that reporting was frequently delayed and much debated. Although individual families' circumstances varied, there were common threads linking their final decisions to notify the police. Families tended to advise the authorities only after the offending became, to some extent, common knowledge and when alternative means of redress were either unavailable or had failed. A girl's pregnancy or suspected pregnancy was the frequent trigger for action. Not only did it alert family members to her sexual activity, but it meant that the wider community would inevitably become aware of it also. Further, for most of these households, it created immediate economic pressure about how to manage the coming baby. Such problems could be alleviated through marriage (if the girl was old enough) or financial assistance from the defendant and negotiations invariably focused on these points. In *R v Horton*,[61] Elizabeth West discovered in December 1901 that she was pregnant to her boyfriend, William Horton. William was reluctant to marry her as he was already supporting his mother and sister. In early January 1902 he gave her money to buy 'medicine' in the hope of inducing an abortion, which failed. She then told her parents, who met with William on three occasions, pressuring him to marry her. On 28 January Elizabeth's father Ansell also paid a surprise visit to William at his workplace. On 1 February William eventually offered to pay Elizabeth's confinement expenses and a small ongoing allowance, but still refused marriage. Ansell said he 'would not hear of such a thing as that' and, on 4 February, he obtained a warrant for William's arrest.[62]

In some cases, of course, neither marriage nor financial assistance was an option. Where the father of a family was the offender, the economic crisis was of the opposite dimension, for if he was removed, his family could rapidly find themselves destitute. In September 1900, Emily Paul notified the police that her de facto husband, Thomas Paul, had sexually assaulted her 13-year-old daughter, Edith Richards. On 20 September Thomas Paul was committed for trial and remanded into custody. On 24 September Edith and her three younger half-siblings were committed to the Department for Neglected Children, Emily

---

60   Statements of Hilda Waterhouse, Winifred Waterhouse, and Sergeant Patrick McManamny, ibid. The jury disagreed in two trials and ultimately the prosecution decided not to proceed. The twins' older sister, Millicent, gave evidence against the girls.

61   Melbourne Supreme Court, 18 March 1902, PROV, VPRS 30/P/0000, Unit 1284, Item 168.

62   Statements of Elizabeth Ann West and Ansell Joseph West, ibid.

declaring that 'she was entirely without means, and could not obtain any work'.[63] In such scenarios, mothers seem often to have reported husbands only when their relationship had already deteriorated, and an assault on a daughter was the final straw.[64] In *R v Merry*,[65] for example, Cecilia and Thomas Merry had apparently had a volatile relationship for some years, Cecilia complaining that Thomas did not earn enough to keep her, forcing her to take in sewing, and Thomas that her daughters — his stepdaughters — were disrespectful.[66] When Cecilia walked in on Thomas on top of her 15-year-old daughter, Beatrice Frazer, on Christmas morning 1903, she threw him out and took Beatrice to the police.[67] Similarly, in *R v Dunkley*,[68] 14-year-old Elsie Jude was raped by her stepfather, Charles Dunkley, but was frightened to tell her mother because 'he [stepfather] was in the habit of hitting her [mother] and I thought he might murder her if I told her'.[69] When a neighbour advised Annie Dunkley of Elsie's allegations, she took Elsie to the police, later telling her husband that, 'I could forgive anything you've done to me but not to my daughter'.[70]

Expectations and outcomes

Women like Cecilia Merry and Annie Dunkley reported assaults on their daughters in outrage and anger, presumably hoping that their husbands would be exposed and punished for their misdeeds. Desire for punishment was certainly one reason to bring offending to the attention of the authorities, but it was often only part, and sometimes a relatively minor part, of the overall decision. Economic considerations loomed large in pre-court negotiations, but most families do not seem to have expected that bringing the defendant to trial would itself lead to damages or any financial reward. Indeed, if the man or boy was convicted or imprisoned, they would not be able to claim any ongoing assistance from him at all for the life of the gaol term. This might explain why the Howes family held out for so long in *R v Leftley*, waiting until well after the birth of the baby before reporting the case. Only when it became absolutely certain that Harry Leftley was not going to provide for their daughter did they finally notify the local police. On the other hand, some families did subsequently bring maintenance proceedings against a defendant, in which a conviction for

---

63   *R v Paul*, Melbourne Supreme Court, 15 October 1900, PROV, VPRS 30/P/0000, Unit 1228, Item 414; 'Police Intelligence', *Age* (Melbourne), 25 September 1900, 5.
64   Louise Jackson comes to the same conclusion in her discussion of nineteenth-century Yorkshire and Middlesex cases, see Jackson, 47–48.
65   Melbourne Supreme Court, 15 February 1904, PROV, VPRS 30/P/0000, Unit 1346, Item 22.
66   Statements of Thomas Merry and Beatrice Frazer, ibid.
67   Statement of Beatrice Frazer, ibid.
68   Melbourne Supreme Court, 15 February 1903, PROV, VPRS 30/P/0000, Unit 1312, Item 9.
69   Statement of Elsie Jude, ibid.
70   Statement of Nellie Jude, ibid.

carnal knowledge could be useful, indeed essential, evidence. Daniel Peddie, father of 14-year-old Marian Peddie, does not seem to have tried to negotiate with 17-year-old William Sievers when he discovered that he had impregnated his daughter.[71] Nevertheless, on 17 September the North Melbourne Police Court made a maintenance order against William, noting that he had recently been convicted of 'intimacy' with Marian.[72]

More often, the threat of punishment was held over defendants' heads to try and force them to provide financial compensation or, in some cases, to stop the behaviour. Most of the witnesses in these cases were evidently aware that carnal knowledge of an underage girl was an offence punishable by a term of imprisonment. Mothers and fathers claimed repeatedly that they had warned young men that their daughters were under 16 and defendants sometimes made enquiries themselves. In *R v Weatherdon*,[73] Arthur Weatherdon asked the complainant, Josephine Barrett, with whom he had been 'walking out', how old she was. Josephine, an orphan, told him she thought she was 16, although she added that she had once been told that she was a year younger. Arthur was evidently satisfied with the first reply and persuaded her to come and live with him in furnished rooms.[74] In *R v Watson*,[75] 15-year-old Eileen Fogg, also an orphan, lived with her aunt and uncle, Elizabeth and Joseph Morris, in the seaside town of Sorrento. In December 1905 Elizabeth Morris suspected that her niece might be pregnant and took her to the doctor, who confirmed that she was between five and six months pregnant. Eileen then disclosed that she had had a sexual relationship with three men, including James Watson. The Morrises duly attended on James and his mother, Joseph Morris advising James that 'it was not a simple case of maintenance [but] … a criminal case and it might be very serious for him' if he did not co-operate.[76] In a very different set of circumstances, when Giacomo Bombardieri told his brother-in-law Giovanni Plozza to stop assaulting his daughter, he also used the law as a backup, warning Plozza 'if you don't stop I will give you a summons'.[77]

Above and beyond any desire for punishment or economic reward, however, a major expectation, reiterated again and again, was that a hearing would restore the reputation of a girl and her family in the eyes of the public. Involvement in extramarital sexual activity, whether it was consensual or not, exposed a girl, and by extension her relations, to community condemnation. There were frequent references throughout these cases to the shame that families experienced when

---

71   *R v Sievers*, Melbourne Supreme Court, 17 August 1900, PROV, VPRS 30/P/0000, Unit 1224, Item 342.
72   'Police Intelligence', *Age* (Melbourne), 18 September 1900, 6.
73   Melbourne Supreme Court, 22 February 1900, PROV, VPRS 30/P/0000, Unit 1208, Item 96.
74   Statement of Elizabeth Barrett, ibid.
75   Melbourne Supreme Court, 23 February 1906, PROV, VPRS 30/P/0000, Unit 1411, Item 22.
76   Statement of Joseph Morris, ibid.
77   Statement of Giacomo Bombardieri, *R v Plozza*.

they became aware of their daughters' situation. These feelings did not vary noticeably even with very young children. We will recall in *R v Thomas Brown* that Alice Anderson was reluctant to report a sexual assault on her very small girl 'for the child's sake'.[78] Girls who had been the subject of unwanted sexual advances felt the same humiliation. In *R v Francis Hendry*,[79] Bessie Martin had been raped by a family friend, a sailor who sometimes slept at their house. She told the Williamstown Police Court that, 'I never made a complaint as I did not want to disgrace them all'.[80] This sense of shame no doubt stopped many families from reporting incidents at all. For those who did, the trial was envisaged as a way to shift responsibility back onto the young man involved, by insisting that he was the dominant and/or coercive figure in the relationship. It also provided an opportunity for a family to assert (or re-assert) their own respectability. In both *Leftley* and *R v Sievers* the parents emphasised that the sexual relationship had occurred in otherwise 'respectable' contexts. In *Leftley*, Blanche Howes's mother told the court that Harry Leftley had assaulted her daughter when she was 'coming home from business', and she was not otherwise allowed out at night.[81]

The twin aims of penalising the defendant, while exonerating the complainant and her family, were rarely achieved by the court process. Scholars like Jill Bavin-Mizzi and Constance Backhouse have emphasised the multiple legal and practical barriers young girls in carnal knowledge cases faced at all stages of the court process. These included the rules of evidence, which discriminated against uncorroborated evidence, the often offensively masculine atmosphere of the courtroom and the social attitudes, held by lawyers and magistrates alike, which assumed that sexually active young women, especially working-class girls, were morally untrustworthy.[82] We have seen already that, overall, significantly less than half of the defendants in these cases were found guilty of the principal charge, although if guilty pleas and convictions for lesser charges are included, about 53 per cent of defendants were convicted of a charge. Breaking down the results in the Victorian cases between 1900 and 1906 supports the view that class, gender, and occasionally racial attitudes, significantly influenced outcomes at trial.

Carnal knowledge cases, as we have seen, usually involved working-class parties of the same social standing, hardly surprising when complainant and defendant were often either related or intimate acquaintances. In only eight cases out of the 68 was there a significant variation from this pattern. Two cases involved girls who might be described as either middle or lower middle class and working-class

---

78   Statement of Alice Anderson, *R v Thomas Brown*.
79   Melbourne Supreme Court, 12 December 1906, PROV, VPRS 30/P/0000, Unit 1438, Item 495.
80   Statement of Elizabeth Martin, ibid.
81   Statement of Mary Howes, *R v Leftley*.
82   Backhouse, 86–88, 107; Bavin-Mizzi, *Ravished*, 10–13.

defendants. Catherine Bazeley was a baker's daughter from Leongatha whose father had employed the defendant as an apprentice. Lucy Hill was a farmer's daughter from Sorrento and the defendant was a labourer on the property.[83] Generally, however, middle-class girls did not appear in this jurisdiction. In six other cases, the complainant was working class and the defendant middle or lower middle class. The typical social standing of the complainant created an immediate distance between the parties and magistrates or judges hearing the case, lawyers involved and possibly the jury members, for whom there was still a property qualification in this period.[84]

When the parties did not stand on an equal footing, the girl's class position does seem to have influenced the outcome of the trial. In all but one case when working-class girls brought charges against middle-class defendants they were unsuccessful, regardless of the strength of the evidence. In *R v Orr* Margaret Green, a state ward, complained that she had been raped by her employer's son, William Orr. William made admissions to the police, but he was not convicted.[85] In *R v Whitley*,[86] 13-year-old Sarah Turner alleged that Charles Whitley, a teacher at the local state school, had sexually assaulted her whilst she was employed cleaning his home. When Sarah's mother took her to a local doctor he refused to examine her, not believing her complaint against a man in Charles's position.[87] Although the prosecution produced a witness who had seen Charles entering the house at the relevant time, Sarah admitted under cross-examination that she had had a subsequent sexual relationship with another boy, which no doubt helped to further exonerate Charles.[88] The one exception was *Upton*, discussed above, when there was an abundance of corroborating evidence linking working-class Gertrude Furzer with the middle-class (and married) Herbert Upton. Conversely, both the cases in which girls made complaints against a man of lesser social standing ended in convictions. In *R v McPherson*, for example, 12-year-old Catherine Bazeley was sexually assaulted by, and became pregnant to, Neil McPherson, her father's employee who had lived with them. Catherine said nothing about the incident until her mother noticed her pregnancy five months later, and both parents admitted that they had not observed anything at the time.[89] These might have been damning factors in other cases, but Neil was convicted.

Whether parties came from urban or rural areas had a noticeable effect on the statistics. A significantly higher percentage of matters from rural areas ended in

83   *R v McPherson*, 16 September 1901, Melbourne Supreme Court, PROV, VPRS 30/P/0000, Unit 1264, Item 433 and *R v Swift*, Melbourne Supreme Court, 15 October 1902, Unit 1305, Item 503.
84   *Juries Act* 1890 (Vic), s 5.
85   Statement of Margaret May Green, *R v Orr*.
86   Melbourne Supreme Court, 15 July 1901, PROV, VPRS 30/P/0000, Unit 1251, Item 243.
87   Statement of Sarah Turner senior, ibid.
88   Statement of Sarah Turner junior, ibid.
89   Statement of Catherine Mary Bazeley, *R v McPherson*.

acquittal than the average across all regions (16 out of 24, or 66.6 per cent). One rural defendant pleaded guilty to the principal charge and one pleaded guilty to a lesser charge, so only five were convicted after trial (21 per cent). It would require further study to see whether this was a general pattern or representative only of this relatively small number of subject cases. The types of negotiations were not especially distinctive in the rural transcripts, and we cannot know how many assaults were in fact reported, or how many did not progress past the committal stage. Nevertheless, there are some possible explanations for the differential outcomes in rural matters. Four of the six cases which involved working-class girls and defendants of higher social standing were from rural areas, all of them unsuccessful. Three of the rural cases from 1906 involved the same complainant, Eileen Fogg, who as we shall see below was discredited as a witness because of her relationship with multiple men. In her study of South Australian state wards, Margaret Barbalet has suggested that sexual assault may have been more prevalent in country areas, in part because girls were more isolated.[90] The Victorian cases would not necessarily suggest that sexual assault was more common in the country, but isolation could certainly make a case more difficult to prove, through the absence of corroborating witnesses. Certainly, in at least five of the unsuccessful cases, there was clear evidence of sexual penetration but no evidence beyond the girl's statement identifying the man responsible.[91]

Race or ethnicity was less often a consideration in these trials, as both complainants and defendants were mostly white and English speaking. In three of these cases, however, the defendant's background was not British (or Irish) and this was clearly a factor at trial. Witness statements and investigatory reports indicated that the police and the courts approached these matters differently, and they all ended in conviction. In *Plozza*, the Plozza family were recent Italian migrants and both the investigating officer and jury evidently viewed the whole family as 'less civilised'. When Giovanni Plozza was convicted of incest, the jury recommended mercy 'on account of his being a foreigner and probably ignorant of the law'.[92] The same assumptions seem to have been at work in *R v Keefe*.[93] Isaac Keefe, an Aboriginal boy from Coranderrk station near Healesville, was accused of assaulting seven-year-old Emma Patterson, a 'half caste'.[94] Unusually, Isaac's first trial was suspended so that he could be legally represented, but

---

90 Margaret Barbalet, *Far From a Low Gutter Girl: The Forgotten World of State Wards, South Australia 1887–1940* (Melbourne: Oxford University Press, 1983), 90–91.

91 *R v Carlsen*, Melbourne Supreme Court, 15 February 1900, PROV, VPRS 30/P/0000, Unit 1208, Item 93; *R v Lamb*, Melbourne Supreme Court, 15 February 1901, Unit 1241, Item 66; *R v Cummings*, Melbourne Supreme Court, 15 August 1902, Unit 1298, Item 393; *R v Hyle*, Melbourne Supreme Court, 15 April 1904, Unit 1352, Item 117; *R v Manverton*, Melbourne Supreme Court, 16 May 1904, Unit 1357, Item 230.

92 *R v Plozza*, notation on brief.

93 *R v Keefe*, Melbourne Supreme Court, 10 December 1902, PROV, VPRS 30/P/0000, Unit 1309, Item 568.

94 Statement of Constable William Henry Hocking, ibid.

his guilt was assumed from the outset and he duly confessed, so the trial was a formality only. In *R v Abdullah*[95] members of a local working-class family pitted themselves against the defendant, Chaudri Abdullah, variously described as 'Indian' or 'Hindoo'. Fifteen-year-old Blanche Blight complained that Chaudri, her brother-in-law, had raped her. Blanche's older sister Miriam had married Chaudri's older brother Miyan Abdullah without the consent of their father, James, and the assault took place at Miyan's shirt factory where Blanche worked. The relationship, and Miyan's superior financial circumstances, evidently rankled James Blight immensely and he could barely contain his wrath at having to let Blanche work in an environment 'full of Indians and Hindoos'.[96] The jury perhaps sympathised for, despite much debate about a possible alibi, Chaudri was eventually convicted of carnally knowing Blanche.

Of course, whatever the class or ethnic background of complainant and defendant, a girl's reputation still remained relevant. As in rape trials, sexual knowledge was a weapon and, while the prosecution might enquire about a defendant's situation, they were far more interested in that of the girl and her immediate family. In such circumstances, Ruby Lever's case against Samuel Pimlott was doomed from the outset. Fifteen-year-old Ruby was living with her widowed mother, Christina Lever, in a notorious slum area of Fitzroy when she complained that Samuel Pimlott, a friend (and, possibly, client) of her mother's, had forced his way into her room and raped her. At trial Samuel gave evidence that 'it was an immoral house and I thought Mrs Lever was a prostitute', although he conceded that Ruby did not have an immoral reputation.[97] Samuel was acquitted. Even without such associations, girls were habitually cross-examined at length on their interactions with other boys; whether they worked in mixed workplaces or went out at night and any prior sexual history. Even young children were not immune from this line of questioning. Sarah Barber was nine years old when she was raped by her uncle, Charles Thompson. The Crown Solicitor's Office demanded extra information from the police about Sarah's school attendance, 'truthfulness' and whether she was allowed out on the streets.[98] Consent was not a defence in carnal knowledge cases, unless the defendant was younger than the complainant, and relations with others were also legally irrelevant, but both were recognised means of obtaining jury and judicial sympathy for defendants. Eileen Fogg, from Sorrento, confessed

95 *R v Abdullah*, Melbourne Supreme Court, 15 August 1900, PROV, VPRS 30/P/0000, Unit 1223, Item 326.
96 Statement of James Blight, ibid.
97 *R v Pimlott*, Melbourne Supreme Court, 22 May 1900, PROV, VPRS 30/P/0000, Unit 1216, Item 215.
98 Police Queries and Answers, *R v Thompson*, Melbourne Supreme Court, 18 October 1904, PROV, VPRS 30/P/0000, Unit 1367, Item 393.

to sexual relations with three boys. Her aunt Elizabeth Morris subsequently brought action against all three but, despite admissions confirming Eileen's version of events, they were all acquitted.[99]

Conclusion: Using the law

Carnal knowledge cases that were heard in the Melbourne Supreme Court between 1900 and 1906 were familiar affairs. The vast majority of complainants knew the defendants, often intimately, and court proceedings took place amidst a complex network of family and community relationships. In many of these cases, law functioned as a secondary mechanism for regulating sexual relationships. Most families understood by 1900 that carnal knowledge was a crime and that they had the right to prosecute. The decision to engage with the judicial system, however, frequently came only after private negotiations had failed, or where settlements were impossible in the circumstances of a particular case. Negotiations reflected gender and power balances within families and communities. Fathers or male family members customarily initiated legal proceedings, with women taking charge only if men were unavailable. Respect for parental or familial authority was such that young women outside the protection of a family were significantly less likely to report, or have their case taken up by others, including state agents. Girls themselves rarely had the influence, or courage, to take such a step independently. Once other family members had become involved, decision-making power no longer rested with the young woman concerned, although she might continue to play a role in discussions. The decision to prosecute was much more likely if complainant and defendant stood on an equal social footing. When the defendant was of a higher social class, both reporting and conviction were significantly less likely. It was also, overwhelmingly, a white working-class jurisdiction. Middle-class girls appeared in only two cases and ethnic minorities also very rarely.

When working-class families and their friends did report carnal knowledge cases to the police, they apparently did so on the expectation that a trial would punish a defendant and restore respectability to the girl and her family. These expectations revealed the limits of their understanding of the legal system, for even when a hearing led to the defendant's conviction, it did not usually salvage the reputation of either the young complainant or her associates. Girls' moral characters were examined in far greater detail than those of defendants, invariably to their detriment. When exploring the regulation of sexual conduct, we are nevertheless reminded repeatedly that these people were not simply the

---

99   *R v Skelton*, Melbourne Supreme Court, 23 February 1906, PROV, VPRS 30/P/0000, Unit 1412, Item 33; *R v Watson*, Melbourne Supreme Court, 23 February 1906, Unit 1411, Item 22; *R v Hibbert*, Melbourne Supreme Court, 23 February 1906, Unit 1412, Item 34.

subjects of intervention. In the majority of cases, discretion to prosecute rested with family members rather than state agents. At most points in the process, working-class families, if not young girls themselves, retained a large degree of agency and their choices to use the law were based upon social and moral, rather than legal, imperatives. Transcripts of carnal knowledge cases allow us to listen to the voices of working-class communities at the turn of the twentieth century 'in their own words', with all their emotion, anxiety and distress. By listening to these voices, we can track attitudes to gender, class, sexuality and morality as they played out in everyday life and in the legal system. We can also chart the reach of the regulatory state, by unpicking the complex dynamics informing crucial decisions to make the private public, or by engaging with the legal system in the first place.

Reading Past Cases of Child Cruelty in the Present: The Use of the Parental Right to Discipline in New Zealand Court Trials, 1890–1902

Debra Powell

In 2003 the United Nations Children's Fund (UNICEF) annual report on child welfare focused its concerns on the physical maltreatment of children, and published a league table of fatal child abuse statistics that placed New Zealand among the worst performing Organisation for Economic Cooperation and Development (OECD) nations.[1] Among its recommendations was the ending of legal sanctions (as enshrined in section 59 of the *New Zealand Crimes Act 1961*) that allowed for the hitting of children in the name of discipline.[2] Since that time, the topic of child punishment has generated significant anxiety and debate amongst child welfare advocates, doctors, educators, journalists, politicians and the general public.[3] Jane and James Ritchie, psychologists from the University of Waikato in New Zealand, were the first to suggest a link between the country's high levels of societal and domestic violence and the physical disciplining of children.[4] In 1979, acting on the findings of their groundbreaking study on the use of physical punishment in the home, the Ritchies made a submission to parliament advising 'the elimination from statute of any provision that permits the right to employ physical force in the correction and training of the young'.[5] Not only was their submission disregarded, but the response they encountered surprised them in its aggression — they had, by their own account, uncovered a firmly embedded 'cultural pattern' which, when threatened, provoked a strength of feeling 'so beyond reason and rationality as to indicate the social equivalent of a personal neurosis'.[6]

---

1   UNICEF, 'A League Table of Child Maltreatment Deaths in Rich Nations', Innocenti Report Card Issue No. 5 (September 2003), Innocenti Research Centre, Florence, http://www.unicef-irc.org/publications/pdf/repcard5e. pdf accessed 14 May 2011. With Hungary, New Zealand's abuse fatalities were singled out as being six times higher than the average rate for the leading countries. Only Mexico and the United States rated higher.

2   *Statutes of New Zealand*, 1961, No. 43, Crimes Act, Section 59; Innocenti Report Card Issue No. 5, 22–28. The report identifies the hitting of children by parents or carers as the most common form of violence in the industrial world.

3   For a comprehensive timeline of events relating to child discipline laws see Beth Wood, Ian Hassall and George Hook, *Unreasonable Force: New Zealand's Journey Towards Banning the Physical Punishment of Children* (Wellington: Save the Children New Zealand, 2008), 33–50.

4   Jane and James Ritchie, *Spare the Rod* (Sydney: George Allen and Unwin, 1981), 105–22.

5   ibid., 132.

6   ibid., viii.

In June 2007, however, the Ritchies' vision came to fruition with the passing of the *Crimes (Substituted Section 59) Amendment Act*, which effectively removed the defence of 'reasonable force' for the purpose of correction, for parents charged with assaulting their children.[7] During the course of the 2007 campaign, those seeking the full repeal of Section 59 met with the same welter of intense emotion that the Ritchies had encountered almost 30 years earlier.[8] It had become clear that the issue of child discipline was one that still 'cuts deep[ly] into the national psyche'.[9]

While proponents of repeal positioned it as a necessary step towards developing a domestic culture of non-violence towards children, opponents focused their concerns more narrowly on the criminalisation of the disciplinary smack.[10] The resulting debates, which were played out extensively in the public media, focused almost exclusively on the removal of the parental right to discipline their children as they choose.[11] Among those who continue to believe in physical punishment as part of 'good parental behaviour', the resistance to change has been intense.[12] The complex range of responses to repeal, however, belied the simplicity of its original aim: to remove the special legal defence available to parents who were prosecuted for significant assaults on their children, thereby affording children the same legal protection from physical assault as adults (or indeed, as animals).[13] As the bill's sponsor, Green Party MP, Sue Bradford stated during its first reading:

---

7   With the 2007 amendment to s. 59 of the Crimes Act, New Zealand became the 18th country to revoke legal provisions allowing for the physical punishment of children.

8   The first reading of the bill called for full repeal by removing s. 59 from the statute books. Compromise led to amendment in the form of a convoluted rewording that nevertheless removes the parental right to strike a child for the purpose of correction.

9   Sue Bradford, 'Crimes (Abolition of Force as a Justification for Child Discipline) Amendment Bill', First Reading, Parliamentary Debates (*Hansard*), vol. 627, 22086, http://www.parliament.nz/en-NZ/PB/Debates/Debates/b/1/6/47HansD_20050727_00001406-crimes-abolition-of-force-as-a-justification.htm accessed 27 April 2011.

10   Hence the popular terminology promulgated by the media who referred (and continue to refer) to the discourse surrounding the bill and subsequent amendment as the 'anti-smacking debate'.

11   British child welfare historian Harry Hendrick notes that the welfare of vulnerable children has more often been focused on adult, societal concerns, or, as Bronwyn Dalley says, on 'what adults consider children require, rather than children's needs' (Harry Hendrick, *Child Welfare: England 1872–1989* (London and New York: Routledge, 1994), 257; Bronwyn Dalley, 'Deep and Dark Secrets: Government Responses to Child Abuse', *Past Judgement: Social Policy in New Zealand History*, eds, Bronwyn Dalley and Margaret Tennant (Otago University Press, 2004), 178).

12   The bill for the repeal of s. 59 received more public submissions than any other piece of legislation in New Zealand's history (Wood, Hassal and Hook, 8). Moreover, a well-funded but obfuscatory campaign by repeal opponents led to a national referendum in which 80 per cent of respondents (from a voter turnout of around 50 per cent) disagreed when asked whether 'a smack as part of good parental correction should be a criminal offence'.

13   'Crimes (Abolition of Force as a Justification for Child Discipline) Amendment Bill', First Reading. A related aim was to bring New Zealand law into line with the United Nations Convention on the Rights of the Child, which s. 59 effectively stood in breach of.

I do not understand at all why it is illegal in New Zealand to beat my spouse, another adult, a policeman, or even an animal harshly with a horse crop or a piece of wood, but it can be legal to do the same thing to my child. It seems to me that section 59 of the Crimes Act is a relic of English nineteenth century law and thinking, which said that children were simply the property of their parents and were subject to their total control and to harsh physical discipline. At that time the same applied to wives, servants and horses. Strangely, it is only children to whom this quaint but dangerous law still applies.[14]

This chapter seeks to shed some light on the longer history of this 'quaint but dangerous' legislation by investigating its practice in the New Zealand courts at the turn of the twentieth century. Given the current strength of feeling, it is surprising that the laws relating to child discipline and child abuse have so far received little attention from New Zealand's social and legal historians.[15] This chapter implicitly suggests that their investigation is crucial to our understanding of current debates, and the anxieties that surround them. In tracking the history and context of early child welfare legislation in the courts and in communities, this chapter reveals that late-nineteenth and early twentieth century contemporaries struggled similarly to negotiate the tensions between notions of parental control and parental abuse. It appears that attempts to balance the rights of parents to discipline and punish, and the need to legislate against parental violence and abuse have long been fraught with difficulties. To uncover the ways people imagined parental discipline and control, the chapter examines these issues using a microhistorical approach. This method, using the close reading of legal files from court trials and their media reportage, derives from social and cultural historical modes of analysis that are also relevant to legal–historical scholarship. I contend that the interpretation of historical court narratives might contribute fresh ways of seeing our present struggles over the place of physical punishment both within families and before the law.

The two case studies I have selected to illustrate this theme took place nine years apart. In 1893 Kate Donovan was charged under the *Children's Protection Act 1890* with 'ill-treating' her son by beating him with a stock whip.[16] In 1902 Harriet Drake was tried under the *Criminal Code Act 1893* for the manslaughter of her daughter, who died following a 'severe beating'.[17] While vastly different in terms of charges and outcomes, and in the social classes of the accused, the case trials share similarities. Each involved extreme parental violence

---

14   ibid.

15   An important exception is Sally Maclean's research into the historical use of s. 59 in child cruelty cases tried in the Christchurch Courts (Sally Maclean, 'Child Cruelty or Reasonable Punishment? A Case Study of the Operation of the Law and the Courts 1883–1903', *New Zealand Journal of History* 40, no. 1 (2006): 7–24.

16   'Parental Castigation', *Wanganui Chronicle*, 19 September 1893, 2.

17   *The King v Drake, Gazette Law Reports,* Court of Appeal, 22 (1902), 145–49.

perpetrated by a mother on an eight-year-old child. Both the accused women argued that their actions were carried out as part of good parental discipline and turned to the legal defence of reasonable force for the purposes of correction. Both trials relied heavily on evidential testimony provided by friends, family and community. Above all, these case trials illuminate the contradictions and tensions surrounding the emerging ideas of child abuse and child protection that could be discerned at social, legal and governmental levels.

Beginning with the first case, this chapter goes on to consider the significance of early legislative responses and the emergence of agencies concerned with the issue of child welfare. The investigation of the second case trial is followed by an exploration of the peculiar tensions borne from the need to prosecute against such abuses in what, I argue, was an innately violent society.

Kate Donovan, a deserted wife and mother, was reported to be the first to be charged under New Zealand's *Children's Protection Act 1890*.[18] Those attending the Auckland Police Court trial in 1893 heard from neighbour, Ellen Clark, how she had witnessed eight-year-old Daniel being whipped and beaten so severely by his mother, that the sight of the boy's body 'nearly made her faint'.[19] Attracted by the child's screams, Ellen had peered in through the windows of the house, attempted to force the locked door and threatened to 'call a policeman', while Daniel's older sister ran pleading for someone to stop her mother from killing the boy.[20]

In court Kate Donovan stated that she did not consider the whipping too severe, insisting that the boy had grossly misbehaved himself by 'interfering' with the five-year-old daughter of a neighbouring family.[21] Daniel himself was called to testify before the court, and responded to the first line of questioning by declaring that 'he knew if he did not tell the truth he would go to burning fire'.[22] He told the court that his mother had beaten him for 'locking a little girl in her room', and doing 'naughty things to her', though he maintained that it had been his sister Mary who had locked them in the room and that he had been accused unfairly.[23]

Counsel for the defence, in an impassioned call to reason, attempted to shift the focus to the witness Ellen Clark, who, it was noted, had only lived alongside the defendant for one week. Was she in the habit of peering into people's windows? Had she never beaten her own little boy? The Bench, it was pointed out, frequently censured parents for not controlling their children,

---

18 'Parental Castigation', 2.
19 'A Terrible State of Things', *Observer* (Auckland), 16 September 1893, 3.
20 ibid., and 'People are not Satisfied', *Observer* (Auckland), 21 October 1893, 2.
21 'Parental Castigation', 2.
22 ibid.
23 ibid.

yet, 'unfortunately there were persons who would try to interfere with parents when they tried to control their children. The question was: what were parents to do?'.[24]

The magistrate himself physically examined Daniel and found that his body was 'covered with wales' and that the child 'could hardly turn his head'.[25] Nonetheless, he admitted to finding himself in 'a difficult position' as Kate was a deserted wife with sole care of her children and reliant on outdoor relief in the form of Charitable Aid. Moreover, he personally took no issue with the use of a whip as punishment for the boy's alleged misdeeds and 'fully agree[d] that children must be controlled'.[26] On the question of whether the punishment was 'reasonable' under the circumstances, the magistrate, however, declared himself to be of the opinion that the 'the boy had been punished too severely for his tender years'. Kate Donovan was found guilty of ill-treating her son. She was fined 40 shillings and returned home with Daniel in tow.[27]

Four weeks later, Daniel's name again turned up in the official records, this time in a coronial report. The post-mortem carried out on Daniel's body showed that his sudden death had been caused by a fracture of the skull.[28] The inquest, which took place at the bar of the Rob Roy Hotel in Freemans Bay, heard a confusion of testimonies in which Daniel's mother, neighbours, and other witnesses told conflicting stories. The boy had eaten poisoned oranges, or had fallen and hit his head on a fence; he spent the morning at school with his sister, or else he spent it lying on a stranger's couch bleeding from a head-wound.[29] Letters to the editor of the Auckland *Observer* suggest that there was a degree of unease among those familiar with the case, and at least one writer was prepared to suggest a connection between the boy's violent, sudden death and the ongoing violence in the Donovan household.[30] Such concerns appear to have been put to one side at the coroner's inquest. Instead, those attending heard from neighbours like Annie Melrose who came forward to offer positive accounts of Kate's maternal character. Annie deposed that she had 'always found [Mrs Donovan] kind and affectionate towards her children and only beat them when they were naughty', and added in reference to the earlier indictment for child cruelty, that '[h]er whole affair was only a bit of spite'.[31] Despite claiming to be 'dissatisfied' with the variously opposing points of evidence, the coroner's

---

24   ibid.
25   ibid.
26   ibid.
27   ibid.
28   Coroner's Inquest Report: D. Jnr Donovan, J46Cor 1893/645 (Micro U 5400), Archives New Zealand, Wellington. The report also noted signs of neglect in the form of intestinal worms and bodily sores.
29   ibid.
30   'People are not Satisfied', 2.
31   ibid.

jury gave Kate Donovan the benefit of the doubt. They found that 'no evidence was forthcoming to show how the fracture was caused', and an open verdict was brought in on Daniel's death.[32]

Daniel Donovan's story, inconclusive and open-ended as it is, nevertheless illustrates something of the tensions between notions of 'parental guidance' and the reality of physical violence, and highlights the significant challenges encountered by a society grappling with rapidly changing attitudes around the care and welfare of children. These changing ideals were driven by a 'reconceptualisation' of the notion of childhood, which took place throughout the western world from around the mid-to late-nineteenth century.[33] While the rising awareness of children's issues informed child welfare policy and practice in New Zealand, the path between shifting ideologies and legislative change was not always direct. In England, an obvious need for child protection legislation had been uncovered by reformers associated with child welfare organisations such as the National Society for the Prevention of Cruelty to Children, and England's *Prevention of Cruelty to, and Protection of, Children Act*, which was introduced there in 1889, came about as a result of the long and concerted efforts of those associated with the Society.[34] In New Zealand, however, there had been no such agitation for reform. Isolated concerns about parental violence or mistreatment were muted and, before the turn of the century, passed largely without comment. New Zealand legislation, enacted in 1890, just one year after the introduction of the English act, was, in the words of New Zealand government minister the Hon. Dr Pollen, 'simply a copy of [the] statute which had been passed by the Imperial Legislature in its last session'.[35] The honourable minister argued against the 'slavish' adoption of such measures when 'there was no necessity, to his mind, for encumbering our statute-book, which was already greatly over laden with laws that could have no immediate beneficial operation'. For Pollen and others, the object of the Act, which was 'the prevention of cruelty to and better protection of children', was an extraneous issue as 'the conditions

32   ibid.
33   The awareness of children's issues took place across a range of Western countries. Paris held the first international conference on child welfare in 1882 and, in that same year, the state of Massachusetts pioneered a law to protect children from cruelty and neglect. A second conference, which was held in Florence in 1896, was the catalyst for the formation of the International Congress for the Welfare and Protection of Children (Lionel Rose, *The Erosion of Childhood: Child Oppression in Britain 1860–1918* (London and New York: Routledge, 1991), 235). On the shift in ontological thought around child life see for instance, Hendrick, 21–37; George Behlmer, *Child Abuse and Moral Reform in England 1870–1908* (Stanford University Press, 1982), 44–77; Viviana Zelizer, *Pricing the Priceless Child: The Changing Social Value of Children* (New York: Basic Books, 1985), 11; and Dorothy Scott and Shurlee Swain, *Confronting Cruelty: Historical Perspectives on Child Protection in Australia* (Melbourne University Press, 2002), 9–10.
34   Behlmer gives a detailed account of the origins and passage of the English Children's Protection Act, commonly known as the 'Children's Charter', in *Child Abuse and Moral Reform*, pp.78–119.
35   Children's Protection Bill, *New Zealand Parliamentary Debates*, vol. 97, 3 July 1890, 260–61.

for which the act was intended to provide had practically no existence in this colony at all'.[36] However, it was unanimously agreed that it was 'better to prevent evil from asserting itself than to attempt to cure it after it had arisen'.[37]

Those looking to official figures might be forgiven for coming to such conclusions: even in the wake of a severe depression in the economy in the 1880s and 1890s, few cases of child cruelty came to official notice. Under the terms of New Zealand's *Children's Protection Act 1890*, intentional ill-treatment or neglect of a child was punishable by a fine of up to one £100 or up to two years imprisonment, and a magistrate could order the removal of a child or children from the family home.[38] While these provisions nominally included 'any offence involving bodily injury to the child', enshrined within the Act was the common law defence of 'reasonable punishment'.[39] Section 14 held that: 'Nothing in this Act contained shall be construed to take away or affect the right of any parent, teacher, or other person having the lawful control or charge of a child to administer reasonable punishment to such child'.[40]

As this chapter shows, the practice of physically striking a child to cause shock and pain as punishment, and the belief in its necessity and efficacy, was firmly entrenched in *Pākehā* (non-Māori) society, and therefore the boundaries of what might be considered 'reasonable punishment' proved slippery to define.[41] As a corollary the law was never heavily enforced. Indeed, in the eight years between 1892 (when the annual police reports began recording returns) and 1901, only 35 cases of child cruelty or neglect had been tried in New Zealand's courts of law.[42]

Despite government assertions that New Zealand children were not yet in need of protection, societies and agencies concerned with the welfare of vulnerable children were formed in the larger urban centres, and were kept extremely busy

---

36   ibid.

37   ibid.

38   *Statutes of New Zealand*, 1890, no. 21, Children's Protection Act, ss. 3 and 7, 78, 80. Before the 1890 Act, child cruelty cases involving violence were charged under the *Crimes Act 1867* as assault, assault causing grievous bodily harm or assault causing actual bodily harm.

39   *Children's Protection Act*, Section 79(a), 80.

40   *Children's Protection Act*, s. 14, 83. This same provision could also be called on for those charged with the assault of a child under the 1893 *Criminal Code Act* (s. 68). The defence of reasonable parental punishment was carried over into the 1908 *Crimes Act* (s. 85), and repeated with minor amendments in s. 59 of the 1961 *Crimes Act*.

41   The research carried out by the Ritchies in the 1960s and 1970s showed smacking to be the prevalent disciplinary method, with just over half of parents surveyed reporting that they hit their child once a week or more (Ritchie, 27). Figures from a more recent study suggest this figure may have been conservative. A 2006 study by the Dunedin Health and Development Research Unit found that 71 per cent of a sample group of 26-year-olds experienced physical punishment *on a regular basis* throughout their childhoods. Jane Millichamp, Judy Martin and John Langley, 'On the Receiving End: Young Adults Describe their Parents' Use of Physical Punishment and other Disciplinary Measures during Childhood', *Journal of the New Zealand Medical Association* 119, no. 1228 (27 January 2006), http://www.nzma.org.nz/journal/119-1228/1818/ accessed online 12 May 2011.

42   Maclean, 10–11. Maclean notes, as do historians transnationally, that trials were more likely to focus on neglect than abuse, as 'cruelty was more difficult to define and reach a consensus on'. See also Hendrik, 30–31.

in their work among families. Throughout the 1890s, Societies for the Protection of Women and Children (or the SPWC) were established in Auckland, Wellington and Dunedin, and the Children's Aid Society was founded in Christchurch.[43] The SPWC employed 'lady visitors' working in semi-professional positions to call into the homes of the poor to assess their needs. The group focused their efforts primarily on the work of 'compelling husbands and fathers to recognise and discharge their duties', which essentially meant following up cases of unpaid maintenance for deserted women and children.[44] Nevertheless, some attempts were made to address the problems of child neglect and domestic violence when incidences were brought to their attention. The process by which concerned citizens could report such incidences was explained in Otago's *Daily Times*:

> Every case brought under the notice of the Society is investigated by the chairman, who is in attendance at a certain place one hour every day for that purpose. Having investigated a case he decides what steps should be taken with regard to it. As a rule, a letter from the secretary is sufficient to produce the desired effect; but when necessary the Society has recourse to the law.[45]

It was understood that communities regulated and kept watch over their own members and, while a number of cases were reported to local societies by the police, it was expected that incidences of abuse or neglect would be identified and reported by individuals living within neighbourhoods:

> No active steps are taken by the committee to find out such cases as the Society deals with. The mere knowledge of the fact that a society exists for the protection of women and children causes people outside of it to bring cases under its notice.[46]

And, to some extent, this strategy was successful. In 1900 in the Coromandel district, northwest of Auckland, a local doctor reported such a case to the Auckland SPWC after local police declined to take action against Alfred Elmore for the excessive 'punishment' of seven-year-old Thomas Johnstone, who was in his charge.[47] Although Elmore received a paltry £2 fine for his acts, the efforts of the SPWC in taking the case to court were rewarded by the public discussion that followed about the frequency and levels of violence used to punish children. Figure 1 shows a journalistic representation of the case, which was published for the readers of the *Auckland Observer*. The narrative describes the judicial leniency in this case as 'an outrage in the name of justice' and goes on to illustrate the unease that this case generated among local residents in the Coromandel community.

---

43 Maclean, 21.
44 'Society for the Protection of Women and Children', *Otago Daily Times*, 11 February 1899, 8.
45 'Society for the Protection of Women and Children', *Otago Daily Times*, 13 February 1899, 3.
46 ibid.
47 'A Fiendish Story: How Children are Treated at Coromandel', *New Zealand Freelance*, 18 August 1900, 6.

N. Z. Observer

Alfred George Elmore, of Coromandel, reduces torture to a science, and takes his seven-year-old orphan brother-in-law from a warm bed and gives him a cold bath. Alfred: 'This will harden his weak and puny body.

'Now, there's nothing like the rod to train a child of tender years, when applied feelingly. There comes the blood—rather thin and colourless.

'So a good rubbing with a rough towel will help the circulation and tease the flesh a bit when it scrapes the cuts. Ah! Ah! this is great exercise on a bitterly cold night. Hullo! What's up with the child?'

Dr Cheeseman (to Alfred): 'Something wrong with this poor, delicate child? I should imagine there was. There are eighteen bruises and marks on his body. Nine of them have broken the skin and drawn blood.' And this was six days after the thrashing.

Alfred before the Coromandel Court for cruelty to the child. J.P's.: 'Well, Mr Elmore, you've been rough on the child. We really disapprove of your conduct for perpetrating those fiendish tortures, so we fine you two pounds and costs.'

Thamesites: '———! This is red-hot, and a disgrace to our mining townships. What is Coromandel thinking of when they let a fiend like that loose?'

A GROSS SCANDAL.—THE SCIENCE OF TORTURE.
A SCANDAL AND AN OUTRAGE ON THE NAME OF JUSTICE.

Figure 1: The *Auckland Observer* comments on the judicial leniency afforded to Alfred Elmore after excessively 'disciplining' seven-year-old relative Thomas Johnstone ('A Gross Scandal — The Science of Torture', *Observer*, 18 August 1900, 20).

Such media commentary, however, was extremely uncommon and the scarcity of reportage or observation on the issue of child cruelty suggests that public discussions about the vulnerability of children were measured and infrequent. The physical welfare of children in their own homes was an issue that remained heavily veiled by powerful social conventions, which prevented interference into the private sphere of families and into the parent–child relationship in particular. Despite the confidence of the SPWC that incidences of cruelty would be 'brought to their attention', it is clear that cases like that of Thomas Johnstone were among only a small minority of instances of child neglect or abuse that were actually reported to social agencies or legal authorities. Witness testimonies taken from events that resulted in prosecutions commonly reveal evidence of prior or ongoing neglect or violence, and a marked reluctance by neighbours to involve those outside of the immediate community context. The Donovan trial provides evidence that those living within communities who did intervene when they believed the line between chastisement and cruelty was crossed, risked public censure. Moreover, neighbour Ellen Clark testified in court that she had witnessed Daniel being beaten more than once in the week that she had lived in Freemans Bay — it might be presumed, then, that others were aware of ongoing violence in the Donovan household, yet only one other person from the Freemans Bay community was prepared to serve as a witness against Daniel's mother in a court of law.[48] While a measure of self-policing certainly did take place in New Zealand communities, evidence from trial records detailing cases of fatal violence suggests that individuals struggled, and at times failed, to address long-standing and extreme cases of abuse occurring within their neighbourhoods.

Popular understandings of the root causes of child neglect and cruelty, and just where such problems might be found, further veiled abuse occurring within families. While such issues were widely believed to have been problems of the poor, those working in the area of child protection had come to recognise children's vulnerability across class boundaries. George Behlmer notes that the London Society for the Prevention of Cruelty to Children argued strongly that child cruelty was 'unrelated to economic status'.[49] Representatives of Scotland's equivalent society, the Royal Scottish Society for the Prevention of Cruelty to Children, agreed, declaring that they 'wished the Society had the right to investigate the homes of the better classes as well as the homes of the poor, as they might often find cases which surprise them very much'.[50] The New Zealand trial of Harriet Drake, who, in 1902, was indicted for the manslaughter

---

48 Maclean's study of child abuse trials processed in the South Island courts between 1883 and 1903, similarly found that 'much child abuse went unreported or was not prosecuted', Maclean, 11.
49 Behlmer, 94.
50 Lynn Abrams, *The Orphan Country: Children of Scotland's Broken Homes from 1845 to the Present Day* (Edinburgh: John Donald, 1998), 210.

of her eight-year-old daughter Dorothy, may have been seen as a case in point. The weight of the medical evidence in this case, coupled with the fact that the woman accused of manslaughter was the matriarch of a 'well-known and highly-respected' middle-class family, attracted considerable public interest in the trial.[51] Unlike Daniel Donovan's case, there was little ambiguity surrounding the death of Dorothy Drake. The description of the injuries on the child's body left few in doubt that she had died of 'shock' after being 'disciplined' by her mother and two older sisters.[52] Dorothy's punishment, allegedly given after the child's refusal to recite a verse of poetry, was administered with a supplejack and a triple-lashed riding whip and appeared to have taken place systematically over the course of an afternoon.[53] A post-mortem report left no doubt as to the viciousness of the assault on the child, noting that the extent of the bruising meant that a piece of unbruised skin as wide as a shilling could not be found. A deep depression on the right side of the child's head carried the marks of the metal handle of the whip and the inside of the scalp showed extensive bruising. Of note was the existence of old wounds and scars consistent with ongoing beatings.[54]

As a manslaughter case, Harriet was tried under the *1893 Criminal Code Act*, and her defence relied almost exclusively on the parental right to reasonable force.[55] Section 68 of the Act reads:

> Section 68 (1) It is lawful for every parent or person in the place of a parent, or schoolmaster to use force by way of correction towards any child or pupil under his care; Provided that such force is reasonable under the circumstances; ... (3) The reasonableness of the force used, or of the grounds on which such force was believed to be necessary, shall be a question of fact and not of law.[56]

Dressed throughout the proceedings in deep mourning, Harriet argued that her actions were those of any responsible and loving mother — Dorothy had been a stubborn and disobedient child and in need of parental correction. The prosecution presented evidence, however, to show that Harriet was motivated by malice towards Dorothy that had existed since her birth. Witnesses were produced who were willing to attest to ongoing neglect and cruelty on the part

---

51 'Evidence at the Inquest', *Evening Post* (Wellington), 30 June 1902, 2.
52 Coroner's Inquest Report: Dorothy Drake, J46Cor 1902/456-829 (Micro U 5426), Archives New Zealand, Wellington. Harriet Drake's defence counsel's suggestions that Dorothy's death may have been due to concussion from an earlier fall, or even haemophilia, were unable to gain traction in the face of Harriet's admission that she had given the child 'a severe thrashing'. *Evening Post* (Wellington), 16 August 1902, 5.
53 ibid.
54 ibid.
55 *Statutes of New Zealand 1893*, Number 56, Criminal Code Act (s. 68).
56 Criminal Code Act 1893 (s. 68). This section was replicated with some slight rewording in s. 59 of the *Crimes Act 1961*, and remained in place for parents prosecuted for assault on their children until the 2007 amendment.

of Harriet towards her daughter.[57] Notably, these witnesses were outsiders, who were no longer immediately associated with the local community of Otaki — an ex-domestic servant; a sister-in-law from Eltham who had fostered Dorothy for two and a half years; and an ex-labourer on the Drake family farm. From among those within the community, however, there was a markedly different response. A long line-up of defence witnesses from the Otaki district attested to the respectability of the Drake family and to Harriet's affection for her children and devotion to her domestic duties.[58] Harriet's husband, Arthur, stood by his wife resolutely, insisting that: 'a warmer-hearted or more self-sacrificing woman there could not be … she was entirely devoted to her household, and lived solely for the benefit of the children, who were very fond of her'.[59]

Harriet's defence counsel, Mr Skerret, spoke at length on the temperament and upbringing of the accused woman, and stressed that while the consequences of her act were shocking, it could not be suggested that they were intended or contemplated.[60] The act itself, he argued, was not one of deliberate or designed cruelty, but occurred in an outburst of passion. He appealed for mercy for 'a woman who had brought up her children in a creditable manner, and discharged her duty as a loving mother, and whose remaining seven children should not be left without a mother's loving attention and devotion'.[61] Given the evidence of the physical injuries detailed in the coroner's report and Harriet's own admission that she had beaten her daughter severely, it is unsurprising that she was found guilty of the manslaughter of her child. Mr Skerret's appeals in Harriet's defence did not, however, fall on deaf ears. The jury delivered their verdict with a unanimous recommendation to mercy in order to indicate to the judge their preference for a light sentence. Nevertheless, the sentencing judge, Justice Edwards, was pragmatic. He informed the court that, '[t]hose who give way to their passions and allow themselves to use unrestrained violence towards young children must learn that the punishment which will follow will be a severe one'.[62] Harriet Drake was sentenced to six years with hard labour in Wellington's Terrace Gaol.

Undaunted, Harriet's defence counsel called for the case to go before a Court of Appeal. Mr Skerret argued that the prosecution's use of evidence relating to the mother's prior attitude towards the child had been both irrelevant and prejudicial.[63] He contended that 'it had been established by the evidence already adduced by the Crown, that the occasion was a reasonable and proper occasion

---

57 'Charge of Manslaughter', *Evening Post*, 15 August 1902, 5.
58 'The Case for the Prosecution Closed', *Evening Post*, 16 August 1902, 5.
59 'The Drake Manslaughter Case: A Severe Sentence', *Evening Post*, 9 December 1902, 5.
60 ibid.
61 ibid.
62 ibid.
63 *The King v Drake*, Gazette Law Reports, Court of Appeal, 22 (1902), 145.

for parental correction; that the only questions for the consideration of the jury was whether the punishment was excessive, and whether, if excessive, it had caused death, or had caused actual bodily harm'.[64] In deciding the question of what is meant by 'force reasonable under the circumstances' in such a case, Mr Skerret felt strongly that all argument must refer solely to the occasion of the correction.[65] It was on this basis that the case was brought before the appeal judges. The parameters of what might constitute 'reasonable' force remained vague, however, and particularly so as they were to be considered in the context of the middle-class family home. When explaining his decision to allow the contested evidence, Justice Edwards demonstrated a keen awareness of this fact by repositioning his stance within the framework of a less emotive set of circumstances. He asked his fellow Court of Appeal judges to consider this:

> If, for instance, a lad of seventeen, a scholar at a public school, should deliberately set himself to destroy the discipline of the school, and, after repeated mild punishments and kindly warnings, should be guilty of a further act of insubordination, it is plain that the schoolmaster would be justified in inflicting — nay, that in the interest of the offender himself he ought to inflict — a much more severe punishment in respect of such an act of insubordination than would be reasonable if such act stood alone. ... Under such circumstances ... it would be impossible to exclude evidence of the prior acts which rendered a severe punishment 'reasonable under the circumstances'. So, if a high spirited boy had fallen under the displeasure of his schoolmaster, and had been wilfully goaded into acts of insubordination ... and the schoolmaster availed himself of such an act of insubordination as an excuse for administering a flogging to the boy, it would, I think, be impossible to reject evidence as to the prior matters, which would establish that the motive ... was not the maintenance of discipline, but was the gratification of private malice. ... The use of force by way of correction by a parent stands in exactly the same position.[66]

While the circumstances of the case in question presented an altogether more complex picture, the Court of Appeal judges unanimously agreed in principle with Justice Edward's argument. They found that the testimony of Crown witnesses demonstrated that 'what was done was not honestly done by way of correction at all, but was done vindictively, and that the pretence that it was done for the purpose of correction was merely colourable'.[67] If, as Justice Williams pointed out, 'the mother was animated by dislike' and 'took the

---

64 ibid.
65 ibid., 146.
66 ibid., 149.
67 ibid., 147.

occasion of a slight offence to cruelly beat [the child], then the force would not have been honestly used for the purpose of correction, and the defence must fail'. What the appeal judges had actually accomplished was a shift in focus which allowed them to avoid a debate about the 'reasonableness' of the parental force used to 'discipline' an eight-year-old child who had died as a result. In reopening the question of whether the force used had actually been carried out as part of parental correction, and by dismissing the appeal on that point, recourse to the second arm of the defence (whether the force used was reasonable) became unnecessary. Harriet's conviction was left to stand.[68]

If the definitions of cruelty proved difficult to define in such case trials, this was grounded in their taking place within a culture of violence that existed despite the claims of parliamentarians. A deep contradiction lay behind the system whereby the courts themselves sentenced parents under the *Child Protection Act* and the *Criminal Code Act* for the use of excessive violence towards their children, while simultaneously rebuking others for failing to control their wayward offspring. Judges regularly commented on the need for physical punishment to be carried out by parents to stem the flow of delinquent children being brought before them. Indeed, those who were guilty of the 'evils of laxity of home discipline' were said to be culpable of 'a crime against their children'.[69] On sentencing 14-year-old Martin Murphy for the indecent assault of an eight-year-old girl, in 1900, Justice Denniston commented that 'if all boys and girls of that age who committed indecency were brought up [before the court] they would have their docks full'.[70] 'It was a pity', he said, 'to see so young a lad convicted'. In the judge's opinion, it should have been, 'another case for domestic discipline ... a sound thrashing by the boy's father would have been the commonsense solution of the case'.[71]

The law further encouraged and promoted physical punishment by sentencing children to be flogged or birched by the police. The *Criminal Code Act 1893* gave no minimum age for physical punishment using the birch or whip, and flogging using a cat-o'-nine-tails could be carried out from around the age of 16.[72] On sentencing 15-year-old James McLaren in 1888, a Dunedin judge mused: 'It is difficult to know whether a boy of this age ought to be flogged with the "cat" ... a good birching cannot hurt; it will inflict pain but it cannot be suggested

68   ibid.
69   'Juvenile Depravity', *Hawkes Bay Herald,* 27 February 1889, 2.
70   'Supreme Court', *Timaru Herald,* 7 February 1900, 3.
71   ibid.
72   *New Zealand Statutes 1893,* no. 56, Criminal Code Act, s. 14, 325–26. Newspapers carry reports of judicially sanctioned corporal punishment being carried out on very young children. For example, in 1875, a Thames court sentenced eight-year-old John Quadri to be privately whipped and incarcerated for 24 hours in the local prison after he was found guilty of stealing a fowl 'to the value of two shillings' ('This Day', *Thames Star,* 17 December 1875, 2). Judicial flogging was finally abolished in New Zealand with the *Crimes Amendment Act 1941.*

there is any cruelty about it'.[73] This was certainly not the opinion expressed in a 1937 article in the *British Medical Journal*, where a medical doctor condemned the punishment — in which a boy was stripped, then tied hand and foot to a tripod and beaten with a heavy bundle of birch twigs soaked in brine — as inhuman and barbaric.[74] By English law, police surgeons were required to be on hand to check the condition of the heart between each stroke of the birch, and to administer treatment afterwards, and it was noted that it would require 'around three days' for a child to be fit to attend school following such a punishment.[75] Accounts of judicial birching in New Zealand suggest that the experience diverged in severity and application and was subject to significant regional variation.[76] A correspondent in the *Wanganui Chronicle* described the 'instrument of punishment' used in the judicial flogging of boys in Wellington as a rod of 'blood-curdling' appearence, which had been 'purposely split for about half its length into a number of tails, and is there bound with cord to prevent it splitting further, the tails being bound also at the ends'.[77] Obviously disturbed by the brutality of the practice, he went on to describe 'the case of a boy who was beaten so severely [by the instrument] his screams could be heard from the closed cell by the watch-house (where the "birching" was inflicted) to the other side of Lambton Quay'.[78]

Predictably though, newspaper accounts of incidences of larrikinism and youth crime were regularly accompanied by correspondence from concerned citizens insisting on the 'healthy and stimulating laying on of birch and leather' to combat the 'rising problem' of moral laxity among the youth of the day.[79] The view appears to have been widely held that '[i]f parents so neglect their children as to allow them to become a menace to the well-being of society, then the State must in self-defence take charge of those children and endeavour to fill the place of parents'.[80] Such correspondents may have gained a measure of satisfaction from an 1895 ruling, where fatherless Thomas Thompson was spared a conviction by the judge who declared that if someone from the boy's neighbourhood would whip him with 'ten good strokes of the birch', the offence would be expiated. A newspaper article describes how a volunteer from the

---

73   'Supreme Court', *Otago Daily Times*, 12 April 1888, 2. McLaren was sentenced to six months imprisonment with hard labour, and privately whipped with 20 strokes of the birch rod.
74   'The Birching of Children', *British Medical Journal* (20 March 1937): 618–19.
75   ibid.
76   See John A. Lee's autobiographical account of his childhood experiences of judicial flogging in late-nineteenth century Dunedin (John A. Lee, *The Children of the Poor* (Christchurch: Whitcoulls, 1973), 231–33).
77   'Juvenile Offenders', *Wanganui Chronicle*, 1 May 1913, 5.
78   ibid.
79   'Juvenile Probation', *New Zealand Truth*, 27 January 1923, 4. See also 'Juvenile Depravity', *Hawkes Bay Herald*, 27 February 1889, 2.
80   'Juvenile Depravity', 2.

neighbourhood agreed, 'amid roars of laughter from a crowded court'.[81] Such evidence puts the hesitancy of juries and judges to condemn parental abuse, when presented in the guise of discipline, in a clearer light.

Historians of child protection legislation have shown how fledgling governmental concern for neglected and vulnerable children in the nineteenth century was effectively deflected by a social focus on the delinquent and criminal child.[82] A dualistic view of children as both victim and threat influenced legislation enacted throughout western countries and, in New Zealand as elsewhere, any government apprehension concerning the problem of parental neglect or cruelty centred not on the problematic family, but was projected outward, to the threat to societal stability that unsupervised and undisciplined children might engender.[83] In New Zealand, the passage of the *Children's Protection Act 1890* promised to prevent cruelty and 'better protect' children, however, the need to protect the rights of children to bodily safety was effectively trumped by the need to protect the rights of parents to physically punish. Trial records demonstrate that the violent actions of parents who appeared before the courts of law on charges of 'cruelty' were never trivial, and significant physical injuries to children were not uncommon in such cases. Nevertheless, as Sally Maclean has shown, there was a great deal of inconsistency in the verdicts pronounced on those tried for the maltreatment of children.[84] The two hearings considered here, one tried under the *Children's Protection Act 1890* and the other under the *Criminal Code Act 1893*, resulted in convictions, though neither demonstrates an uncomplicated evaluation or understanding of the criminal actions under consideration. Rather, they provide evidence of complexity and uncertainty, as judges, juries and community members struggled to come to terms with the meanings of 'violence', 'discipline', 'reasonableness' and the boundaries of parental 'force'.

The events discussed in this chapter took place during a period of social and political flux, when emerging ideologies surrounding child welfare and the rights of the child were coming into conflict with the inviolability of the family unit and ongoing concerns about child delinquency and criminality. The tensions that resulted from seemingly incompatible and contradictory beliefs around the issue of discipline were manifested not only at the social and intra-community levels, but also at the institutional level, within the provinces of government

---

81   'Stratford and Ngaire', *Hawera and Normanby Star*, 26 October 1895, 4.

82   See Hendrick, 7–12; Scott and Swain, 4; Bronwyn Dalley, *Family Matters: Child Welfare in Twentieth Century New Zealand* (Auckland University Press, 1998), 15–16.

83   I refer here particularly to the passage of the *Neglected and Criminal Children Act 1867* which enabled provincial councils to establish industrial schools in which children, who were judged to be either delinquent or neglected, could be detained. Included in the Act is the ruling that a boy of any age attempting to abscond from an industrial school would receive a 'private whipping' in punishment. *Statutes of New Zealand 1867*, No. 14, Neglected and Criminal Children's Act, s. 46, 172.

84   Maclean, 15.

and law: government ministers introduced child protection legislation while confidently denying the need for it; the courts, forced to censure some parents for their excessive use of violence, continued to rebuke others for not punishing enough; members of the public were moved to indignation when cases of child cruelty did come to light, yet few were willing to speak up against violence occurring among the families living within their own communities.

The recent twenty-first century debates surrounding child discipline laws, questions of public intervention in cases of suspected abuse, and the policing of private life and families, demonstrate that such tensions remain far from resolved. The defence of reasonable force to correct children's misbehaviour can no longer be used in court, although parents retain the legal right to use force in certain circumstances. In 2009, a government-ordered review found that the new law was working well and, the following year, the New Zealand police reported that the legislative change had had only a minimal impact on their activities.[85] Nevertheless, the public discussions on child discipline continue.[86] It is my contention that a clear understanding of the historical antecedents of these issues can only assist in their resolution. It is therefore imperative that new directions continue to be taken in legal historical research by asking hard questions about the private worlds of home and family, and how private behaviours have been codified and moderated by the law.

85   Review of New Zealand Police and Child, Youth and Family Policies and Procedures relating to the *Crimes (Substituted Section 59) Amendment Act*, 1 December 2009, http://yesvote.org.nz/files/2009/12/s59-report-to-prime-minister.pdf accessed 10 September 2011; and New Zealand Police, 6th review of Crimes (Substituted s59) Amendment Act 2007, 12 March 2010, http://www.police.govt.nz/news/release/22547.html accessed 10 September 2011.
86   See, for instance, the release of a documentary in July 2011 that challenges the findings of the Government review of the new legislation, http://www.radionz.co.nz/news/national/80224/family-first-challenges-review-of-child-discipline-laws accessed 10 September 2011.

Women, Children and Violence in Aboriginal Law: Some Perspectives From the Southeast Queensland Frontier

Libby Connors

Aboriginal writers, Jackie Huggins, Michael Dodson, Rosemary van den Berg, Lester Irabinna Rigby argue that the extent of research conducted in Aboriginal lands and on Aboriginal people since British invasion in the late 1770s, is so immense it makes us one of the most researched groups of people on earth . . . Indeed, in some social science disciplines we are over-researched and this has generated mistrust, animosity and resistance from Aboriginal people.[1]

Unlike the other social sciences, and despite Henry Reynolds's call for historians to write the story of the 'other side of the frontier' more than 30 years ago, Australian colonial historians have been slow to take up the challenge of Aboriginal-centred history. Bound by the limitations of overwhelmingly white and unsympathetic source materials, attempting to interpret Aboriginal frontier actors is fraught with methodological difficulty for the historian. Scholarship on missions and reserves from later periods which have been able to draw on Aboriginal writing and oral history have been tackled with greater confidence and are now being supplemented by evocative histories by Aboriginal scholars,[2] but Aboriginal frontier histories remain underdeveloped. Postcolonial approaches, with their interest in indigenous subjectivity, should have stimulated greater interest in Aboriginal views of the colonial past but here, too, the influence on Australian historiography has been mixed. Bain Attwood's book on the Batman treaty concluded that Aboriginal views of the 1830s were impossible to recover and so, only the Aboriginal protest movement of the 1970s was considered as

---

1   Karen L. Martin, 'Ways of Knowing, Ways of Being and Ways of Doing: A Theoretical Framework and Methods for Indigenous Re-search and Indigenist Research', *Journal of Australian Studies*, no. 76 (2003): 203.
2   Rachel Perkins and Marcia Langton, *First Australians* (Melbourne University Press, 2010). The literature on missions is too immense to cover here but Robert Kenny, *The Lamb Enters the Dreaming: Nathanael Pepper and the Ruptured World* (Melbourne: Scribe, 2007) is groundbreaking. Some of the best examples of reserve histories from Queensland include David S. Trigger, *Whitefella Comin': Aboriginal Responses to Colonialism in Northern Australia* (Cambridge University Press, 1992); Thom Blake, *A Dumping Ground: A History of the Cherbourg Settlement* (Brisbane: University of Queensland Press, 2001); Joanne Watson, *Palm Island: Through a Long Lens* (Canberra: Aboriginal Studies Press, 2010).

part of the study of that important experiment of land purchase.[3] The best work in the field of Aboriginal-centred colonial history has come from Sydney where Inga Clendinnen, Keith Vincent Smith and Grace Karskens have been prepared to interrogate and sift the white sources to recover Aboriginal voices and actions in histories that are deservedly celebrated for their multi-layered and vivid retelling of colonial foundations.[4]

The task, however, is not easy and it presents formidable methodological problems, as Aboriginal and history critics have highlighted. This chapter uses some of the evidence from Moreton Bay to respond to some of the more complex and controversial aspects of traditional law that have surfaced in the Sydney histories, regarding the level of violence directed at wives and children. It briefly outlines some of the criticisms that have been made of Clendinnen's *Dancing with Strangers* (2003), notes how Karsken's *The Colony* (2010) overcomes some of the earlier work's limitations but also where it concurs regarding some contentious aspects of Eora society; it then briefly outlines the evidence from Moreton Bay regarding just two aspects of traditional society — Aboriginal marriage and attitudes to children — before drawing some conclusions about contextualising traditional law in Australian historiography.

Despite its deserved celebration for recovering the importance of Bennelong's role as a cross-cultural diplomat and negotiator in the founding of New South Wales, *Dancing with Strangers* was subject to staunch criticism from Aboriginal scholars, one of whom argues that it 'render[s] invisible and dematerialise[s] contemporary flesh-and-blood Aborigines'.[5] There was concern about Clendinnen's portrayal of gender relations as being marked by excessive violence.[6] It was argued that an effect of the work was to reproduce a view of Aboriginal women as the abject beasts of burden that was so favoured by nineteenth-century anthropology, a representation well and truly rejected by anthropologists by the 1980s.[7] Another concern was that its timing affirmed a right-wing representation of Aboriginal community dysfunction that justified

3   Bain Attwood (with Helen Doyle), *Possession: Batman's Treaty and the Matter of History* (Melbourne: Miegunyah, 2009).
4   Inga Clendinnen, *Dancing with Strangers* (Melbourne: Text, 2003); Keith Vincent Smith, *Bennelong: The Coming in of the Eora: Sydney Cove 1788–1792* (Sydney: Kangaroo Press, 2001); Vincent Smith, *King Bungaree: A Sydney Aborigine Meets the Great South Pacific Explorers, 1799–1830* (Sydney: Kangaroo Press, 1992); Vincent Smith, *Wallumedegal: An Aboriginal History of Ryde* (Sydney: Ryde City Council, 2005); Grace Karskens, *The Colony: A History of Early Sydney* (Sydney: Allen and Unwin, 2010).
5   This is part of Philip Morrissey's critique of Inga Clendinnen's *Dancing with Strangers*. See Philip Morrissey, 'Dancing with Shadows: Erasing Aboriginal Self and Sovereignty', in *Sovereign Subjects: Indigenous Sovereignty Matters*, ed., Aileen Moreton-Robinson (Sydney: Allen and Unwin, 2007), 69.
6   Clendinnen, 146–51, 159–67.
7   See Les Hiatt's summary of the anthropological debates on the status of women in L.R. Hiatt, *Arguments about Aborigines: Australia and the Evolution of Social Anthropology* (Cambridge University Press, 1996), 57–63; Nancy M. Williams and Lesley Jolly, 'From Time Immemorial? Gender Relations in Aboriginal Societies before "White Contact"', in *Gender Relations in Australia: Domination and Negotiation*, eds, Kay Saunders and Ray Evans (London: Harcourt Brace Jovanovich, 1992), 9–19.

the Northern Territory Intervention, as introduced by the Liberal government of John Howard. Shoni Konishi contends that the problem lay in Clendinnen's failure to consider how the assumptions and values of late-eighteenth-century ideas about civilisation infused the writings of the First Fleet officers; these works on which the author placed so much reliance were unreliable as they sought to represent Aboriginal gender relations as the polar opposite of that valued by refined and civilised late-eighteenth-century gentlemen.[8]

Karskens avoids such a reductionist view of traditional society by covering the broader span of Aboriginal individuals and communities over time, rather than telescoping on moments of internal discord. Karsken's does not reject the white primary sources, with their collaborating data, but better contextualises them so that conflict and brutality, by both white and black individuals and communities, can be understood as cause and effect, heightened by new geographies. Nonetheless, the description of domestic discord and an incident of murderous payback carried out upon a six- or seven-year-old girl repeats evidence that is also presented by Clendinnen and disturbs the representation of the apparent integrity of Aboriginal law.[9] It is this which needs to be critically examined by looking at the comparable evidence from other parts of the continent.

Part of my original interest in the topic of indigenous women in southeast Queensland was stimulated by the contrast with the circumstances of indigenous women in Sydney. The primary sources are derived from a period 30 to 50 years later and, unfortunately, they are not as extensive as those produced by the members of the First Fleet. There are, however, a number of sympathetic sources that offset the official and antagonistic settler documents. While none of these sources is flawless — the main counter-discourse came from missionaries who were bound by their own cultural assumptions of Christian moral superiority — they provide a contrast that allows a more balanced reconstruction of the events of the frontier period. Fortunately, the European sources are supplemented by the knowledge of Gaiarbau, a member of the Jinibara or Dalla[10] who, as a man in his 80s, related a great deal of information about traditional life to L.P. Winterbotham between 1950 and 1957.[11] The result is some intimate information that is, albeit, still very fractured by being embedded in the male perspective.

8   Shino Konishi, '"Wanton with Plenty": Questioning Ethnohistorical Constructions of Sexual Savagery in Aboriginal Societies, 1788–1803', *Australian Historical Studies* 39, no. 3 (September 2008): 356–72.
9   Karskens, 442, 460.
10   Gaiarbau gave the name of his people as 'Jinibara' but I have generally used the term 'Dalla' as it and 'Gubbi Gubbi' are the names by which the traditional owners of the Blackall Ranges identify today. Where possible I have used the names for traditional owners as given by the Foundation for Aboriginal and Islander Research Action, but the missionaries' nomenclature does not always match that in use today, and historic terms are retained to minimise confusion.
11   Gaiarbau's story of the Jinibara tribe of southeast Queensland (and its neighbours). Collected by L.P. Winterbotham, MS 45 / MS 429, Australian Institute of Aboriginal and Torres Strait Islander Studies (AIATSIS).

The stereotype of Aboriginal brutality towards wives, as promulgated by sources based around Sydney, had become so entrenched in colonial discourse that the marooned convicts who gave us the first recorded evidence of gender relations in the north were taken aback by the level of sympathy and affection shown between husbands and wives. At the same time, they recorded women's participation in communal meetings and group fights, which, along with other evidence, confirm women's ready engagement in hand-to-hand combat. Clendinnen's and Karsken's use of the term 'warrior culture' seems the best way to categorise this aspect of hunter-gatherer society for a modern audience.

One of the earliest accounts from the Moreton Bay region comes from John Uniacke, a member of the crew that accompanied surveyor-general John Oxley in 1823. Left on board the main vessel moored near Bribie Island while Oxley went exploring up river, Uniacke was in a position to record discussions with rescued shipwreck survivors Thomas Pamphlet and John Finnegan, who had been living with traditional owners around the bay for several months. Their accounts challenged the prevailing view of female subjugation in Aboriginal society:

> The women are far more fortunate than those in the neighbourhood of Sydney, where they are abused in the most cruel way by the men, and where the marriage ceremony consists of seizing the bride and beating her till she is senseless. Pamphlet assured me that, during his residence among these natives (nearly seven months) he never saw a woman struck or ill treated except by one of her own sex ... The women that I saw were far superior in personal beauty to the men, or, indeed, to any natives of this country whom I have yet seen. Many of them are tall, straight, and well-formed.[12]

Oxley's party had arrived in Pumicestone Passage, on the northwest side of Moreton Bay, just two days after a major meeting had taken place to settle intertribal matters, a circumstance that allowed Finnegan to give Uniacke a fresh and vivid account of proceedings. He related how, after two days' travel he, and the tribe by which he had been adopted, arrived at the meeting place where the participants 'were so numerous, that I could hardly count them ... (for there were many tribes assembled to see the fight)'. The contests — for this was an opportunity to settle a number of outstanding grievances, not just a dispute between 'two tribes' as Finnegan had expected — took place about two and a half kilometres from the village and encampment; there 'the multitude' assembled around the perimeter of a specially constructed large sunken pit. The first fight Finnegan was permitted to witness was between two women:

---

12 Uniacke's narrative of Oxley Expedition 1823 cited in J.D. Lang, *Cooksland in North-Eastern Australia* (London: Longman, Brown, Green and Longmans, 1847), 410.

I there saw a woman of my tribe, and one of another, fighting desperately with sticks. The battle did not, however, last long, as they appeared to be quite in earnest, and in five minutes, their heads, arms, etc, being dreadfully cut and swelled, our woman was declared the conqueror, the other not being able any longer to oppose her. The victory was announced by a loud shout from all parties, and the Amazonian combatants were immediately carried away by their respective friends.[13]

Pride in one's kin group, physical prowess and personal bravery were prized as much by the women as by the men; there was no point in a woman initiating a legal challenge if she was not prepared to stand her ground forcibly. This 'Amazonian' culture, shocking to European observers, was an intrinsic part of life and the system of law in southeast Queensland. Finnegan's account made clear that the fights were supervised and governed by rules of fair play, with a halt called to proceedings when those rules were deemed to have been breached. Tom Petrie, who had travelled and periodically lived with local Aboriginal people since a small child, also told his daughter of how women not only fought to settle disputes, but would sometimes contribute to major battles between their menfolk from the outer fringes.[14]

Women with childcare responsibilities were not spared the tensions of these contests but had to be prepared to retreat with the children and give up their ground in the event of their men being routed. Finnegan gave a personal example of this as his lack of bushcraft left him at a decided disadvantage at this great fight. The Bribie Island 'chief' who had accepted him into his tribe insisted on introducing Finnegan to the other chiefs; he needed to gain a commitment from the other tribes not to molest Finnegan should the Bribie Islanders not prevail. Indeed, the fight did go against the Bribie Islanders and Finnegan was forced to withdraw with the women and children. He was unable to keep up with his companions, however, and his lack of bushcraft soon saw him surrounded by the Bribie Islanders' opponents, who laughed at him as they overtook him.[15]

Some 18 years later, but still before the opening of the district to settlement, two of the German missionaries who had established a mission at Nundah in 1838, were invited by the local Aboriginal people to travel with them to a fight and festivities for several groups of traditional owners. They came from across the region to gather at Toorbal, on the northwest side of Moreton Bay. Like Finnegan

---

13 'Account of a Fight Among the Natives of Moreton Bay Witnessed by John Finnegan' cited by Lang, ibid., 411–15.

14 Constance Campbell Petrie, *Tom Petrie's Reminiscences of Early Queensland* (Melbourne: Lloyd O'Neil, 1975 [facs of 1904]) 46.

15 'Account of a Fight Witnessed by Thomas Pamphlet' cited in Lang, 410–11, 413–14.

before them, the missionaries were aghast at the ferocity of the women's formal contests. Reverend Christopher Eipper wrote a description for their Presbyterian supporters in Sydney, which was printed in the *Colonial Observer*:

> In the afternoon our attention was suddenly arrested by a great noise, caused by beating sticks together, and as we saw all the women run with their long and pointed sticks, which are used in digging dangum; we ran also to ascertain what this meant. But what a scene did we behold! The whole of the women were engaged in a regular battle; it was quite overwhelming to look at this fight of women, than which no contest of men could be fiercer; some actually had froth before their mouth. Each had her antagonist, who parried her blow by holding her stick between her fingers over her head; and then immediately returned the stroke, which was parried in the same way; when they got close together, they took hold of one another, each endeavouring to throw the other down.

'Some had their fingers and elbows bleeding when we arrived'; Eipper continued and so the two young missionary men sought to disrupt the fight, much to the annoyance of the older women who 'were very much displeased, and pointed their spears at ours; yea one threw it at Mr E'. Not only did the young Christians fail to understand the authority of the older women, they also failed completely to understand a warrior culture in which it was accepted that disputes were settled by resort to arms. The next morning they were shocked to see two women fighting 'whose husbands were quietly looking on ... we separated them, threatening that we should tell the Commandant of their quarrels'.[16]

A culture based on warrior values was also much more accepting of informal violence between men and women and between husbands and wives than contemporary standards allow. Unlike the castaways, the German missionaries did witness incidents of domestic violence but seemed as much struck by the women's vocal objections to their treatment as by the assaults. This warrior culture was oral as well as physical and one reason for the 'froth before their mouth', as Eipper had phrased it, was that challenges and fights were preceded by the angry public issuing of a complaint and challenge followed by verbal jousting which sometimes averted a physical showdown while, at other times, it heralded the onset of a fight in earnest.[17] On one occasion the missionary Niqué recorded how a woman, who was knocked down by a man after she provoked him, was not only not submissive, but continued to challenge him by singing

---

16 *Colonial Observer*, 21 October 1841, 23.
17 'Such was the eagerness of all to listen to what was spoken on such occasions, that whenever any one was heard to speak in that way after the evening meal had been taken, we scarcely could get any information from our neighbours or guides of the cause of the quarrel'. *Colonial Observer*, 14 October 1841, 10.

a war song at him for 'about half an hour'.[18] A vocal wife also reprimanded her husband at length when he struck her for eating his roast potato, a new delicacy courtesy of the missionary guests.[19]

A scolding is obviously not as effective an expression of power as physical force but it would be wrong to assume female subjection as a result. The missionaries were struck by the desire of the men to impress their women, and the obvious affection between married couples that was often displayed. On one of their excursions to Toorbal, young Ningy Ningy guides escorted the missionaries over to 'Yarun', the local name for Bribie Island. Circumstances forced them to stay overnight but, before returning to their own village, Eipper recorded that 'as the [Ningy Ningy] were young men they were very particular to dress themselves carefully before they made their appearance again in the camp, significantly replying to our enquiry, why they did so, *the ladies* will see us'.[20] Anthropological work has established that the system of betrothals worked in the interests of the older men and women and increased competition among young men and unbetrothed females for the prize of a marriage partner.[21]

One of the most important contributions from the missionaries is the context for some of the violent exchanges that they witnessed, and how traditional society managed violence and set limits on its expression. The young German evangelists worked closely with Deciby, a Ningy Ningy man whom they referred to as the 'King of Toorbal' and who frequently stayed at the group of cottages the missionaries constructed for their regular indigenous visitors. The camp and gardens — known by a local name of Girkum — were on the other side of Kedron Brook, opposite the missionaries' own thatched cottages and planted fields. Clearly a man of some stature, Deciby was an important diplomatic go-between for the missionaries and many of the traditional owners to the north of Brisbane. Deciby's standing was presumably also high among the women because, although he had a wife and a newborn son, he committed adultery with the wife of Wogan, a prominent local man who was well-known in Brisbane and at the mission.[22] When informed of his wife's actions, Wogan approached

18   Journal of the Brethren Niqué & Rodé who were Itinerating Among the Natives at Umpie Boang from the 12 of March to the 31st 1842, entry for 25 March, Lang Papers Mitchell Library (ML).
19   *Colonial Observer*, 28 October 1841, 27.
20   *Colonial Observer*, 21 October 1841, 23. Emphasis in original. This report also included discussion of a man's great concern for his sick wife; other references to spousal affection or concern are evident in *Colonial Observer*, 11 November 1841, 42 and 'Mission Diary', entry for 15 January 1842, Lang Papers, ML.
21   Hiatt, 67–71 covers the debates concerning benefits to mothers-in-law of the bestowal system.
22   Wogan was well known in Brisbane and Ipswich and featured regularly in newspaper reports after 1842. He may have been an elder since the missionaries referred at times to the 'Wogans' meaning a number of other men who may have been his tribal or biological brothers. It is not clear from any of the accounts whether he was Yaggera, Turrbal or Ningy Ningy and his ready movement between Girkum, Toorbal and Brisbane indicate the high level of interaction between the Brisbane, Ipswich and Bayside peoples. For other references to Wogan see *Colonial Observer*, 14 October 1841, 10; 28 October 1841, 27; 18 November 1841, 51; *Sydney Morning Herald*, 7 April 1846, 3; Lang, 398–99.

the camp late one summer night to confront Dambir Dambir, his wife, but he did not go alone. He brought with him his brother, Borungado. Wogan found his wife and brought her to his own hut where he was armed with his club and shield; Dambir Dambir was also prepared with her digging stick, which she used to shield herself from her husband's blows. Wogan, however, soon knocked her to the ground at which point 'all the women' of the camp intervened, shielding Dambir Dambir from the blows of the waddies of Borungado and Wogan with their sticks. The missionaries believed that, if they left the scene, Wogan and Borungado intended to kill Dambir Dambir, although it is not clear how this could have been accomplished given the role of the other women of the camp.[23]

Was this normal women's business to intervene to protect Dambir Dambir, or was Dambir Dambir fortunate to have her tribal sisters there that night? Gaiarbau gave another revealing account of how marital cruelty was managed. He assigned key roles not to the women of the tribe but to the victim's mother and her brother. According to Dalla protocol, a secret message was sent to the headman of the wife's tribe; the headman then organised for her brother to bring her back to her family. The brother had to carry a specially painted spear, which was adorned with the white cockatoo feather that had been presented to the girl's mother upon her marriage. The headman of the husband's tribe, upon seeing the brother, would allow him to approach his sister. If she took the spear she would be led away to her own people where it then became the responsibility of her brothers to maintain her. This system was essentially a form of divorce, for the wife was required to leave behind any children and neither husband nor wife were permitted to remarry during the other's lifetime. Social harmony prevailed, however, for according to Gaiarbau, 'All this was done by consent of the Bora and caused no fight'.[24] So it would be unfair to characterise Dambir Dambir's assault as typical since there were formal mechanisms to protect wives. Despite the pre-eminence of fighting skills in traditional culture, women's security was safeguarded through their kin and through women's culture.

The descriptions of women's fighting and their lack of subservience to husbands mirror the Sydney material closely. What is new are the insights from Gaiarbau that, in the north at least, there were formal processes for limiting spousal violence. The lack of similar practice in Sydney could be a result of the smallpox epidemic's impact on local traditions, a local variation peculiar to southeast Queensland, or a bias of the extant sources.

It raises similar uncertainties over the interpretation of the apparent payback killing of the six- or seven-year-old female child near Sydney Domain in

---

23 Monday 7 – Tuesday 8 March 1842, Extracts from the Diary of the German Mission to the Aborigines at Moreton Bay from the 25th December 1841 to the 13 of May 1842, Lang Papers, ML.
24 Gaiarbau's story of the Jinibara tribe of southeast Queensland (and its neighbours). Collected by L.P. Winterbotham. MS 45 / MS 429, AIATSIS, 29–30.

circa 1795–96, which also indicates starkly different relationships to those in existence at Moreton Bay. In reports of their northern journeys, the German missionaries had commented on the evident affection for children that was displayed by the traditional owners. The tears shed by Aboriginal fathers, uncles and grandfathers on being reunited or parting from small children indicates demonstrative affection for children was a part of everyday manners in southeast Queensland.[25] Furthermore, traditional law enforced respect for infant dead to the full extent. In 1829 the convict runaway, James Davis, witnessed the lawful killing of his companion John Downes who had emptied a dilly he had found in a tree of its bones. After long communal debate the coastal tribe insisted on full punishment for his sacrilege, for he had disturbed the bones of a dead child.[26]

Gaiarbau outlined the system of discipline for children as it operated in the 1870s, and later, in his interview with Winterbotham. A mother and her brothers were responsible for the oversight of children; a common chastisement was to be hit on the legs with sticks which is consistent with Petrie's story of the 'beating' of his youthful companion Wamgul by a 'gin'.[27] When a mother's or uncle's rebuke proved to be insufficient, the mother could appeal to the tribal council, which would enforce the 'smoking' of the child to drive out the evil spirit that was presumed to be responsible for the behaviour. It was a ritual that was also applied to adults and, according to Gaiarbau, thoroughly scared children, who lived in dread of it.[28]

There is no mention of payback applying to children and Gubbi Gubbi oral history affirms that it was unheard of.[29] From February 1842, in the aftermath of the mass poisoning at Kilcoy Station, a pattern of Aboriginal payback can be identified across the region, culminating in a mass attack on Gregor's Station near Caboolture in October 1846. This attack caused outrage in Brisbane, for it was the first time that a white woman, Mary Shannon — a female servant, who was killed alongside her pastoralist employer, Andrew Gregor — had been the victim of an Aboriginal attack in the north. Perhaps more remarkable, however, was that none of the four children, all under 11 years of age, who lived on the station were harmed.[30] Under a system of payback it would seem logical that children might be seen as a target for law enforcement, given that Aboriginal

25   See entry for 10 June 1842 in Karl W. Schmidt, Report of an Expedition to the Bunya Mountains in Search of a Suitable Site for a Mission Station (Translated by Dr L. Grope and edited and notated by P.D. Wilson, F.S. Colliver and F.P. Woolston), Acc. 3522/1 and 3522/2, Box 7072, John Oxley Library; also Journal of the Brethren Eipper and Hausmann During their Residence at Umpie Boang from 22nd November to 3rd December 1842, entry for 23 November 1842, Lang Papers, ML.
26   Lang, 420; Brisbane Courier, 27 October 1923, 19.
27   Petrie, 143–45.
28   Gaiarbau, 78.
29   Discussion with Gubbi Gubbi community historian and descendant of Dalaipi, Alex Bond, 26 February 2011.
30   For an account of the attack see Libby Connors, 'A Wiradjuri Child at Moreton Bay', Queensland History Journal 20, no. 13 (2010): 775–86. Ten-year-old Aboriginal boy, Ralph Barrow, and the three daughters of Thomas and Mary Shannon, five-year-old Margaret, four-year-old Mary Ann and two-year-old Eliza, were living on the station in 1846.

children were reported to be among the dead at Kilcoy,[31] but here they were consciously excluded from violence, despite a score or more of Aboriginal people raiding the station while the only remaining adult station worker fled for his life.

There was one attack on a white child by two Aboriginal men in Ipswich in April 1843 that needs to be considered in this context. The two-year-old child of a blacksmith went missing and her body was found, badly mutilated, six days later. From February to April 1843 there had been payback attacks on Kilcoy, Durundur and Eales stations but, other than the timing, these were markedly different adult-male-to-adult-male situations, comprising surprise spearings that were undertaken with local Aboriginal support. This attack on a child did not have local Aboriginal support: Aboriginal women, unaware of the intentions of Jacky Jacky, one of the perpetrators, had called out to him and his accomplice Peter when they abducted the child, been aggressively rebuffed and then reported them to the police. This suggests that there was no communal discussion of grievances, no agreed guilty party and no agreement about an appropriate punishment, all of which were standard features of local payback deliberations. The *Sydney Morning Herald* report gives only one hint — it described Jacky Jacky as 'the complete terror of his tribe'.[32] Jacky Jacky may have been a feared medicine man, a *gundir* in the language of the Dalla, and the murder of the child part of an act of sorcery, although this interpretation does not fit easily either. The *gundir* or 'medicine man' held great power and esteem. In southeast Queensland, the position was not confined to men for Gaiarbau knew of three women who had held this post.[33] The awe and authority held by these 'doctors' was described by Petrie who gave the Turrbal name as 'Turrwan'.[34] Because they had the power to use magic for good or ill, to bring rain and storms and to set a curse upon an enemy and to release them from it, *gundir* contributed an emotional and spiritual aspect to the intertribal politics of the region that often left them outsiders, people apart.[35]

It is possible to reconstruct historical events to provide Jacky Jacky with cause — there is documented evidence of his grievances with a convict who had taken an Aboriginal woman from Oxley Creek to the penal settlement in

---

31   Only three individual victims of the poisoning were ever identified — the three sons of Pamby Pamby, who had adopted Davis into his tribe. Davis and Bracewell both reported to Commissioner Simpson that women and children were among the victims. Commissioner Simpson to Colonial Secretary, 30 May 1842, Return of Mr Petrie from Excursion to the North, letter no. 42/4284 in CSIL: Moreton Bay 1842, 4/2581.2, 30 May 1842, Return of Mr Petrie from Excursion to the North, letter no. 42/4284 State Records of New South Wales (SRNSW).
32   *Sydney Morning Herald*, 19 April 1843, 3; entry for 25 January 1843, General Diary of the German Mission from 23 January to 18 July 1843, Lang Papers, ML.
33   Gaiarbau, 52.
34   Petrie, 29–30; see also Uniacke in Lang, 408.
35   Gaiarbau, 51–5; Petrie, 29–30.

December 1841.[36] The readiness with which Aboriginal information was given to the Ipswich police, however, and with which Jacky Jacky and Peter were surrendered, all suggest the killing was not sanctioned by the Yagerra.

As we struggle to reconstruct the processes of communal decision-making from brief and fragmented source material, the difficulty of interpreting situations such as the death of the blacksmith's child at Ipswich or the young Aboriginal girl in the Domain will arise again. Without the brief references to Aboriginal opposition to Jacky Jacky's attack in a *Sydney Morning Herald* report, the circumstantial evidence would have weighted an interpretation favouring payback. Construing the brutal death of a European child as an act of Aboriginal law in its historical context is not impossible: just as on the Cumberland Plain, night raids on camps of unsuspecting Aboriginal families by white settlers became more frequent in the decade following the opening of the northern region in May 1842, although the first openly admitted case in which an Aboriginal child and three women were killed was not until November 1848.[37] Where on such raids children were not killed outright but orphaned, we have accounts of Europeans returning home with Aboriginal children who became the first of many informal stolen generations, long before any official policy was in place in the twentieth century. Shirleene Robinson has sought to identify as many of these children in Queensland as possible and the unfree and unpaid conditions under which many of them survived.[38]

We could just as easily further historicise such retaliatory conduct by Jacky Jacky with reference to the excesses of the British criminal justice system between 1788 and 1840. The age of criminal responsibility was just seven years in the eighteenth century, and remained at eight years of age in British law until 1963 when it was raised to ten.[39] Children as young as seven were subject to the severity and callousness of a legal system that included execution, although most of these children escaped the gallows[40] only to find themselves transported

36 Andrew Evans: Charged with Disobedience of Orders and Neglect of Work, 21 December 1841, *Book of Trials*, Queensland State Archives.

37 Commissioner Rolleston on the Darling Downs reported the incident and his inability to find a single witness who would identify those responsible. Commissioner Rolleston to Colonial Secretary, 28 November 1848, L/no. 48/14088 and enclosure in CSIL: 1848 CCL (2) 4/2812 SRNSW.

38 Shirleene Robinson, *Something like Slavery: Queensland's Aboriginal Child Workers, 1842–1945* (Melbourne: Australian Scholarly Publishing, 2008).

39 'The Age of Criminal Responsibility in England and Wales', House of Commons Library, Standard Note, SN/HA/3001, p. 2. Available at: http://www.parliament.uk/briefingpapers/snha-03001.pdf accessed 26 February 2011.

40 Michael Stern and Richard Clark are attempting to catalogue all children and youths hanged in Great Britain from the seventeenth to the twentieth centuries on their Capital Punishment UK website. See: http://www.capitalpunishmentuk.org/child.html accessed 26 February 2011.

to New South Wales.[41] Contextualising British law's cruel indifference to the plight of the child serves to undercut any accusation of reproducing anew a colonial discourse of the savagery of traditional society.

Such contextualisation is not necessary in the case of the attack on Moore's child because the evidence, although light, points in the opposite direction towards an assault that was unsanctioned by Jacky Jacky's Yaggera people. The evidence from the north suggests that Aboriginal law was far better at protecting its people from excessive cruelty than British law of the same era. As historians reconsider the colonial sources to tell Aboriginal-centred histories of the frontiers, broader patterns of traditional ways of managing one another, outsiders and intruders will be discerned. Perhaps then we will be able to explain the 'stable core, a sense of rightness in one's skin'[42] that marks the persistence of Aboriginal identity and Aboriginal ways of viewing the world through such immense change. Close and critical reading of existing flawed primary sources can de-centre European interests and concerns and shift the critical gaze to the unnamed women who fill their background. The integrity of women's lives in traditional society is a useful starting point for this venture into the realm of Aboriginal sovereignty.

Acknowledgments

This paper draws in part on work published in 'Women on the South-East Queensland Frontier', *Queensland Review* 15, no. 2 (2008): 19–37.

---

41   Robert Holden has identified three convicted children on the First Fleet, six aged between nine and 12 years of age on the Second Fleet, and five sentenced to transportation as late as 1837 (Robert Holden, *Orphans of History* (Melbourne: Text, 1999), 3, 22).
42   Karskens, 435.

III. Law as Theory and Practice

How to Write Feminist Legal History: Some Notes on Genealogical Method, Family Law, and the Politics of the Present

Ann Genovese

> Genealogy does not oppose itself to history as the lofty and profound gaze of the philosopher might compare to the molelike perspective of the scholar; on the contrary, it rejects the metahistorical deployment of ideal significations and indefinite teleologies. It opposes itself to the search for 'origins'.

Michel Foucault, 'Nietzsche, Genealogy, History' (1971)[1]

> We are arguing for a political perspective in historical research and writing, a suggestion which must disturb every academic vigilant in pursuit of the 'value-free' ... It is only by seeking and recognizing political relevance in history that we can bring it more directly into the battle of ideas ...

Sally Alexander and Anna Davin, 'Feminist History' (1976)[2]

What is the purpose of feminist legal histories, and how can we write them, especially in Australia in our own times? In this essay I explore, in the spirit of dialogue, how we might confront the tension between legal history's intellectual traditions, and the political effects of law's legacies in the present. This question of method is an important inference in this collection's conversation about 'who owns the legal past'. My premise is that for many legal history projects, especially in a settler-colonial state like Australia, writing about law historically requires a conscientious identification of law's present paradoxes, discontinuities, and iterations. To this end, this chapter will be in three parts. First, a description of the historiographical problems I have encountered in my current project, which is an account of how feminism and law met in the 1970s. Second, a consideration of what genealogy as a particular theory and method for writing can offer feminist histories of the present in light of those problems;

---

1   Michel Foucault, 'Nietzsche, Genealogy, History', in *The Foucault Reader*, ed., Paul Rabinow (New York: Pantheon Books, 1984), 77.
2   Sally Alexander and Anna Davin, 'Feminist History', *History Workshop* 1 (Spring 1976): 6.

and lastly, to turn to some of the questions of limits or anxieties that such an approach entails, when one of the political constituents of the present is spoken in the narratives and archives of law.

Problems: Writing Australian histories of 'feminism' after 1970

My research project on feminism and family law after 1970 aims, in a macro sense, to understand current cultural and public discourse about feminism as a historical question. Feminism, in its 1970s formations, sought to question the gendered bases of how society operated, and to imagine a different, utopian future. Now, in the twenty-first century, feminism is resented or miscast, viewed as a battle for equality that has been won, or a revolution that promised much and delivered little. My political project is to understand how so many came to see feminism in this way, and with what consequences. Making theoretical and historical sense of how feminism is understood as simultaneously a malevolent success and a malignant failure drives much current feminist scholarship.[3] As Angela McRobbie, to take just one example, writes in *The Aftermath of Feminism*, that feminism in its post-1968 expression was a manifold 'self organised politics, taking place from the ground up, a kind of disputatious and contentious force, especially in matters of sexuality and family life', bearing enormous potential for social change. Yet that potential, she argues I think correctly, is what has also, in our own times, caused 'anxiety, concern and pre-emptive action, on the part of those bodies, institutions and organisations which do not wish to see established power and gender hierarchies undermined'.[4]

It is difficult, however, to write about feminism's very recent past. In one sense, this is a difficulty for all historians of the late twentieth century — our 'period' is often unfathomable (even within historical scholarship itself) as 'history'. As Tony Judt has argued, this miasma about the recent past is pervasive:

> The 20th Century is hardly behind us, but already its quarrels and its dogmas, its ideals and its fears, are slipping into the obscurity of mis-memory. Incessantly invoked as 'lessons', they are in reality ignored and untaught. This is hardly unsurprising. The recent past is the hardest to know and understand.[5]

---

3 This is a point made by many. For an important discussion, see: Marian Sawer, 'Populism and Public Choice in Australia and Canada: Turning Equality-Seekers into "Special Interest"', in *Us and Them: Anti-Elitism in Australia*, eds, Barry Hindess and Marian Sawer (Perth: API Network, 2004), 33–56. Also see, Ann Genovese, 'Worlds Turned Upside Down', *Feminist Review* 95 (2010): 69–74; Margaret Henderson, *Marking Feminist Times: Remembering the Longest Revolution in Australia* (Bern: Peter Lang, 1996).
4 Angela McRobbie, *The Aftermath of Feminism* (London: Sage Publications, 2009), 2.
5 Tony Judt, *Reappraisals: Reflections on the Forgotten Twentieth Century* (New York: Penguin Press, 2009), 4.

This is particularly the case when feminism (of the 1970s and 1980s) is evoked as a category of historical enquiry. Feminism in this sense is not directly interchangeable with *feminist history writing*. The latter has a been a key technique and practice of feminist politics since the 1970s[6] and, as Sally Alexander and Anna Davin note in the epigraph to this chapter, it challenged the certainties of method and intent of historiography in order to expose the causes and shapes of women's absence, resistance or oppression.[7] The former, interrogating Australian feminism — itself a subject of feminist history — has of course played a part in that praxis. For example, Barbara Caine's history of the Victorians,[8] or Marilyn Lake's work on the internationalism of the 1920s and 1930s and beyond,[9] both demonstrate how earlier 'waves' of feminism have been written about to interpolate the political and historical form and content of the writer's own times. But, maybe because of the rapidity of social change since the 1970s, or its sheer scale of impact (Agnes Heller calling 1970s feminism 'the greatest and most decisive social revolution of modernity'),[10] or because those who *were* there are still very much present in the present, writing about feminism since the 1970s as a historical subject is often distinctively fraught. As Meaghan Morris has explained, the fact that feminism in this period occasioned social change 'while at the *same time* contesting the very bases of modern thinking about what constitutes "change"' induced 'intense strain, almost a kind of overload, in historical articulation'.[11] Margaret Henderson in *Marking Feminist Times* specifically explores that 'intense strain' through an Australian history of the cultural texts (film, histories, memoir, fiction) that were written by those present in the 1970s, to speak to their own unease about contemporary feminist politics. Henderson's account argues that, because present '[f]eminist cultural memory is being made in a counter-revolutionary time',[12] there is tension between the historical remembrances (and mis-remembrances) produced by those who took part, and those who want to relate the archives produced by feminist groups in the 1970–90s to the manifestations of feminist disorder in the present.[13]

---

6   See Ann Curthoys, 'Historiography and Women's Liberation', *Arena* 22 (1970): 35–40; Alexander and Davin.

7   See, in general, Ann Curthoys and John Docker, *Is History Fiction?* (Sydney: University of New South Wales Press, 2006), 154–79.

8   Barbara Caine, *Victorian Feminists* (Oxford University Press, 1992).

9   Of course Marilyn Lake also interpreted her own time, in the broader historical narrative. See Marilyn Lake, *Getting Equal: The History of Australian Feminism* (Sydney: Allen and Unwin, 1999); also see Margaret Henderson's response to Lake in Henderson, 38.

10   Agnes Heller, 'Existentialism, Alienation, Postmodernism: Cultural Movements as Vehicles of Change in Patterns of Everyday Life', in *Postmodern Conditions*, eds, Andrew Milner, Philip Thomson and Chris Worth (New York: Berg Publishers, 1990), quoted in Henderson, 13.

11   Meghan Morris, *Too Soon Too Late: History in Popular Culture* (Bloomington and Indianapolis: Indiana University Press, 1998), quoted in Henderson, 11.

12   Henderson, 14.

13   See ibid.; also see Ann Genovese, 'Writing The Past as Politics', *Lilith: A Feminist History Journal* 17 (2008), lilith.org.au/the-journal/lilith-17-2008/Genovese accessed September 5, 2011.

Despite these difficulties, there *is* important critical scholarship, such as that by Henderson, Natasha Campo, or Monica Dux and Zora Simic, that determinedly makes recent Australian feminism itself the object of historical inquiry.[14] This work, however, speaks through the traditions of cultural and social history. To position recent feminism as a category for *legal* history is a less familiar practice, entailing not only similar difficulties but also additional ones. The similarity lies in the fact that feminisms' recent engagements with and through law are usually written about in feminist legal scholarship as 'lessons' (in Judt's sense). These 'lessons' offer a means by which to compare feminist legal reform progress over the past 30 years, which tightens the bind and allure of teleological histories.[15] Notably, and as a general exception in Australia, Margaret Thornton has identified and written about feminism as constitutive of legal historical narratives (for example, *Dissonance and Distrust*) in a way that does not overcommit to the success/failure script.[16] Perhaps because of this recognition, Thornton has also suggested how hard it is, in Australian feminist legal scholarship, to think about the recent and local as anything but normalised. In her 2004 essay 'Neoliberal Melancholia', she describes this phenomena as 'myopia': the inevitable loss of ability by individuals or communities to focus on what is nearest to them.[17] I agree with her, but would also emphasise that this has consequences: it becomes incomprehensible to render strange or uncertain that which is accepted; and, at the same time, it becomes acceptable to 'mis-memorialise' legal feminism's immediate past in the present. Although there is a wealth of feminist legal scholarship in Australia and internationally which is committed to viewing doctrinal or theoretical developments in law through a gendered history,[18] there is, with few exceptions, a reluctance to understand the part played by legal feminism's own institutional forms, and *epistemic* engagement with the object of its critique: the law. This is a point also made in the genealogical jurisprudence of legal scholar Maria Drakopoulou, who has argued, for example, that modern legal feminist thought is so 'fuelled by a yearning for change', by a desire to

---

14   Henderson; Natasha Campo, *From Superwomen to Domestic Goddesses: The Rise and Fall of Feminism* (Bern: Peter Lang, 2009); Monica Dux and Zora Simic, *The Great Feminist Denial* (Melbourne University Press, 2008).

15   See, for example, *Australian Feminist Law Journal* 20 (June 2004).

16   Margaret Thornton, *Dissonance and Distrust: Women in the Legal Profession* (Oxford University Press, 1996). I have also written to these questions, see: Genovese, 'Family Histories: John Hirst v Feminism, in the Family Court of Australia', *Australian Feminist Studies* 21 (2006): 173–96; Genovese, 'Madonna and/or Whore?: Feminism(s) and Public Sphere(s)', in *Romancing the Tomes: Popular Culture, Law and Feminism*, ed., Margaret Thornton (London; Sydney: Cavendish Publishing, 2002), 146–64. Also see Dorothy E. Chunn, Susan B. Boyd and Hester Lessard, eds, *Reaction and Resistance: Feminism, Law, and Social Change* (Vancouver: UBC Press, 2007), which approaches these issues from a Canadian perspective.

17   Thornton, 'Neoliberal Melancholia: The Case of Feminist Legal Scholarship', *The Australian Feminist Law Journal* 20 (2004): 20.

18   See Diane Kirkby, Dealing With Difference: Essays in Gender, History and Culture (Melbourne University Press, 1997); Kirkby, ed., Sex, Power and Justice: Historical Perspectives on Law in Australia (Melbourne: Oxford University Press, 1995); Rosemary Hunter, ed., *Rethinking Equality Projects in Law: Feminist Challenges* (Oxford: Hart Publishing, 2008).

expose, critique and reform the 'phallocentric nature of the political, ontological and epistemological commitments' of law,[19] that feminism 'necessarily registers a lack' in itself.[20] Drakopoulou seeks, as a response, to understand the practice of feminist jurisprudence itself as a 'phenomena', that shifts in its formations, and which must be held to account in how it 'colours the seemingly neutral technology of reform'.[21]

There is therefore an additional difficulty of using feminism as a category for recent legal history that is not present for social or cultural histories. To argue for a history of law that is also unsettled, or at least unsettling, because of its interactions, dominations by, or contaminations with other cultural or political ideas, is always difficult. This is because of the tendency of law to be legocentric,[22] to view the only sustainable historical narratives as those that mimic law itself: common law, stages of legislative reform, legal theory, which often do not speak to the contentious archive that feminism produces. Legal history, when reflecting on or summarising what has been achieved or what has not worked as it should in terms of reform, does not relish looking outside of itself to the communities and cultural contexts with which it interacts to look for explanations. It especially does not easily view that external history as of importance to itself[23] (A point to which I will return.) Feminist legal scholarship, although a branch of critical legal praxis which could potentially engage in the cultural context or 'outside' of its own traditions, is reluctant to do so if the 'outside' is the unruly yet dynamic cultural histories of Australian feminism, from where it emerged.[24] As a result, feminist legal scholarship in Australia seems often unwilling to ask how, and when, 'our positions work in the same register of the political rationality … which they purport to criticize'.[25]

---

19   Maria Drakopoulou, 'Feminism, Governmentality and the Politics of Legal Reform', *Griffith Law Review* 14, no. 1 (2008), 330.
20   ibid., 331.
21   ibid., 334.
22   I have developed this point through conversations with Patrick Wolfe, who is in turn deploying the famous quote from Alexis de Tocqueville, 'Scarcely any political question arises in the United States that is not resolved, sooner or later, into a judicial question'. Alexis de Tocqueville, *Democracy in America* (Ware, Hertfordshire: Wordsworth Editions Limited, 1998), 123.
23   See Robert W. Gordon, 'Introduction: J. Willard Hurst and the Common Law Tradition in American Legal Historiography', *Law & Society Review* 10, no. 1 (Fall 1975): 9–56.
24   Genovese, 'A Radical Prequel: Historicising the Concept of Gendered Law in Australia', in *Sex Discrimination in Uncertain Times*, ed., Margaret Thornton (Canberra: ANU E Press, 2010), 47–73.
25   Wendy Brown, 'Genealogical Politics', in *The Later Foucault*, ed., Jeremy Moss (London: Sage Publications, 1998), 40.

Problems: Writing Australian histories of (family) 'law' after 1970

In order to attempt to contextualise legal feminism through its *episteme*, I chose to explore the recent and disruptive history of Australian family law. This is not because I wish to offer an account of the reformist 'phases' of the *Family Law Act* (1975) Cth, to gauge if they provide signposts of legal responsiveness (or not) to a changing society. In my legal history, I have focused on family law and its archive because it has carried most transparently the story of the political responses to and incursions by feminism into law, since the late 1960s. Specifically, and in summary: The 1975 Act was intended by the state as a break with a non-cosmopolitan past, a progressive commitment to recognise people's sexual and personal freedom through a 'caring' court. This new streamlined jurisdiction, a flagship of modern Australian values and governance in many ways, was accompanied by a raft of other measures that replaced older forms of moral or economic control over families with new ones. Under the new regime of the 1970s, which involved the intersection of family law with child support, state based protections against domestic violence, welfare and tax law, families could be socially identified, protected, and prosecuted. The move to modernise Australian family relationships, however well intentioned, led to diffuse forms of scrutiny and regulation of individual men, women and children. The personal battles between individuals in court — battles read specifically through shifting social and political ideas of gendered fairness, because of the critical praxis of feminist knowers, and actors — became translated into legal doctrine, and legislative presumptions. Rights, interests, needs, and freedoms that were grounded on sexed identities began to have a legal limit.[26] My point is that feminisms and law in this period are not parallel but constitutive. Feminists in the 1970s and 1980s robustly debated the definition of the family in relation to the state and its premises, leading to the development of specifically feminist legal thinking and critique.[27] These ideas inevitably made their way into family law reform processes. The performance and construction of legal feminisms can therefore be understood as a specific expression of what, in an American idiom, can be called Left Legalism. An outcome of lawyers' engagement with critical politics from the late 1960s, Left Legalism was intent on enabling political questions of minority groups to become legal ones.[28] This is I think a phenomena

---

26 See Genovese, 'Family Histories'; Genovese, 'National Legislation and Transnational Feminism', in *Feminist Theory & Activism in Global Perspective: Feminist Review Conference Proceedings* (2010), e99–e155.

27 For three examples: Martha Fineman, *The Illusion of Equality: The Rhetoric and Reality of Divorce Reform* (The University of Chicago Press, 1990); Regina Graycar and Jenny Morgan, *The Hidden Gender of the Law* (Sydney: Federation Press, 1990); Carol Smart, *The Ties that Bind: Law, Marriage, and the Reproduction of Patriarchal Relations* (London; Boston: Routledge and Kegan Paul, 1984).

28 Wendy Brown and Janet Halley, 'Introduction', in *Left Legalism/Left Critique*, eds, Wendy Brown and Janet Halley (Durham; London: Duke University Press, 2002), 1–37. David Kennedy makes a similar point

that has also arisen in Australia, despite having a different experience, and meaning of 'legalism' itself. It is no accident, for example, that the direct confrontation of the state by Indigenous politics' over the issue of land rights, since the 1970s, has become, increasingly, a series of questions for courts, or has, at least, been read through law. The same could be said of feminist projects.

Janet Halley and Wendy Brown, respectively legal and political theorists, in their edited collection *Left Legalism/Left Critique* explore this phenomenon in detail. They argue that critical legal praxis took seriously the legal realist point that law is politics by other means, but never anticipated the extent to which the reverse proposition would become increasingly dominant.[29] Their analysis is useful as a way of interpreting law as a historical question, and practice, in later modernity. It infers that the rise of legalism as a form of politics has meant that the particular space which was carved out by lawyers in the 1980s, lawyers who were committed to gender or sexuality based challenges to liberal legalism's traditions, has been undermined. This demands close archival attention in any feminist history of the recent past. The space for politics in law, imagined as a Trojan horse for feminists in the 1970s and 1980s, is now wide open: the *ressentiment* expressed by fathers' rights groups, for example, appropriates the same strategic language as the feminist groups that they critique. This renders feminist arguments — those that contest law's operation on gendered grounds — as potential poisons, and as vulnerable. If they want to have any voice at all, feminists must play in the demarcated spaces set up by family law, yet they are susceptible to being denigrated as a 'femi-nazi plot'.[30] The problem that emerges, and the one that drives my project, is that contemporary life 'is so saturated by legalism' that it is often difficult to imagine alternative ways of deliberating feminism's response to law, or even imagining when the very rhetoric of 'equality' or 'rights' inferred a political response. Embeddedness of both feminist thinking within law, and thinking about feminism through law, make it difficult to address material or philosophical problems that are predicated in an ever shifting formulation of gender. As Brown and Halley put it:

> As we incessantly refer our political life to the law, we not only sacrifice opportunities to take our inherited political condition into our own hands, we sacrifice as well the chance to address at a more fundamental or at least far reaching level various troubling conditions which appear to require address.[31]

---

about international law in the same volume: David Kennedy, 'When Renewal Repeats: Thinking against the Box', 373–419.

29 Brown and Halley, 19.
30 Genovese, 'Family Histories'.
31 Brown and Halley, 20.

For me, therefore, 'family law' is not only a constantly contested jurisprudential and policy space, but also a history of the present. In telling this narrative, I do not seek to 'add in' histories of feminism to what John Dewar has called family law's 'normal chaos',[32] nor to reposition ideas about what or how to constitute feminist legal theory through a gendered critique of family law's operation.[33] My point is slightly different, although informed by those other scholarly spaces. Family law offers to my project a complex archive of later modernity, through which to expose, and consider as contingent, the effects that liberal legalism has had on feminism as a political force which set out to contest it.

Genealogy, and how it matters for feminist histories of the present

But how can we actually write a politically and culturally located feminist legal history? It is one thing to offer a summary of my argument in this context, quite another to write this story in a historical form. I want to avoid teleology as a narrative frame, as it is the telling of feminism's present as a story positioned on a 'success' or 'failure' or 'lessons' axis that is the problem. My search for an alternative approach has led me to a re-engagement with genealogy as a method for writing history of the present. As Foucauldian scholars Andrew Barry, Thomas Osborne and Nikolas Rose have argued, genealogy can be viewed as a specific method for scholarly enquiry in later modernity; it helps us to destabilise the perceived inevitability of the present and to 'bring into view the historically sedimented underpinnings of particular "problematizations" that have a salience for our contemporary experience'.[34]

The very idea of writing histories of the present is not only an exercise to diagnose our own times. Friedrich Nietzsche in *On the Genealogy of Morality* (1887) took the idea of writing of the subjective experience of knowledge as a way to destabilise the certainty of forward-looking Enlightenment projects. For example, he insisted that values experienced were not inevitable, that they served purposes that may not be immediately clear, and that they required 'deciphering', or 'artful questioning' instead of chronicling, with the aim being

---

32   John Dewar, 'The Normal Chaos of Family Law', *Modern Law Review* 61, no. 4 (July 1998): 467–85.

33   See, for example, Alison Diduck, *Law's Families* (London: Lexis Nexis, 2003).

34   Andrew Barry, Thomas Osborne and Nikolas Rose, 'Introduction', in *Foucault and Political Reason: Liberalism, Neoliberalism and Rationalities of Government*, eds, Andrew Barry, Thomas Osborne and Nikolas Rose (University of Chicago Press, 1995), 5.

to reveal them as not common place, but historically contingent and variable. Nietzsche called this genealogy and described it as the way into 'a secret garden, the existence of which no one suspected'.[35]

These were ideas that were of course attractive to historical (and political) theorists throughout the twentieth century, including, in different ways, Benedetto Croce, and Hannah Arendt.[36] But, of course, it is the scholarship of the 1970s and 1980s itself, especially that of Michel Foucault alongside feminist historians like Joan Scott, who asked contemporaneous questions about the function of gender as a category of historical analysis and knowledge,[37] which grounded genealogy as a historical practice in later modernity. These scholars sought to make sense of how Enlightenment traditions constructed political subjects yet, at the same time questioned the then dominant form of liberal critique: Marxism. What Foucault, for example, did in projects like *Discipline and Punish* (1977) was to take Nietzsche's idea that knowledges are inherently capable of various perspectives, and Croce's idea that the historian writes out of the interests of the present, and developed them into a 'sociology of knowledge'.[38] History, in these terms, became an analysis of power in the present: its deviations, ruptures, and insidiousness.

In his 1971 essay 'Nietzsche, Genealogy, History', for example, Foucault offers his account of the purpose and intent of genealogy as methodological politics and practice. He replaces the traditional search for total history — the 'constants' of 'traditional history'[39] with 'effective' history,[40] 'which seeks to dispel the chimeras of origin'.[41] The point of this effective history is to 'introduce discontinuity into our very being'[42] to show the differences and disruptions of the uncertain past and, therefore, the uncertain present. Effective history is history of the present, it 'shortens its vision to those things nearest to it … it reverses the surreptitious practice of historians, their pretensions to examine things furthest from themselves … It studies what is closest, but in an abrupt dispossession'.[43] Foucault importantly, is not speaking in this essay as an abstract philosopher: genealogy is a 'tactical weapon' not a conceptual

---

35   Friedrich Nietzsche, *On the Genealogy of Morality* (1887), ed., Keith Ansell-Pearson, trans., Carol Diethe (Cambridge University Press, 2007), 5.

36   Benedetto Croce, 'History and Chronicle' (1917), as discussed in Curthoys and Docker, 91–93, and in Hayden White, 'The Abiding Relevance of Croce's Idea of History', *Journal of Modern History* 37 (June 1963): 109–24; Hannah Arendt, 'The Modern Concept of History', *The Review of Politics* 20, no. 4 (1958): 570–90.

37   Joan Scott, *Gender and Politics of History* (New York: Columbia University Press, 1988); Michel Foucault, *Discipline and Punish: The Birth of the Prison*, trans., Alan Sheridan (London: Penguin Books, 1977).

38   Curthoys and Docker, 186.

39   Foucault, 'Nietzsche, Genealogy, History', 80.

40   ibid., 87.

41   ibid., 80.

42   ibid., 88.

43   ibid., 89.

construction of fixed meaning, as Mariana Valverde has described.[44] Nor in turning to genealogy as a method is he suggesting in any way the substitution of material or archival engagement for wilful theoretical disturbance. On the contrary: Foucault's genealogies are always over archived: the archive rather than being a contained or linear investigation of key events, institutions or individuals, 'demands endless erudition',[45] it becomes sprawling and ever expanding, in order to expose and understand the conditions of accident and how contingencies appear. The point is that the genealogist sets out to study 'numberless beginnings whose faint traces and hints and colour are readily seen by an historical eye'.[46] What Foucault offers in 'Nietzsche, Genealogy, History', and in his histories, is both a method for *and performance* of how to write history of the present.

Genealogy can, however, be viewed as a dangerous practice.[47] It can be treacherous for the writer, as there is no road map in, or out, of the sprawling archive, (Nietzsche's 'secret garden') and the very artful questions asked at the start of an inquiry must, irresolutely, be shifted as a result. The danger is also that because by necessity genealogy speaks against the grain of the time in which it is written, the kind of knowledge that may be exposed is '[of a] kind that is not [necessarily] desired'.[48] Further, as Wendy Brown argues in her essay on the political intent of Foucault's genealogical method, 'Politics without Banisters' (2001), genealogy is a practice that is necessary for 'stalled' projects like feminism. Brown argues, I think rightly, that genealogies are often viewed as potential political dead ends, rather than as openings. This is because, unlike traditional political or narrative history, which desires to explain something in particular, and in which 'legitimate political positions' flow directly from their endpoint of 'objective' or 'systematic' political critiques,[49] genealogies proscribe nothing. They seek no totalising transformation besides disruption of what is thought of as so normalised as to be unworthy of comment (for example: 'human rights means progress'). Yet, genealogy features instead 'forthrightly contingent elements of desire, attachment, judgment and alliance as the compositional material of political attachments and positions'.[50] Foucault called genealogy 'ontology of the present' and, as Brown suggests, this offers something to feminism. It is something quite different, she argues from 'ontologically grounded politics', it is instead a '[c]ritical ontology of the present [which could] be precisely what productively disrupts or "cuts" the tight relation between constructions of identity and

---

44   Mariana Valverde, 'Specters of Foucault in Law and Society Scholarship', *American Review of Law and Society* 6 (2010): 45.
45   Foucault, 'Nietzsche, Genealogy, History', 77.
46   ibid., 81.
47   Or legacy; see ibid., 82.
48   Wendy Brown, *Politics out of History* (Princeton; Oxford: Princeton University Press, 2001), 97.
49   ibid., 118–20.
50   ibid., 119.

normative political claims in the contemporary political rationality'.[51] This is a point also made by Drakopolou, who exhorts specifically feminist legal politics to shift 'away from the relentless effort to establish links between how things are and how they ought to be … and [to become] concerned instead with trying to identify why things are as they are and not as they were before'.[52] It is for this reason that history of the present offers not just a way of engaging in scholarly disorientation, or even visiting secret gardens. It is an important practice for projects like feminism, which do seem stalled, or trapped because, as a practice, an act of writing, Brown reminds us:

> [G]enealogy reorients the relationship of history to political possibility: although the political possibility is constrained by its histories, those histories are themselves tales of improbable, uneven, and unsystematic emergence, and thus contain openings for disturbance.[53]

Is genealogy intelligible to law and its history?

But, to write history in those terms, it is necessary to consider how the contemporary political rationality is already given narrative form. And, as noted, the role law itself plays in shaping our own times cannot be gainsaid. It constitutes the political relations for a project like feminism in our present, and surreptitiously demands stories of progress, (and therefore moralising about success/failure) when attempting to write of that relation. So, the real dilemma in attempting a history of the present predicated on asking about the contingent relations between feminism and family law, is not only feminism itself, as described in the first part of this chapter, but the law: both historicising it, and at the same time making it the constitutive subject of a broader political and historical narrative.

One aspect of this dilemma is the question of whether a genealogical approach, drawn as a method from Foucault, and when used to critique law's doctrinal institutional (or in my case, cultural) presence, is recognisable within Foucault's own work on law. This is a criticism raised by Ben Golder and Peter Fitzpatrick in their recent book *Foucault's Law* (2009). Although there has been an important tradition developed in critical legal and sociological scholarship that uses the practices of genealogy,[54] Golder and Fitzpatrick describe such scholarship (including the work of Valverde and Rose) as 'appropriative' and 'occasioning

---

51   ibid.
52   Drakopoulou, 'Women's Resolution of Lawes Reconsidered: Epistemic Shifts and the Emergence of the Feminist Legal Discourse', *Law and Critique* 11, no. 1 (2000): 71.
53   Brown, *Politics*, 103.
54   See, for example: Valverde, *The Age of Light, Soap, and Water: Moral Reform in English Canada, 1885–1925* (Toronto: McClelland and Stewart, 1991); Jacques Donzelot, *The Policing of Families*, trans., Robert

a certain conceptual violence to Foucault's broader arguments and critical focus'.[55] This is because, in their own book, they seek to assert that within Foucault's corpus of work is a discernable and conceptually whole philosophy of law. I think such assertion misjudges the purpose of Foucault's own project, as described above, as it attempts to convert 'the juridical' from practices disturbed by genealogy as constitutive of problems inherent in liberalism, into theories of philosophical completeness that mimic the Enlightenment practices that Foucault sought to render uncertain.[56] But, as I align myself with these 'appropriative' scholars, who are interested in understanding genealogy as a historical practice that questions law's intent and effects, as opposed to a jurisprudence, I want to consider two problems specific to the concerns and practices of legal history, and to ask whether genealogy can in fact be intelligible to law because of those traditions.

The first, as already mentioned, is the problem of legal history's own method and intent. The dominant legal historiographical practice is what critical legal historian Robert Gordon described in 1975 as the common law tradition, in which legal history's method and intent is to justify law's teleology.[57] This is regardless of whether history is invoked to write scholarly accounts of law's development, or invoked judicially to make sense of what is empirically questionable in the experience of those who stand outside the law. This is important to question, in all nation states, where the archives that enable this 'legal history' are, in a spirit true to Ranke and to Hegel, those of the institutions of the state itself, especially the courts. Such archives, and the teleologies of national progress that they assume and produce, are of particular concern to legal historians in settler colonies like Australia and New Zealand. We only need to re-read, for example, the cumulative judgements in the *Yorta Yorta* decision, or even *Mabo* (which used history to expose *terra nullius*, yet to sidestep sovereignty), to see how that works in practice.[58] What is absent from such traditional legal histories, histories that law both creates and can recognise, is their conscious challenge to law: they offer no room for alternative accounts of law, or a more open past. Genealogies of law, by contrast, openly challenge and contradict that tradition as they aim to distort the inevitability of the history of law itself. To make a case for genealogies as histories of the present where law's own authority and function is not contained or certain in its legitimacy, opens the very real possibility that

---

Hurley (New York: Pantheon Books, 1979); Carol Smart, *Feminism and the Power of Law* (London; New York: Routledge, 1989); Jeffrey Minson, *Genealogies of Morals: Nietzsche, Foucault, Donzelot and the Eccentricity of Ethics* (New York: St Martin's Press, 1985).

55 Ben Golder and Peter Fitzpatrick, *Foucault's Law* (New York: Routledge, 2009).

56 Valverde argues that Golder and Fitzpatrick are trying to 'recuperate Foucault for the grand European philosophical tradition within which Heidegger looms large': Valverde, 'Specters', 45.

57 Gordon, 'Introduction'.

58 For commentary on Gordon's thesis in the Australian context, as well as these cases, see Ann Curthoys, Ann Genovese and Alexander Reilly, *Rights and Redemption* (Sydney: University of New South Wales Press, 2008), 140–43 and Chapters Two and Three, which discuss the *Mabo* and *Yorta Yorta* decisions respectively.

one of the intended audiences for such histories — the community of law, as opposed to the community of which law is a part — can be dismissive of, or deaf to, the political intent and challenge.

The second, interrelated problem, is that of narrative. This concerns how genealogical interrogations that are intended to destabilise the present can ever account for law while, at the same time, trying to suggest law's current function in our society has escaped its boundaries. That is, law becomes the site of critique of minority rights politics but, at the same stroke, is exposed as a means by which those groups must endeavour to contest their subjecthood. Historicising law as a response to present political conditions means unsettling law's origins, yet also potentially acquiescing to law's role in liberal societies. This is hard to write, as Gordon noted presciently in 1980s, as:

> [making an historical case about] the fundamentally constitutive character of legal relations in social life is a lot easier to understand [and research] when made about slave or feudal societies than about liberal societies, as in liberal societies differences of legal status are not supposed to define social relationships, but merely to channel and facilitate them.[59]

Writing this story becomes increasingly difficult the closer we are to our own times, again, as already noted in relation to histories of feminism. Legal historians are always implicated in law: as both critics and participants, in ways we cannot always choose. The writing of law as a constitutive rather than isolated part of a general history of later modernity means the legal historian, if engaged in genealogy, can unsettle the very narratives they inhabit, potentially leaving their projects exposed as irrelevant to the triumphalism of law's progress.

And yet, despite these limits, it is undeniable that we — the 'we' here being those of us who gather to write and research legal history, have as a discipline sought to meet the challenges we make. The opening up of legal history as a field of enquiry or critique that enables a different understanding of what law does in culture and society, to whom, and how, was, like feminism and legalism, *also* possible because of the philosophical and historical turns of modernity itself. Legal history as practice is therefore also produced by the conditions I seek to understand, and has as a result become difficult to describe and contain. It is no longer the handmaiden to precedent, the provenance of Frederick Maitland's enclosed legal scholar.[60] It has prised open the back of the common law's ticking clock, most importantly — as already noted — in work concerned with understanding law's implications in the settler-colonial

---

59   Robert W. Gordon, 'Critical Legal Histories', *Stanford Law Review* 36, no. 1/2 (January 1984): 104.
60   Frederick William Maitland, *Essays on the Teaching of English History* (Cambridge University Press, 1901).

project.[61] Despite the suspicion of many jurists, the political nature of much historical writing about law's violence over indigenous peoples, as well as their resort to its protections, *has* exposed a contingent nature of law, and produced significant political rethinking. Regardless of what other historical work we do, for many, if not most, legal historians in settler-colonial states in the present, myself included, there is a constant questioning of what laws must or can mean, that is never separated from the interrogation of dispossession. This does not eradicate the internal pull of law's own promises, but the political question of injustice and Aboriginal people has made us work harder to cut another tight relation between constructions of legal history and law itself, as genealogy suggests we might.

To conclude: I think legal history as a practice must bring these insights to bear on all work that questions the nation state in various guises. The epistemological step in relation to settler–indigenous histories and the law demands nothing less: that is the paradigmatic example of how law operates, not its exception, and as such it suggests possibilities for perspectives that unsettle the effects legalism has had on minority politics. Although we need to be vigilant about our own traditions, I want to be optimistic that the political questions and practices, including those embodied by legal feminism, that seem normalised, underexposed or resisted can be understood as adventitious and also situated. How to write a legal history in which feminism operates as category and as a political question is, then, to descend into the sprawling archives of both the cultural politics of feminism, and its constitutive response in domestic law, and to make visible how it is implicated and embedded in complex national as well as disciplinary pasts. I have predicated my 'legal history' on political pamphlets as well as cabinet documents relating to the writing of legislation; I have conducted oral histories with feminist activists as well as judges; I have read the letters of an earlier generation of father advocates alongside the 'canon' of women's liberation literature. The point is that the narratives that are opened by this uncertain archive may infer contingent possibilities for feminisms, as well as vary our understanding of law, in the unsettling contemporary moment. Genealogy's value, as Foucault said, is as a 'curative' or 'antidote' to the poisons of its own time,[62] and this is something that ought to resonate with legal historians today as we 'discover that truth or being does not lie at the root of what we know and what we are, but the exteriority of accidents'.[63]

---

61 For example: Shaunnagh Dorsett, 'Mapping Territories', in *Jurisprudence of Jurisdiction*, ed., Shaun McVeigh (Oxford: Routledge-Cavendish, 2007), 137–58; Julie Evans, *Edward Eyre, Race and Colonial Governance* (Dunedin: Otago University Press, 2005); Paul McHugh, *Aboriginal Societies and the Common Law: A History of Sovereignty, Status and Land* (Oxford University Press, 2004); Lisa Ford, *Settler Sovereignty: Jurisdiction and Indigenous People in America and Australia, 1788–1836* (Cambridge, Mass: Harvard University Press, 2010).

62 Foucault, 'Nietzsche, Genealogy, History', 90.

63 ibid., 81.

Spain's 'pact of silence' and the Removal of Franco's Statues

Aleksandra Hadzelek

Introduction

The Spanish Law of Historical Memory, passed in 2007, is an important milestone in addressing several issues that have remained unresolved since the death of Franco, 32 years earlier. The law calls for, among other important provisions,[1] the removal of all Francoist symbols from public buildings and spaces. Franco was highly visible in the public sphere, using his own images to legitimise his rule, not unlike other dictators, contemporaneous or historical. But, what makes Franco's case so interesting, is that he remained present in the public sphere for decades after his death, due to a 'pact of silence' that Spanish society agreed upon at the time of transition to democracy. In Giles Tremlett's words:

> for almost four decades [after his death] General Francisco Franco was someone Spaniards could not escape. He was there in school books, church prayers, statues, plaques, street names and thousands of other reminders of a violent insurrection that led to a vicious civil war. Now his face and name are being erased from public view.[2]

The reactions to the removal of statues, from the most publicised Madrid event in 2005 to a stream of other removals following the passing of the 2007 law, illustrate the divisions that are still present in Spanish society with regard to its recent past, and they encapsulate the main attitudes towards the re-evaluation of that past. At the core of these attitudes lies the period of transition from dictatorship to democracy, when any memories that might have provided an alternative to the official version of history, as supported by the old Francoist regime, were effectively silenced. Current attempts to revive those memories, considered by many people to be both necessary and urgent, are labelled dangerous and against the spirit of reconciliation by spokespeople of the

---

1   It condemns Franco's regime, recognises all victims of the war and violence on both sides of the conflict, annuls prior legislation, offers government assistance in identifying victims buried in clandestine mass graves, prohibits political events at *Valle de los Caídos* (Valley of the Fallen, burial place of Franco and a monument to nationalist soldiers who perished in the war), and grants Spanish citizenship to descendents of Republican exiles from the Civil War, as well as surviving members of the International Brigades.

2   Giles Tremlett, 'Franco's Face and Name Erased from Public View in Spain', *Guardian*, 6 October 2009, http://www.guardian.co.uk/world/2009/oct/06/franco-name-erased-spain accessed 2 September 2010.

opposing camp. What some see as the necessary exposure of still open wounds to the light of day in order to heal, others see as the reopening of wounds that have already healed.

Franco's iconography

Few images remain of Franco in his early years, before his spectacular military career lifted him from the unknown to a ruthless leader of the Moroccan campaign, to the leader of the insurgency that toppled the Spanish Republican government, to the victor of a three-year bloody civil war and the first military confrontation between fascism and the rest of the world.[3] The images that appear after the end of the war hardly resemble the shy and plain looking boy from the early years of his training at the military academy.[4] Franco the victor, the saviour of Spain from all things evil, made regular and heavily orchestrated public appearances all over the country,[5] which were then broadcast as newsreels — carefully prepared sets of 'news' for the Spanish public, the only news that it was regarded as acceptable for Spaniards to see and hear, as they were now safely under the protection of the *caudillo*.[6] The broadcasts were under tight government control and presented an image of the dictator at ease in a variety of situations: gentle family man with his wife and daughter; pious Catholic coming out of mass; thoughtful head of government in consultation with his advisers; and, ultimately, a firm military commander in full control of his troops and his country.

For Franco, his own images were part of an extensive propaganda machine, designed and implemented in an effort to legitimise his rule, as is often the case with dictatorships. Along with newsreels, public displays such as posters, busts and statues of Franco were being erected all over Spain from the very early

---

3   The Spanish Civil War is also often referred to as the 'Little World War' as it was the first direct confrontation between fascism and communism, on the eve of World War II.

4   The website http://www.generalisimofranco.com has the most extensive gallery of photos of Franco available on the internet, and it includes some lesser known pictures of him from the early years, as well as the more iconic images of Franco as a saviour of the Spanish nation, which were widely circulated and publicised as part of the propaganda machine of the regime.

5   The public image of Franco while he was in power is in stark contrast with the image of General Salazar, the military dictator of neighbouring Portugal. While ideologically both Franco and Salazar represented right wing politics, fascism and defence of Catholicism against the communist threat, Salazar did not appear in public as much as Franco, and his appearances were not as carefully prepared by his advisers to project the image of imperial grandeur to which Franco aspired. The comparison between the two personalities is the topic of an excellent Portuguese documentary from 2004 (*Franco and Salazar*, produced by Jaquin Vieira and Fernanda Bizarro) but, surprisingly, it has not yet been examined in a dedicated academic study in Spanish or English.

6   Similarly to Hitler referring to himself as Fuhrer, and Mussolini as Il Duce, Franco decided to call himself 'Caudillo de España, por la gracia de Dios': 'the "great leader" of Spain, by the grace of God'. The term caudillo originated in 19th century South America, and has strong connotations of military authoritarian power, often of populist nature and based on personality cult.

days of his rule. Jesús De Andrés[7] dates the commissioning of the first one,[8] a bust to be placed in Salamanca's main square, to November 1936[9] — only a few months after the beginning of the insurgency on 18 July, and in the midst of a brutal war with, at that point, no clear winner. The first equestrian statue was commissioned by the *Servicio Nacional de Prensa y Propaganda* (National Service for Press and Propaganda) in 1938. Diverting resources to iconography in such early stages of his rule is a powerful sign of Franco's obsession with his own image and his aspirations to grandeur, but it also reflects the cult of the leader, essential to fascist ideology, and the role of iconography in a conflict that was fought on the propaganda front almost as much as on the battlefield.[10] What sets Spain aside from other fascist and authoritarian regimes of its time is the persistence of the iconography in the public sphere for decades after the dictator's death, as well as its society's inability or lack of willingness to, until recently, seriously address the human rights abuses of the Franco era.[11]

Francoism or fascism

Whether Franco's regime was actually fascist is contentious and subject to an ongoing debate. Most academic literature from the 1970s and 1980s, especially by non-Spanish scholars, avoided the classification of Franco and his regime as fascist, preferring instead the more benevolent term of 'Francoism' that did not invite direct comparisons with other fascist regimes of the early twentieth century. Stanley G. Payne,[12] Paul Preston[13] and Christopher J. Ross[14] all focus on the ideological aspect of the Franco regime and point out that it was not 'purely fascist' and that it distanced itself from fascism due to international pressure.[15]

7 Jesús De Andrés, 'Las estatuas de Franco y la memoria histórica del franquismo', (Bilbao: Asociación de Historia Contemporánea, 2003), http://www.ahistcon.org/docs/Santiago/pdfs/s1g.pdf accessed 1 July 2011.
8 De Andrés, ibid., points out that, already in October 1936, a decision was made to erect a statue in El Ferrol, Franco's birthplace, but it was not actually carried out until 1967.
9 The bust was installed on 1 October 1937, while the war was not officially over until 1 April 1939.
10 De Andrés. 'Las estatuas', offers an interesting analysis of the aesthetics of the various monuments in the context of the three widely accepted stages of the dictatorship, as well as the impact of international circumstances, such as the fall of Nazi Germany, on the symbolic meaning of different elements of sculptures, thereby demonstrating Franco's understanding of the symbolism behind the public use of his images.
11 For an excellent introduction to a discussion on human rights abuses in the Franco era, in the context of the 'pact of forgetting' and the politics of memory, see Madeleine Davis, 'Is Spain Recovering its Memory? Breaking the Pacto del Olvido', *Human Rights Quarterly* 27, no. 3 (August 2005): 858–80, and Carlos Jerez-Farrán and Samuel Amago, eds, *Unearthing Franco's Legacy. Mass Graves and the Recovery of Historical Memory in Spain* (University of Notre Dame Press, 2010).
12 Stanley G. Payne, *The Franco Regime, 1936–1975* (Madison: University of Wisconsin Press, 1987).
13 Paul Preston, *Franco: A Biography* (London: HarperCollins, 1993).
14 Christopher. J. Ross, *Spain 1812–2004*, 2nd ed. (London: Arnold, 2004).
15 Referring to the 'New State', Ross says that 'the name he [Franco] gave it emphasised its affinity with fascism, as did the special status enjoyed by the Falange. Short for 'Falange Española de las Juntas de Ofensiva Nacional Sindicalista' or FE JONS (Spanish Phalanx of the Assemblies of the National Syndicalist Offensive) from its founding in 1933 to 1937, and 'Falange Española Tradicionalista de las Juntas de Ofensiva Nacional

On the other hand, many Spanish historians from the late 1970s and through the 1980s insist on the classification of Franco's regime as fascist.[16] António Costa Pinto observes that 'the debate "fascism-authoritarianism" has, during the past decade, lost its ideological content in both Portugal and in Spain'.[17] Instead, the most recent literature seems more preoccupied with the issue of violence applied heavily by the Franco regime, particularly in the immediate post-war period. Peter Anderson, who calls Falange 'the Spanish fascist party led by Franco'[18] points out that:

> only in recent years have historians uncovered conclusive evidence that reveals the massive scale of the Francoist repression. One of the conclusions these historians have drawn from their research is that Francoism formed an important component within the European totalitarian and fascist movements of the mid-twentieth century period.[19]

Javier Rodrigo supports the above argument that a comparative analysis of fascist movements in twentieth-century Europe indicates the fascist nature of Franco's regime.[20] It can be argued that the use of a 'fascist' categorisation of the Franco regime is in sync with leftist political ideas — Vyacheslav Molotov insisted on that categorisation throughout the post-war negotiations, and even convinced the Allies to adopt it in the text of the Potsdam Agreement.[21] The association of Franco with fascism was present during his rule in the minds of his Republican opponents, and represented as such by the Republicans in exile. Those who had fought in the Spanish Civil War on the side of the Republic, had

---

Sindicalista' or FET JONS (Spanish Traditionalist Phalanx of the Assemblies of the National Syndicalist Offensive) from 1937 when Franco combined the original Falange with the Carlist party and assumed its leadership. It was the only legally permitted political party in Spain while Franco was in power. Although to a large extent a reflection of Franco's own ideas, its economic policy also had fascist overtones' (ibid., 99–100). He agrees that Falange played an important part and fascist symbols such as the salute were adopted (ibid., 100–02) but points out that 'As soon as it became clear that the western democracies were going to prevail in the World War, Franco began to downplay the fascist side of his regime' (ibid., 102).

16 For example: Juan Marsal, *Pensar bajo el franquismo: Intelectuales y politica en la generacion de los años cincuenta* (Barcelona: Ediciones Península, 1979); Raúl Morodo, *Los orígenes ideológicos del franquismo: Acción Española* (Madrid: Alianza Editorial, 1985) and Julio Rodríguez Puértolas, *Literatura fascista española* (Madrid: Akal, 1986).

17 António Costa Pinto, 'Elites, Single Parties and Political Decision-making in Fascist-era Dictatorships', *Contemporary European History* 11, no. 3 (2002): 437, note 29.

18 Peter Anderson, 'Singling Out Victims: Denunciation and Collusion in the Post-Civil War Francoist Repression in Spain, 1939–1945', *European History Quarterly* 39, no. 7 (2009): 16.

19 ibid., 22. Also see Ángela Cenarro, 'Matar, vigilar y delatar: la quiebra de la sociedad civil durante la guerra y la posguerra en España (1936–1948)', *Historia Social* no. 44 (2002): 65–86, for an interesting perspective on the participation of civil society in the violence and terror, through right-wing mobilisation and other tactics that were employed to engage the 'good Spaniards' in the oppression characteristic of the New State.

20 Javier Rodrigo, 'La naturaleza del franquismo: un acercamiento desde la perspectiva comparada de los fascismos europeos', in *Universo de micromundos*, eds, Carmelo Romero and Alberto Sabio (Zaragoza: Institución Fernando el Católico, 2009), 47–62.

21 See Enrique Moradiellos, 'The Potsdam Conference and the Spanish Problem', *Contemporary European History* 10, no. 1 (March 2001): 82–89.

fought a war against fascism. Supporters of the Republican version of history are strongly opposed to the classification of Franco's regime as Francoist instead of fascist. According to Vicenç Navarro:

> its replacement by the term Francoist represents a successful conservative project of representing the regime only as *caudillista* while in reality it brings together all the characteristics of a fascist regime. And not only at the beginning but until the end.[22]

Navarro's firm conviction that the regime maintained its fascist characteristics until the end is in contrast to many scholarly opinions that argue that Franco distanced himself from fascism as early as 1942.[23] Peter Pierson analyses Franco's policies and appointment of specific people to crucial posts as a way of gaining international acceptance, especially from the United States, and proposes that Franco manipulated the make-up of the government and the external appearances of his regime to appease the international community. 'To appeal to the Catholic world, Franco stressed Spain's Catholicism and downplayed the role of the Falange.'[24] Stanley Payne in his 1987 work identifies the reforms of 1967–68 as the final phase of the defascitization of the regime,[25] and reiterates in 2011 (quoting David W. Pike[26]) that 'in 1945 Franco was almost universally denounced as "the last surviving fascist dictator", and would never entirely escape "the Axis stigma". Nonetheless, most scholars conclude that the Spanish regime was not intrinsically fascist, though it included aspects of fascism'.[27] Aristotle A. Kallis analyses an additional category of para-fascism that could be applicable to 'a larger category of regimes that adapted or aped "fascist" formal and organisational structures, but did not share the revolutionary ideological vision of genuine fascism',[28] including that of Franco's Spain.

Similar disagreements surround the debate on whether Franco's regime was totalitarian. Since Raymond Carr's famous quote, 'Francoism was not a totalitarian

---

22 'su sustitución por el término franquista responde a un proyecto conservador exitoso de presentar aquel régimen sólo como caudillista, cuando en realidad reunió todas las características de un régimen fascista. Y no sólo al principio sino hasta el final.' Vicenç Navarro, '¿Franquismo o fascismo?', *Público*, 7 July 2011, http://blogs.publico.es/dominiopublico/3625/%C2%BFfranquismo-o-fascismo/ accessed 15 November 2011.

23 'The defascistization of the Franco regime began as early as 1942 and proceeded in several stages' (Payne, *The Franco Regime*, 629). 'Franco distances himself from fascism in a variety of ways after 1942, and more rapidly after 1945. Thus, the raised-arm salute was dropped, as was the name "New State". The Falange representation in government was cut, and its presence in public life generally reduced' (Ross, 103). Peter Pierson in *The History of Spain* (Westport, CO and London: Greenwood Press, 1999, 109) also points out the change of name as an important factor in changing the image of the regime, especially in the international arena.

24 Pierson, 161.

25 Payne, 629.

26 David W. Pike, *Franco and the Axis Stigma* (New York: Macmillan, 2008).

27 Payne, *Spain: A Unique History* (Madison: University of Wisconsin Press, 2011), 224.

28 Aristotle A. Kallis, '"Fascism", "Para-Fascism" and "Fascistization": On the Similarities of Three Conceptual Categories', *European History Quarterly* 33, no. 2 (2003): 220.

regime'[29] and Payne's firm conviction that 'the Spanish regime was obviously authoritarian, not totalitarian',[30] a re-conceptualisation of totalitarianism has occurred in global historiography. Anderson, with reference to Abbott Gleason[31] and Sheila Fitzpatrick,[32] points out that:

> ironically this effort to understand Francoism as an important example of European totalitarianism came exactly at the time that historians of other mid-twentieth century terror regimes began to challenge some of the reductions of Cold War totalitarian theory. In this theory ideologically driven regimes control and direct their passive societies in both the public and private sphere through their use of a terror police force that is independent of the society it bends to its own will.[33]

Recently it has been proposed that specific categorisations of the Franco regime should be abandoned as they do not advance or benefit the analysis and debate of emerging critical issues related to the regime. Howard J. Wiarda and Margaret MacLeish Mott refuse the following denominations: 'military dictatorship', 'clerical' or 'theocratic dictatorship' and 'fascist',[34] and posit that one cannot describe the Franco and Salazar regimes 'by employing bumper sticker labels', but rather 'by analysing them carefully'.[35] They refer to Juan José Linz's early work[36] based on a:

> distinction between authoritarian and totalitarian regimes, a distinction that was not always apparent to the victims of these regimes but which is helpful in understanding them. Linz argues that both the Spanish and Portuguese regimes should be understood as occupying an intermediary position, clearly not liberal, but not totalitarian either, and thus in between these two major types — an authoritarian regime that has its own distinctive politics and dynamics.[37]

Navarro, however, who points out Linz's conservative terminology of fascist origins,[38] is convinced that:

29   'In spite of the Fascist trimmings of the early years — the goosestep and the Fascist salute — Francoism was not a totalitarian regime. It was a conservative, Catholic, authoritarian system, its original corporatist features modified over time.' Raymond Carr, *Modern Spain 1875–1980* (Oxford and New York: Oxford University Press, 1980), 165.
30   Payne, *The Franco Regime*, 626.
31   Abbott Gleason, 'Totalitarianism in 1984', *Russian Review* 43, no. 2 (April 1984): 145–59.
32   Sheila Fitzpatrick, 'New Perspectives on Stalinism', *Russian Review* 45, no. 4 (October 1986): 357–73.
33   Anderson, 11.
34   Howard J. Wiarda and Margaret MacLeish Mott, *Catholic Roots and Democratic Flowers: Political Systems in Spain and Portugal* (Westport, CO and London: Praeger, 2001), 48.
35   ibid.
36   Juan José Linz, 'An Authoritarian Regime: Spain', in *Mass Politics*, eds, Erik Allardt and Stein Rokkan (New York: The Free Press, 1970), 251–83.
37   Wiarda and MacLeish Mott, 48–49.
38   '... autores conservadores (procedentes de la misma nomenclatura fascista como Juan Linz)', Navarro, *Tergiversaciones*, 3.

if in Spain there had been a rupture with the dictatorship (as it happened in Eastern European countries) instead of a transition (which was executed under specific division of power, with a very right and a very weak left wing), today we would be speaking of fascism instead of Francoism.[39]

He also warns against considering Francoism a neutral term, given its political and ideological connotations: 'the language that we use is not neutral, nor is the term Francoism that is used to define the dictatorship'.[40]

Madrid statue

The polarisation of academic standpoints on these terms and classifications of the regime are reflected in the public opinion as expressed in press and blogs. The events in Spain's capital, Madrid, in 2005, and the accompanying press coverage, provide a good example of the attitudes towards the dictatorship and its memory that have prevailed in the Spanish society until the last decade. Until then, a seven-metre-tall bronze equestrian statue of Franco stood undisturbed in a square where it had been originally erected in 1959. On 17 March 2005 it was removed, initially without fanfare and with minimal media coverage.[41] A small neo-fascist group protested against the removal of the statue while an even smaller group of supporters of the action cheered on. In an attempt to minimise any possible demonstrations or public debate, the event was not publicised in advance. In fact, the operation was kept secret even from the city authorities, which the mayor of Madrid complained about the next day. The removal occurred in the early hours of the morning, starting at 2 am, supposedly to avoid disturbing traffic. Interestingly, the statue was covered for transport, a clear sign that the authorities were nervous about the removal even at that time of the day. To pre-empt confrontation, there was a heavy police presence and spectators were told to disperse.[42] Except for a few shouts and fascist salutes,

39 'Pero creo que en España, si hubiera habido una ruptura con la dictadura (tal como ha ocurrido en los países del Este de Europa) en lugar de una transición (que se ha realizado en condiciones de gran poder de las derechas y una gran debilidad de las izquierdas), hoy se hablaría del fascismo en vez de franquismo.' ibid., 15.
40 'El lenguaje que utilizamos no es neutro, y el término franquismo, que se usa para definir la dictadura, tampoco lo es.' ibid.
41 The first removal of a Franco statue took place in 1981 in Puente Genil (Córdoba), according to Asociación para la Recuperación de la Memoria Histórica (ARHM, Association for the Recuperation of Historical Memory), while, in Santander, a monument was also removed in 1981, only to be put back in 1983. It was an exact replica of the Madrid statue and was still standing in front of the city's Town Hall in 2005. The removal of the Madrid statue in 2005 is the most significant event of this kind since the death of Spain's dictator, General Francisco Franco, 32 years earlier, save, perhaps, only the removal of a statue in 2002 in the city of El Ferrol, Franco's birthplace, and thus very heavy in symbolism in its own way but not nearly as widely reported in the Spanish or international media.
42 Most sources do not provide any estimates as to the size of the crowd protesting during the actual removal, and concentrate on the demonstration on the following day.

it was uneventful. Until the next day, that is, when people started gathering around the empty pedestal and adorned it with flowers and a Spanish flag, some praying on their knees. A demonstration in protest of the removal, organised by the Spanish fascist party Falange, was attended by approximately 700 people[43] who assembled in front of a large portrait of Franco that had been placed in front of the empty pedestal. One of the iconic images of Franco as a crusader was beamed onto the scaffolding that the authorities had placed there, projecting a virtual presence of Franco where the physical monument of him had stood before. This demonstration was reported in major international media outlets, complete with the image of the fascist salute, and was followed by a heated public debate in the Spanish media.

While international media focused on the resurgence of the Spanish far right, the public debate in Spain took a very different direction, mainly revolving around the issues of memory and commemoration. The opinions of two politicians who were frequently quoted in the Spanish media epitomised the divisions in Spanish society with regard to this particular event, as well as the discord regarding how Spain should deal with its difficult past in general. On the one hand, the leader of one of the ruling parties, Gaspar Llamazares of the *Izquierda Unida* (IU, United Left), declared that, despite the statue being removed in the early hours of the morning, it 'could have been done in the light of the day' as 'there is no shame in removing what is shameful'.[44] In contrast, the opposition, according to Javier Arenas of the *Partido Popular* (PP, Popular Party), considered the removal of the Franco statue an 'unnecessary reopening of wounds' stemming from the Spanish experience of dictatorship, and accused the ruling party of 'hijacking the process of reconciliation'.[45] On the same day, the Catalan edition of *El País* also published a short editorial by Isabel Olesti about a book called *Mujer y exilio 1939* (*Women and Exile 1939*), as well as a talk delivered by its author, Antonina Rodrigo. Olesti finished her editorial with a quote from Rodrigo: 'Franco's death should have opened the doors of history. Instead a pact of silence was agreed upon and nothing happened. And we are left with what they taught us. And the wound remains open'.[46]

---

43 According to estimates in *El País*, Spain's leading newspaper: 'El PP critica la retirada y 700 fascistas protestan ante el pedestal', 18 March 2005, http://www.elpais.com/articulo/espana/PP/critica/retirada/700/fascistas/protestan/pedestal/elpepiesp/20050318elpepinac_10/Tes accessed 10 August 2005.

44 'Aunque comprende que se haya retirado de madrugada para no alterar el tráfico en una ciudad colapsada, entiende que sería "ilustrativo que se pueda hacer a la luz del día", porque "no hay ninguna vergüenza en quitar lo que es una vergüenza: que se mantengan símbolos de una dictadura que se deberían haber retirado hace mucho tiempo."' 'El PP critica la retirada de la estatua de Franco porque puede "abrir heridas" en la sociedad', *El País*, 17 March 2005, http://www.elpais.com/articulo/espana/PP/critica/retirada/estatua/Franco/puede/abrir/heridas/sociedad/elpepuesp/20050317elpepunac_6/Tes accessed 10 August 2005.

45 'Me parece muy mal que el PSOE esté intentando cargarse la reconciliación nacional. ... es un error y abre heridas innecesarias en la sociedad española'. Javier Arenas, interview for the program Mirada Crítica on channel Telecinco on 17 March 2005, http://www.imdb.com/title/tt1925031/

46 'Con la muerte de Franco se tenía que haber abierto las puertas de la historia. Pero se hizo un pacto de silencio: aquí no ha pasado nada. Y nos quedamos con lo que nos contaron. Y la herida sigue abierta.' Rodrigo,

Pact of silence

The 'pact of silence' (*pacto de silencio*) that Rodrigo refers to was an actual political agreement between parties[47] that delayed the removal of statues of Franco, such as that in Madrid, until almost 30 years after his death. It was agreed upon by post-Franco Spanish society in the name of the greater good — that of a peaceful transition to democracy and the regaining of political and economic stability in a country still bearing the scars of the war and facing great uncertainties as to the transition of power upon the dictator's death. The fragility of the peace and the conflicting interests of the various groups that would make a grab for power were on everybody's mind when Franco died in November 1975. He was almost 83 years old and his health had been declining in the last few years of his life, so the end of his rule had been anticipated. The totalitarian regime imposed on Spanish society after the end of the civil war in April 1939 had already softened significantly,[48] and a successor to Franco had been nominated since 1969.[49] However, executions of political opponents were still being carried out as late as September 1975, and emotions were still running high. Many feared that Spain could find itself at the brink of another conflict between the Francoists, who would resort to anything in order to cling to power, and the opposition, who would use the opportunity to seize power and exact revenge.

Nonetheless, a peaceful transition was achieved, in spite of the odds against it, by setting the immediate past aside and moving forward, but at the same time keeping the existing political structure and legal mechanisms. In the words of Salvador Cardús i Ros:

---

in Isabel Olesti, 'Mujer y exilio', *El País*, 17 March 2005, http://www.elpais.com/articulo/cataluna/Mujer/exilio/elpepiespcat/20050317elpcat_3/Tes accessed 10 August 2005.

47   In a strong critique of the debates on historical memory, Payne argues that '"Pact of silence" is simply a propaganda slogan. No such thing ever existed. ...What was agreed upon was not "silence" but the understanding that historical conflicts would be consigned to the labours of the historians and journalists, and that politicians would not make use of them in their parties' mutual competition, which would direct itself to present and future conflicts'. Payne, *Spain*, 251.

48   Wiarda and MacLeish Mott subscribe to the idea of 'soft' dictatorship in the later stages of Franco's rule: 'By the early 1970s such vast economic, social, cultural even political changes had occurred in Spain and Portugal that the two countries were hardly recognizable from what they had been earlier. What had once been "hard" dictatorships were now "soft" dictatorships led by enfeebled old men. These once fierce authoritarian regimes were now tired, out of date, old-fashioned, and hanging on mainly by inertia. It would not take much to topple them.' Wiarda and MacLeish Mott, 59.

49   Franco reinstated the monarchy in 1947 and named himself regent for life. In 1969 he named as heir to the throne the previous king's grandson, Juan Carlos de Borbón, who was enthroned two days after Franco's death and who is still the King of Spain today. Effectively, the successor approved by and groomed by Franco remains as the head of the Spanish state over 35 years after the death of the dictator, although his role in initiating a democratisation process and his firm stand against the attempted coup in 1981 demonstrates an unquestionable departure from Franco's ideology and politics. For an excellent analysis of the figure of the King and his role in the transition process see Paul Preston, *Juan Carlos: A People's King* (London: HarperCollins, 2004).

> The transition is, basically, a process of historical and social amnesia, and the invention of a new political tradition (the contradiction is valid). ... [It] is, in effect, the manufacturing of a great lie ... that had the politically laudable intention of turning the page from an authoritarian to a democratic regime without bringing about a political breakdown and, in the process, achieving the unheard of situation in which the dictatorship's juridico-political framework became the source of legitimacy for the new democratic model.[50]

The end of the dictatorship and the re-establishment of democracy should have made it possible, in theory, to contest the official version of the past, prosecute crimes, and seek reparations for victims. This, however, could have potentially led to purges, retribution, and even another armed conflict. The peace was too precious to Spaniards from both sides to jeopardise, even if it meant that anti-Francoists had to forgo a basic sense of justice. The political compromises achieved during the early transition period were reinforced by the amnesty law proclaimed in 1977, which was deemed necessary for the success of national reconciliation and the possibility of an open dialogue. The amnesty law guaranteed that there would be no legal avenues for the prosecution of crimes committed during the war and the dictatorial regime; however, it did not provide for any sort of public accounting of the abuses committed by those in power during that time. Moreover, the law recognised the continuing validity of the military tribunals from the Franco era and it was not until 1990 that the first capital punishment verdict against a political prisoner was annulled.[51]

The 'pact of silence' not only silenced any attempt to bring to light the violent excesses of the regime; it effectively prevented any legal action to punish those guilty of human rights abuses, as well as any rehabilitation or compensation of victims. Navarro, who moved back to Spain after three decades in exile, is vocal in denouncing the pact of silence and its role in the *transición* that, he said in an interview with Javier Valenzuela, 'was a political pact to erase responsibilities, including the moral ones and the symbolic ones. Besides amnesty it was decided that there should be amnesia'.[52] There was no attempt at a truth and reconciliation commission and, in fact, the term 'reconciliation' signified the

50   Salvador Cardús i Ros, 'Politics and the Invention of Memory: For a Sociology of the Transition to Democracy in Spain', in *Disremembering the Dictatorship: The Politics of Memory in the Spanish Transition to Democracy*, ed., Joan Ramon Resina (Amsterdam and Atlanta: Rodopi), 18–19.
51   While the 1963 verdict was legally annulled in 1990, and the execution of Julián Grimau deemed illegal, in 2002 PP blocked a parliamentary proposal of IU to formally rehabilitate him. In 2005 the IU lodged a similar proposal with the Assembly of the Autonomous Community of Madrid, and it was again successfully blocked by the PP.
52   'La transición', dice, 'fue un pacto político para borrar las responsabilidades, incluidas las morales, las simbólicas. Además de amnistía se decidió que hubiera amnesia.' Javier Valenzuela, 'El despertar tras la amnesia', *El País*, 6 November 2002, http://www.elpais.com/articulo/semana/despertar/amnesia/elpepuculba b/20021102elpbabese_9/Tes accessed 20 September 2010.

pact of silence.[53] In the name of the 'spirit of reconciliation', members of Spanish society were asked to leave the memories of their traumas outside of the public sphere or, as Helen Graham put it, 'those who had been obliged to be silent for nearly 40 years were once again required to accept that there would be no public recognition of their past lives or memories'.[54] Thus, the traumas of the war and the dictatorship were not dealt with collectively; the 'smooth' transition and the 'spirit of reconciliation' did not allow for any blame to be cast, and effectively removed the question of trauma from the public sphere. The political and social changes that Spain underwent from the mid 1970s to the mid 1990s excluded a collective memory of war and oppression and, as Susana Narotzky and Gavin Smith's research concludes, 'exposed in practice the split realities of public and private memories of the past'.[55] In keeping with these split realities, Franco continued to dominate the public sphere with his presence in the form of monuments, street names and even on the coins that were not withdrawn until the 1990s[56] while, for many Republican families, the memories of those killed or persecuted had to remain in the private sphere without public recognition or acknowledgement.

The 'pact of silence' is also often referred to as the 'pact of forgetting' as there was a tacit agreement to forget a war that Spaniards were no longer proud of. Preston points out that years of Franco's indoctrination about a glorious 'crusade of Spanish values against blood-crazed Communist barbarians'[57] dissipated quickly after the transition and, by 1983, an opinion poll showed that 73 per cent of Spaniards regarded the Civil War as 'a shameful period of Spanish history that is better to forget'.[58] Referred to often as 'amnesia' (*amnesia*), 'silence' (*silencio*), 'forgetting' (*olvido*), or 'disremembering' (*desmemoria*), this phenomenon is interpreted in various ways. Michael Richards argues that:

---

53   The Franco regime did not allow the public use of the term 'reconciliation', even by priests. Preston tells of a case where 'the Primate of Spain, Cardinal Gomá, had a pastoral letter censored on August 9th, 1939, for using the word "reconciliation" instead of the officially sanctioned "recuperation"'. Preston, 'Revenge and Reconciliation', *History Today* 39, no. 3 (March 1989): 32.

54   Helen Graham, 'Coming to Terms with the Past: Spain's Memory Wars', *History Today* 54, no. 5 (May 2004): 30. And Paloma Aguilar points out that it also meant that the war veterans on the Republican side were never awarded the pension rights that had been enjoyed for years by the Nationalist veterans (Aguilar, 'Agents of Memory: Spanish Civil War Veterans and Disabled Soldiers' in *War and Remembrance in the Twentieth Century*, eds, Jay Winter and Emmanuel Sivan (Cambridge University Press, 2000), 84–103).

55   Susan Narotzky and Gavin Smith, '"Being *politico*" in Spain: An Ethnographic Account of Memories, Silences and Public Politics', *History and Memory* 14, no. 1/2 (2002): 211.

56   Davis.

57   Preston, *Revenge*, 32.

58   ibid., 33.

'Amnesia', individual and collective, came gradually to be seen as the best medicine for Spain. This prognosis was in line with the generalised and tacit agreement in the 1960s and 1970s that the Civil War had been a tragic act of madness for which all Spaniards were somehow to blame.[59]

In addition to Richards's idea of 'madness' involving the whole of the society, Preston's concept of 'shame' puts the blame on the Nationalists, and Aguilar[60] explores the 'anaesthetic, narcotic' aspects of forgetting when the trauma is in fact very well remembered.

The 'pact of forgetting' could have, in theory, led to the erasure of Francoist-era monuments and symbols, and thus the removal of Franco's statues would have appeared natural in this context of 'forgetting' shameful chapters of Spain's history. Instead, the opposite happened. The transition from Franco's regime to a parliamentary monarchy was conceived on the basis of continuity rather than rupture, thus effectively legitimising the dictatorship. Therefore, glorification of the Republican efforts in the war, exile, and resistance would have gone directly against the spirit of political stabilisation. The Second Republic, overthrown by Franco's uprising, was perceived as being so radically to the left that, according to Aguilar and Carsten Humlebaek, 'during the 1980s [it] was regarded favourably by only 5 per cent or less of the Spanish population and it consistently scored less than the Francoist regime', the popularity of which fell from 21 per cent in 1984 to 8 per cent in 1990. At the same time, acceptance of the current political system in Spain rose from 58 to 76 per cent.[61] While these figures do not directly link the current democracy to the previous regime, they certainly indicate a clear rupture from the legacy of the Second Republic.[62] The reluctance to incorporate any political symbols from that era into the current democracy is such that post-Francoist Spain did not even consider restoring the Republican anthem and, to this day, the Spanish state continues to use the national anthem from the Franco years.

With the amnesty law in 1977, in the famous words of Marcelino Camacho, the spokesman for the Communists, the Spaniards 'buried their dead and their resentments'.[63] The main political players of the transition period accepted and put forward for social approval the idea of closing a certain chapter of Spanish

---

59   Michael Richards, 'From War Culture to Civil Society: Francoism, Social Change and Memories of the Spanish Civil War', *History and Memory* 14, no. 1/2 (2002): 111.

60   Paloma Aguilar Fernández, *Memoria y olvido de la Guerra Civil española* (Madrid: Alianza Editorial, 1996).

61   Paloma Aguilar and Carsten Humlebaek, 'Collective Memory and National Identity in the Spanish Democracy. The Legacies of Francoism and the Civil War', *History and Memory* 14, no. 1/2 (2002): 145.

62   Aguilar and Humlebaek's extensive research 'into the symbolic practices and politics of commemoration of post-Franco Spain' leads them to the conclusion that 'there are many more continuities with the Francoist period than with the Second Republic or with any other previous period'. ibid., 152.

63   'Hemos enterrado nuestros muertos y nuestros rencores.'

history without confrontation so that a political dialogue could begin. The overarching need for stability that dictated Spain's political transition remained present in the society long after institutional changes assured the success of a peaceful political process. Aguilar and Humlebaek quote a Eurobarometer study that collected opinion polls between 1970 and 1992, which demonstrates that:

> The importance that Spaniards accord, even today, to the values of 'peace', 'order', and 'moderation' remains noticeably higher than in other European countries, a phenomenon undoubtedly linked to the memory of the fratricide and the desire to avoid its recurrence. In comparison, of all the countries of Europe, Spain gives highest priority to the value of 'keeping order', with a score of 11 points above the European mean.[64]

The inertia regarding the re-evaluation of the immediate past is in stark contrast with enormous changes in the Spanish social and cultural life, where the *destape* (lifting the lid) effect led to what is commonly referred to as a revolution, but it remained largely within the spheres of lifestyle and artistic expression. On the political level, care was taken not to alienate the major players in either the ruling party or the opposition thus, in theory, allowing all of the main sectors of society to participate in the political process. The hotly debated issues of regionalism and secularism became the most contentious topics in the political arena. Therefore the 'smooth' transition to democracy was deemed a big success, both domestically and internationally, and the 'Spanish model of transition' became a prototype for other fading dictatorships and dissolving totalitarian regimes. But, in view of the persistence of Spanish society in not addressing its difficult past and not breaking the 'pact of silence' or 'pact of forgetting', it is not surprising that the meaning of the term *transición* (transition) itself is widely debated.

Transición

The term *transición* is traditionally used to describe the three-year period between Franco's death in November 1975 and the implementation of the new constitution in December 1978. As many scholars remark, however, the temporal end markers of the transition period are highly debatable. On one end, the beginning of the *transición* could be moved forward to the time when Franco's regime evolved from the harshly totalitarian state of the 1940s and 1950s to a

---

64   The respondents were asked 'Which should be the first aim of your country?' and were given four possible answers: '1. Keep order in the nation. 2. Give the people more voice in government decisions. 3. Fight price increases. 4. Protect freedom of expression.' The European mean for 'keeping order in the nation' was 37.8 per cent, with Spain scoring 48.5 per cent and Denmark (46.4 per cent) and Northern Ireland (45.6 per cent) just behind. The lowest score, 26 per cent, came from Belgium, which scored the highest in Europe (40.6 per cent) for the option 'fight price increases'. ibid., 150.

milder version of an authoritarian regime in the 1960s, considering the seeds of change to have been planted while Franco was still in power. Wiarda and MacLeish Mott posit that 'the post-Franco transition ... had begun even while Franco was still alive'.[65] Raúl Morodo puts forward a concept of *pretransición* (pretransition), to refer to some changes that Franco applied, forced by international pressures to make Spain appear more open.[66] Ofelia Ferrán strongly opposes the idea of a pre-transition on the basis that it would credit Franco for preparing Spain for democracy[67] and points out that executions of political prisoners took place up to the very end of Franco's rule. According to Ramón Buckley, the year 1968 initiated social and cultural changes that laid the ground for the political transition in the 1970s.[68] Some consider the starting date for the transition to be 20 December 1973, when *Euskadi Ta Askatasuna* (ETA, Basque Homeland and Freedom) assassinated Luis Carrero Blanco, groomed by Franco to be his successor.[69] Javier Tusell[70] reminds us that many comparative studies see the Spanish transition as part of a worldwide process named by Samuel Huntington the 'third wave of democratization'.[71]

On the other end, the transition period is sometimes extended until past the *coup d'état* of February 1981, or even the electoral victory of the socialists in 1982,[72] seen as a more stabilising event than the 1978 Constitution. In 1992 Spain hosted the Olympic Games in Barcelona, the International Expo in Seville, and Madrid was the European Capital of Culture; this is sometimes considered the 'real end of transition', the year in which Spain projected itself to the rest of the world as a modern country, and that in the 15 years since the re-establishment of democracy was able to overcome the shadowy past of a civil war and a fascist regime. Some scholars put the ending date of the transition even later: Teresa Vilarós considers it to be 1993 with the signing of Maastricht treaty, which for Spain meant real integration in the European community and the end of isolationism. Rosa Montero posits the 2000 electoral victory of the PP as the true ending of the transition: 'I have a feeling that this is the true end of the

---

65   Wiarda and MacLeish Mott, 69.
66   Specifically, Ley de Convenios Colectivos 1958, allowing some union representation for workers, and loosening up of censorship in Ley de Prensa e Imprenta 1966. Raúl Morodo, *La transición política* (Madrid: Tecnos, 1984).
67   Ofelia Ferrán, 'Memory and Forgetting, Resistance and Noise in the Spanish Transition: Semprún and Vázquez Montalbán', in Resina, 193.
68   Ramón Buckley, *La doble transición: política y literatura en la Espana de los anos setenta* (Madrid: Siglo Ventiuno, 1996).
69   An example is Teresa Vilarós, *El mono del desencanto: una crítica cultural de la transición espanola (1973–1993)* (Madrid: Siglo Veintiuno, 1998).
70   Javier Tusell, 'La Transición política: un planteamiento metodológico', in *Historia de la transición 1975–1986*, eds, Javier Tusell and Álvaro Soto (Madrid: Alianza Editorial, 1996), 109–37.
71   Samuel P. Huntington, *The Third Wave. Democratization in the Late Twentieth Century* (Norman, OK: Oklahoma University Press, 1991).
72   Gregorio Morán, *El precio de la transición* (Barcelona: Planeta, 1991). Morán considers various possibilities for its beginning, but puts its end firmly in 1982's PSOE electoral win.

Transition, the ultimate proof of our democratic maturity'.[73] Joan Ramón Resina puts forward the economic argument, suggesting that market forces rather than any political events were responsible for the transition: 'Spain's insertion into the market economy goes a long way towards explaining the Transition's temporal imprecision and the confusion of those who insist on anchoring it in politically significant events'.[74]

However, as Ferrán points out, 'any historical dates one may try to set for the beginning and end of this variously defined epoch of recent Spanish history are therefore arbitrary and, more importantly, depend on what one is thinking of as having "transitioned"',[75] and warns that 'any effort to delimit and define the transition period will be arbitrary, and subject to ideological constraints'.[76] Increasingly the process of transition is thought of as incomplete until the issue of silence and disremembering of the past is dealt with and can be discussed in the open. Dacia Viejo-Rose quotes the results of a 2000 study of *Centro de Investigaciones Sociológicas* (CIS, Centre for Sociological Research), where half of the respondents answered 'No' to the question, 'Have you forgotten the divisions and resentment that the Civil War created?' and 66 per cent said 'Yes' to 'Although the divisions and resentment of the past are forgotten, the deep mark left by the Franco period is still palpable',[77] and observes that these results occur 'despite consensus on the significant changes that Spanish society had undergone in behavior, attitudes and "moral values"'.[78] But, many scholars and social commentators deem these changes to be insufficient without the accompanying social and political action to bring about a change in attitudes and laws regarding historical memory. Ferrán argues that 'an authoritarian, top-down approach to politics was one of the legacies of the Franco regime. In large measure, this top-down approach characterised much of the transition'.[79] In this, she evokes Carr and Eduardo Subirats who, she says, 'goes so far as to state that, until such a critical recuperation and re-evaluation of the past is undertaken, no real transition will have taken place',[80] and for whom:

---

73 'Tengo la sensación de que éste es el verdadero fin de la Transición, la prueba definitva de nuestra madurez democrática' (Rosa Montero, 'Progresismo', *El País*, 21 March 2000, http://www.elpais.com/articulo/ultima/Progresismo/elpepiult/20000321elpepiult_2/Tes accessed 20 November 2011).

74 Joan Ramon Resina, 'Short of Memory: the Reclamation of the Past since the Transition to Democracy', in Resina, 93.

75 Ferrán, 192.

76 ibid., 193–94.

77 Dacia Viejo-Rose, *Reconstructing Spain. Cultural Heritage and Memory after Civil War* (Brighton, Portland and Toronto: Sussex Academic Press, 2011), 160.

78 ibid., 159.

79 Ferrán, 196.

80 ibid.

a true democracy will have been established only once such a confrontation with the past is undertaken, for only a recuperation of Spain's historical memory will lead to the overcoming of the dangerous 'legacies' of the Franco regime that the transition simply perpetuated.[81]

Breaking the 'pact of silence' is seen here as a necessary step for democracy to truly take root in Spain.

Breaking the 'pact of silence'

This break takes place in the decade of the 2000s, based on background work produced since the mid 1990s, with Aguilar's important study[82] at the forefront of scholarly contributions. In Madeleine Davis's words, this 'unexpected emergence of the belated "memory politics"'[83] in the last decade can be explained by a variety of converging factors, including the surprising win of the *Partido Socialista Obrero Español* (PSOE, Spanish Socialist Workers Party) in the 2004 elections[84] and international pressure to deal with past human rights abuses.[85] A general surge in interest in memory in the 1980s in other European countries such as France and Germany can also be credited. Davis discusses the catalysing effect of the 1996 indictment by Spanish courts of Chilean dictator Augusto Pinochet for crimes against humanity, Pinochet's arrest in Great Britain in 1998 and Spain's request for his extradition that received enormous media attention and inevitably led to parallels between Pinochet and Franco. And in the year 2000 Emilio Silva founded the *Asociación de la Recuperación de la Memoria Histórica* (ARMH, Association for the Reclamation of Historical Memory), the first of many Spanish grassroots organisations that will prove

---

81   ibid., 197. Ferrán returns to the discussion of the place of historical memory in Spain's transition process in *Working through Memory: Writing and Remembrance in Contemporary Spanish Narrative* (Lewisburg, PA: Bucknell University Press, 2007).

82   Aguilar, *Memoria y olvido*.

83   Davis, 862.

84   PP was predicted to win the 2004 election by a landslide, but its actions following the train bombings in Madrid only a few days prior to the elections changed the public opinion in favour of PSOE, led by Rodríguez Zapatero who promised to withdraw Spanish troops from Iraq as part of his electoral campaign.

85   Human rights abuses committed during the war and under Franco's rule started attracting international attention in the early 2000s, and the unwelcome publicity of reports from worldwide organisations such as Amnesty International in the mid 2000s might have aided Zapatero's push for a historical memory law, approved by parliament in 2007. For a discussion of Amnesty International's involvement in the debate and its impact on the political process see Tremlett, 'The Grandsons of Their Grandfathers: An Afterword', in *Unearthing Franco's Legacy. Mass Graves and the Recovery of Historical Memory in Spain*, eds, Carlos Jerez-Farrán and Samuel Amago (University of Notre Dame Press, 2010), 327–44. For a comprehensive analysis of associated legal challenges see Mónica Zapico Barbeito, 'Investigating the Crimes of the Franco Regime: Legal Possibilities, Obligations of the Spanish State and Duties towards the Victims', *International Criminal Law Review* 10 (2010): 243–74.

instrumental in bringing historical memory to public attention and leading to a real eruption of what is today called a movement of recuperation of historical memory (*movimiento de la recuperación de la historia memórica*).

AMRH was initially one man's quest to exhume the mass grave where he suspected his grandfather was buried. After successful identification through DNA testing, the association continued the effort of exhuming mass graves from the Civil War and Franco era and identifying bodies, giving the victims a proper burial and allowing the relatives a sense of closure. Based entirely on volunteers and without any financial support from government agencies, AMRH, which aims to identify the graves of all of the estimated 30,000 'disappeared', has also become a forum for information and discussion through its website, aptly named memoriahistorica.org (http://www.memoriahistorica.org). Celebrating its 10th anniversary in October 2010, AMRH could count the exhumation and identification of 1500 bodies among its achievements, but its impact on society goes well beyond this. ARMH is now credited with initiating a powerful civil society response to the 'pact of silence' that eventually led to a more institutionalised movement for recovering historical memories of the Civil War and the dictatorship.[86]

The internet has acted from the beginning as the medium of choice for activist groups dedicated to recovering the memory of people and events silenced in the official versions of Spanish history. The popular ARMH website has regular updates on the recent developments in the politics of memory in Spain. Archives, testimonies and discussion lists can be found at websites such as *Foro de la Memoria* (Forum for Memory, (http://www.pce.es/foroporlamemoria), *Archivo Guerra y Exilio* (War and Exile Archive, http://www.galeon.com/agenoticias/index.html) and *La Guerra Civil Española* (The Spanish Civil War, (http://www.guerracivil.org). *Equipo Nizkor* (Team Nizkor, http://www.derechos.org/nizkor/eng.html), in its 2004 report on Francoist crimes,[87] proposed the term 'Spanish model of impunity', which is now accepted by the academic community.[88] Some educational institutions have used their web servers to archive documents and host moderated discussion groups, thus forming the *Biblioteca del Exilio* (Library of Exile, (http://www.cervantesvirtual.com/portal/exilio/), as well

---

86 According to Viejo-Rose, 'efforts to create public platforms through which to unearth and share stories from these periods bore fruit in 2004, when a new socialist government began a process termed "the recovery of historic memory"', 160. She specifically mentions ARHM by name, alongside Foro por la Memoria (Forum for Memory), as does Tremlett: 'The work of ARHM, which had begun exhuming mass graves of Francoist Civil War victims in 2000, had much to do with the eruption of *memoria histórica* into the public sphere' ('The Grandsons', 329–30).

87 Equipo Nizkor, 'La cuestión de la impunidad en España y los crímenes franquistas', 2004, http://www.derechos.org/nizkor/espana/doc/impuesp.html accessed 01 July 2011.

88 Sergio Gálvez Biesca, 'El proceso de la recuperación de la "memoria histórica" en España: Una aproximación a los movimientos socials por la memoria', *International Journal of Iberian Studies* 19, no. 1 (2006): 25–51.

as a site named *Memoria del exilio* (Memory of Exile, http://clio.rediris.es/index_exilio.htm) that provides educational materials for teaching and research in history. The rapid proliferation of internet sites, the impressive work of collecting documents and information, and of placing them on open access forums and databases, all demonstrate the scale of engagement of civil society and determination to make public what had remained in the private sphere for too long since the re-instatement of democracy in Spain.

Television played an equally important role in spreading the message to wider audiences. The 2000s saw a large number of documentaries about war, dictatorship and exile being produced by the state television company *Radio Televisión Española*, commercial television channels such as Canal+, publishing houses and research foundations. These documentaries combine previously unknown footage and photographs with interviews with survivors and witnesses. The stories they tell are powerful accounts of the suffering of individuals, families and communities, struggles to keep memories alive during the time of repression, frustration and further suffering when the 'pact of silence' does not allow these memories to become public in the long period of transition and, finally, the challenges and determination to not only preserve the memories of what happened many decades ago but to finally bring them forward to the public sphere and acknowledge their right to form part of the nation's history. When aired on television, these documentaries attracted large audiences and were often rebroadcast due to popular demand. DVDs of these programs were often sold out and the demand has remained steady.

Magazines, weekly supplements to newspapers and other periodicals had an even bigger impact on society, as they reached out to an audience that included moderates, the disinterested, and even those who considered themselves pro-Francoists; in brief, those who would not have otherwise found out about some painful episodes from recent history. In 2002, *El Semanal*, the weekly supplement of the leading Spanish newspaper *El País*, published an emotive account of a former prisoner of a concentration camp. A photo of the camp and the title of the article: '*Yo viví el campo de concentración franquista*' ('I lived through a Francoist concentration camp') screamed from the displays at newsstands all over the country and caused a sensation. Most Spaniards had never heard of Franco's concentration camps, and many would have considered the idea outrageous; however, they were confronted head-on with the harsh truth of the human right abuses of Franco's regime, in a shock treatment that sent waves through the whole society. Many other magazines devoted entire issues to topics such as mass graves from the Civil War and concentration camps under Franco, most putting confronting images on the front page. And it was not a fad; the trend continues[89] as Spanish society goes through an accelerated process of re-evaluating its immediate past and learning the chapters of history that were previously suppressed.

The interest in testimonies and personal accounts of 'silenced' or 'forgotten' memories led to a surge in the publication of autobiographies, memoirs, and fact literature. Faction-style and fully fictionalised novelistic and cinematographic accounts of the war and the dictatorship have also been enormously popular, with Javier Cercas's 2001 'faction' style novel *Soldados de Salamina* (Soldiers of Salamis), an instant bestseller for 40 weeks and selling a million copies in six years, after an initial printing of only 5000 copies,[90] being heralded by many as the real beginning of the 'waking from amnesia' (*despertar tras la amnesia*) that Spanish society has been undergoing for just over a decade now. Cercas's novel is only one of innumerable fictionalised accounts of the war and the dictatorship,[91] many of them produced by Spanish writers who lived in exile while Franco was still in power. The 1990s saw a publishing boom of these literary works that has since continued. Already in 2002, in a very aptly titled editorial, '*El Despertar tras la Amnesia*' (To wake-up from amnesia), Javier Valenzuela reflects on the popularity and success of publications such as Cercas's book, especially among young Spaniards. The historian Santos Juliá contributes an explanation that it is always more interesting, fascinating, even, for a grandson to inquire about a grandfather, than for a son to look at a father.[92] This is mirrored by an abundance of scholarly approaches in the fields of literary studies that, alongside historical and political approaches, contribute to the overall body of literature on the way in which Spanish society is coming to terms with its immediate past.

Similarly, the 2003 movie adaptation of Cercas's novel by renowned director David Trueba,[93] and other motion picture features such as Antón Reixa's 2002 *El Lápiz del Carpintero* (The Carpenter's Pencil), Mexican filmmaker Guillermo de Toro's 2006 *El laberinto del fauno* (Pan's Labyrinth), as well as one the first

---

89 In June 2011, issues of two of the most popular history magazines *Clio* and *La Aventura de la Historia* (The Adventure of History), both had large sections devoted to revisiting those chapters in Spain's history. In *Clio* there is a 12-page spread on the Spanish Fascist Party by historian Xavier Casals ('Las siete vidas de Falange o la odisea del fascismo español', *Clío: Revista de Historia* 10, no. 116 (2011): 26–37), complete with a photograph of Juan Antonio Samaranch, future head of the International Olympic Committee, taking the oath. *La Aventura de la Historia* 13, no. 152 (2011) has a powerful photograph of deceased victims of the War on its cover, and four articles over 35 pages inside: Juan Carlos Losada, 'El Golpe y La Guerra', 62–71; Julio Martín Alarcón, 'Testigos de la Tragedia', 76–9; Enrique Moradiellos, 'Bajo la Lupa de Europa', 72–75; Ángel Viñas, 'La Trama', 56–61.
90 The book has been published worldwide in a myriad of languages and won the Independent Fiction Prize in 2004.
91 Cercas' latest work, *Anatomía de un instante* (The Anatomy of a Moment), (Barcelona: Mondadori, 2009), examines the failed coup d'état of February 1981 and earned him the Spanish National Narrative Award (*Premio Nacional de la Narrativa*) in 2010.
92 'Este interés de la nueva generación se corresponde a la mirada del nieto sobre el abuelo, que siempre es más interesada, más fascinada, más curiosa que la mirada del hijo sobre el padre'. Juliá en Valenzuela.
93 Winner of 2004 Goya Awards.

entries in this boom, Vicente Aranda's 1996 *Libertarias* (Freedomfighters [sic]), are quickly becoming the most studied of contemporary Spanish films: popular fascination with this topic again being matched by academic interest. A television series *Cuéntame cómo pasó* (Tell Me How It Happened), set in the last years of Franco's regime and in the transition period, has been broadcast since 2001 and it is currently in its 13th season, with previous seasons averaging five million viewers and DVDs of past seasons, out of stock for years, just recently reissued.[94]

Del Toro's film, *El laberinto del fauno*, won three Academy Awards in 2007 (for cinematography, art direction and make-up). It is one of many films and novels depicting the Spanish Civil War and the dictatorship era in Spain that found recognition outside of Spain. This, on one hand, confirms the artistic quality of these productions and, on the other, that an historical context can hold attraction for audiences unfamiliar with that context but able to relate to it — it highlights the universality of the fragile and contested boundary between truth and fiction, so often examined and questioned in the contemporary society.[95] The concept of truth is essential to the Spanish process of reclaiming memory: it originally operated on the assumption that there is one unequivocal truth about certain historical events that had been silenced or distorted, and therefore needs to be revealed or corrected. The prevailing terminology used by Spanish commentators in press articles and on dedicated websites was that of 'falsifying the truth' (*falsificar la verdad*) and 'hiding the truth' (*ocultar la verdad*) during the Franco era, 'silence' (*silencio*) and 'oblivion' (*olvido*) in the first 20 years of democracy, and the urgent need to 'unveil the truth' (*desvelar la verdad*) and 'reclaim memory' (*recuperar la memoria*) as a 'blood debt' (*deuda sangriente*) of Spanish society to those who perished or suffered oppression. This emotionally charged vocabulary reflected the high level of frustration and disappointment that was felt by the victims and their families, due to the lack of a concerted political effort to publicly recognise the wrongdoings and rehabilitate the victims. It was accompanied by a flood of specialist history books and articles that adopted a more distanced academic language but departed from the same point of claiming the right for a public recognition of human suffering. By exhuming unmarked graves and collecting the personal testimonies of victims and witnesses, activists and historians alike attempted to make public what had until then remained in the private sphere. Rather than entering into the epistemological debate about truth in history, these works exploited the highly emotional nature of the term *truth* in a society that was only recently opening up to the idea of multiple versions of history coexisting in the public sphere.

94 It has already been subject to scholarly inquiries. An example is Rodolfo Serrano, *La España de Cuéntame cómo pasó : el final de los años sesenta* (Madrid: Aguilar, 2004).
95 In the interpretation of Maja Jaggi, writing for the *Guardian* (2011), Vargas Llosa called *Soldiers of Salamis* (the book) 'magnificent' and 'proof that engaged literature is not dead'.

The generation of Spaniards actively engaging in the process of recovery of historical memory is still heavily influenced by the concepts of *one truth* and *one history*, which prevailed in the Franco-era educational system. Older generations, those whose personal memories and testimonies are collected, are even more conditioned, having lived for decades under a regime that relied on a pervasive propaganda for its legitimacy. Franco's propaganda machine had propagated only one official version of history, one in which Franco saved Spain from the clutches of the Reds, not unlike the crusaders fighting the infidels. As the saying goes, history is written by the victors and, in the case of Francoist Spain, this meant that the victors had not only the monopoly on interpretation of the actual conflict and the events leading to it, but also the right to rewrite other chapters of the past. Therefore, under Franco school curricula,[96] media reports, published books, artistic performances, amongst other forms of public expression, emphasised the glory of Spain's imperial achievements while suppressing knowledge of undesirable historical facts and processes, through strict censorship practices. Preston points out that:

> the Franco regime used a distorted historical memory as a major weapon in its propaganda armoury. History under the Francoist dictatorship was a direct instrument of the State, written by policemen and soldiers, Falangists and priests, invigilated by the powerful censorship machinery.[97]

Besides exploiting the legacies of the Civil War and the Second Republic, Franco used Spain's imperialistic and colonial past to reinforce notions of national unity and glory, especially by reinforcing the concept of a Christian crusade against infidels. Angel Luis Abós, in a study that examined over 200 history manuals used in Spanish schools between 1937 and 1975, considered this 'manipulation of the past' for propaganda purposes. As a result, entire generations of Spaniards grew up indoctrinated not only with a selective historical curriculum, but also had the concept of absolute historical truth embedded in them from very early age. Some beliefs that were fabricated and instilled in that era persist in Spanish society today, mainly due to the lack of an open public debate on Spain's recent history, and the fact that, as Graham points out, the 'coverage of the 1930s and 1940s in school history syllabuses is still frequently patchy or non-existent'.[98] This had an enormous impact on the way in which Spain dealt with the issue of historical memory during the transition in the first place, and in the early stages

---

96 See Juan Luis Abós, *La historia que nos enseñaron 1937–1975* (Madrid: Foca Ediciones, 2003) and José Antonio Álvarez Osés, Ignacio Cal Freire, María Carmen González Muñoz and Juan Haro Sabater, *La Guerra que aprendierion los espanoles: República y Guerra civil en los textos de Bachillerato (1938–1983)* (Madrid: Universidad Autónoma de Madrid, 2000) for comprehensive analyses of Spanish educational curricula under Franco and into early transition, before changes were implemented.
97 Preston, *Revenge*, 31.
98 Graham, 31.

of the process of recuperation of historical memory through the mechanisms discussed earlier, and when previously suppressed information was now being revealed as the supposed *truth*, while the version that had been propagated by the Franco regime got labelled *false* or *a lie*.

Politics of memory

While in the last decade there has been an explosion in popular interest in historical memory, the issue was not at the forefront of Spanish political battles between the Right and the Left as early as one might expect. When it was in power from 1982 until 1996, the PSOE did little to advance the cause of the Republicans and can be credited with only limited achievements as far as reparations to and the rehabilitation of the victims of the war and of the fascist regime.[99] The process then suffered serious setbacks under the government of the right-wing Popular Party between 1996 and 2004,[100] which in turn mobilised activists and academics to continue their research and to organise commemorative events at the local level. ARHM was founded in 2000, just as the PP was re-elected for another term. The return of PSOE to power after the 11 March 2004 Madrid bombings was met with great expectations by the pro-Republicans but, again, the issue of historical memory was upstaged by other urgent and hotly debated social and political issues such as the right of gays to marriage and adoption, and the rights of autonomous regions versus the unity of the Spanish state.

When in September 2004[101] the socialist government announced the creation of a special commission to investigate the victims of the Civil War and Francoism,[102] it appeared that the memory of the Spanish Republic would finally become part of Spain's historical memory through a proper institutional change as a law regarding rehabilitation of the victims and reparations was expected to be proposed sometime in late 2005, preferably before the 30th anniversary of Franco's death, or even on the exact day (20 November). Yet on 12 September, the leader of the Commission, Deputy Prime Minister María Teresa Fernández de la Vega, announced not only that no legislation would be proposed in the near

---

99   As mentioned earlier, from the mid 1980s, some laws were passed regarding reparations to victims, including recognition of time spent in prison as years of work for the purpose of retirement pensions (1984), and provisions for financial compensation for long-term political prisoners of Franco's regime (1990–92).

100   Graham, 30, provides a clear example of PP's political stand on these matters: while denying funding to the ARHM, the government provided financial assistance to the maintenance of the graves of Blue Division volunteers, Spanish fascists who fought alongside the Germans on the eastern front in World War II.

101   Approved on 10 September 2004 and created on 18 October 2004. PSOE rejected similar proposals in June and July 2004, agreeing with the position of the Popular Party, but the General Assembly of PSOE held in July 2004 forced the Executive to take action.

102   Comisión Interministerial para el Estudio de las víctimas de la Guerra Civil y del Franquismo.

future, but also that the project now would include both sides of the conflict and not be used for reopening the wounds but rather to heal them.[103] In a letter to the editor of *El País*, a supporter of the ARHM countered that argument by declaring that 'nobody wants to reopen old wounds, we are only asking for truth and justice'.[104] But the spirit of reconciliation — meaning the pact of silence — prevailed again. Two days after the 30th anniversary of Franco's death, on 22 November 2005, the King celebrated the 30th anniversary of his coronation and, in his speech, he underlined the importance of reconciliation as the key for understanding what was achieved, and the best guarantee to continue ahead with unity, democracy and freedom.[105]

It is not, therefore, surprising that, when the Law of Historical Memory was finally passed in October 2007, it fell short of addressing many issues in a way that would be satisfactory to those engaged in the process of recuperation of memory, and that includes the issue of public displays of Franco's imagery and symbolism.[106] After heated political battle and rejection of various drafts,[107] 'in the end, the Law established that symbols honouring only one side of the war must be removed from all state buildings and recommends that the local governments do the same for all public buildings'.[108] Viejo-Rose points out that 'this was a modified version of the original proposal, demanding that these symbols be removed from all public spaces including church and private property'.[109] The law was expected to deal with all remaining statues of Franco, still on public display at various locations around Spain. It certainly did, in great measure: after the 2005 removal of the Madrid statue, and the one in Zaragoza in 2006, the removals in other cities took place after the law went into effect, in Santander in 2008 and in Ceuta and Valencia in early 2010. In each instance, public demonstrations took place, and the press engaged in the familiar debates

103   'El Ejecutivo ha decidido frenar o al menos ralentizar la ley que preparaba con la idea de buscar un proyecto "ambicioso" que "contiene a los dos bandos y no sirva para reabrir heridas, sino para cicatrizarlas"' (Carlos E. Cué, 'De la Vega frena la ley de memoria histórica para acoger a ambos bandos', *El País*, 12 September 2005, http://www.elpais.com/articulo/espana/Vega/frena/ley/memoria/historica/acoger/ambos/bandos/elpepiesp/20050912elpepinac_9/Tes accessed 20 September 2010).
104   '… aquí nadie quiere reabrir viejas heridas, solo se pide justicia y verdad' (Violeta López de Marcos, 'La memoria histórica', *El País*, 14 September 2005, http://www.elpais.com/articulo/opinion/memoria/historica/elpepiopi/20050914elpepiopi_4/Tes accessed 20 September 2010).
105   'El Rey subrayó que "el consenso, concordia y reconciliación están en la base misma de nuestra constitución, la clave para entender lo mucho que hemos logrado y la mejor garantía para seguir progresando con el esfuerzo de todos, unidos, en democracia y libertad"' (Juan Manuel Pardellas, 'El Rey vuelve a pedir consenso, concordia y reconciliación', *El País*, 22 November 2005, http://www.elpais.com/articulo/espana/Rey/vuelve/pedir/consenso/concordia/reconciliacion/elpepiesp/20051122elpepinac_24/Tes accessed 20 September 2010).
106   José María Abad Liceras examines in detail the various legal challenges associated with the application of the Law to the removal of symbols and public monuments, in *Ley de memoria histórica. La problemática jurídica de la retirada o mantenimiento de símbolos y monumentos públicos* (Madrid: Dykinson, 2009).
107   See Tremlett, 'The Grandsons' for an insightful account on the process of drafting the law and the media responses.
108   Viejo-Rose, 161.
109   ibid.

about 'erasing memory' and 'reopening of old wounds' while displaying — also very familiar by now — images of Franco's horse suspended from the crane that was lifting it for transport into oblivion. The last equestrian statue of Franco on Spanish territory was lifted in August 2010 in Melilla, however, in the same city, another statue of Franco remains on public display despite the Law of Historical Memory. City authorities had originally committed to the statue's removal early in 2010 but then decided to relegate the responsibilities to the Department of Defence, which in turn refused to accept it.[110] In November 2010 the city authorities declared officially that the statue would not be removed because is not against the law: it portrays Franco as commander of the Legion and not as dictator.[111] It seems that Franco's face is still not erased from public view as Spain moves to the next decade and the next government, with the Popular Party winning the election on 20 November 2011.

---

110 'Retiran de Melilla la Última estatua ecuestre de Franco expuesta en España', *El Mundo*, 4 August 2010, http://www.elmundo.es/elmundo/2010/08/04/espana/1280942589.html accessed 25 October 2010.

111 'Melilla apunta que la estatua de Franco no incumple la Ley de Memoria Histórica', *La Gaceta*, 29 November 2010, http://www.intereconomia.com/noticias-gaceta/politica/melilla-apunta-que-estatua-franco-no-incumple-ley-memoria-historica accessed 1 December 2010.

'The sailor is a human being': Labour Market Regulation and the Australian Navigation Act 1912

Diane Kirkby

Labour lawyers wanting to broaden their field beyond the traditional narrowness of the employment relationship do so by employing a concept of regulation that has both economic and social objectives. They have called for law to be seen 'in the wider framework of social relations' with 'a longer time frame for analysis', and for an approach to the field which has an 'eye to both the future and the past'.[1] Their emphasis on the contextual factors impinging on and shaping labour law, its purpose and implementation, provides a compelling argument for historical research. As Michael Quinlan has pointed out, there is a complex interplay between context and purpose that is neither instrumental nor predetermined.[2] Understanding the implementation of law thus requires historical, empirical research, to account for the particularities of its purpose and the unpredictable nature and direction of labour market regulation, which changes over time.

This chapter takes up the challenge to undertake sociolegal research, which expands our understanding of labour regulation. It focuses on the maritime workplace and a process of lawmaking for that workplace which has not previously been studied as it traces the origins and history of the Australian Navigation Act. In so doing, it broadens the field of labour law by accepting the labour market regulation approach which contextualises the employment relationship. It continues an argument for looking outside labour law narrowly defined that was begun in previous work on licensing laws and regulation of the hotel workforce.[3] By looking at laws and their changing formulation, historians can reveal not only law's impact on the workplace in any particular instance, they can also offer perspective on the wider framework of the social history of labouring people.

---

1   Christopher Arup, Peter Gahan, John Howe, Richard Johnstone, Richard Mitchell, Anthony O'Donnell, eds, *Labour Law and Labour Market Regulation: Essays on the Construction, Constitution and Regulation of Labour Market and Work Relationships* (Sydney: The Federation Press, 2006), 11–12.

2   Michael Quinlan, 'Contextual Factors Shaping the Purpose of Labour Law: A Comparative Historical Perspective' in Arup et al, 21.

3   Diane Kirkby, *Barmaids: A History of Women's Work in Pubs* (Cambridge University Press, 1997); Kirkby, '"The Barmaid", "The Landlady", and "The Publican's Wife": History, Law and the Popular Culture of Women's Work in Pubs' in *Romancing the Tomes*, ed., Margaret Thornton (London: Cavendish, 2002), 167–83.

The Australian federal government's announcement in 2009 that it was undertaking a process of reviewing the century-old Navigation Act offers an instance of lawmaking where the larger regulatory approach is particularly pertinent. Importantly, this was only the second time that a Labor government had undertaken to amend this legislation. It followed the 2008 report 'Rebuilding Australia's Coastal Shipping Industry' released by the House of Representatives Standing Committee on Infrastructure, Transport, Regional Development and Local Government, which covered coastal shipping policy then regulated under Part VI of the *Navigation Act 1912*.[4] The purpose of rewriting the legislation was to implement the International Labour Organisation (ILO) Maritime Labour Convention (MLC) 2006 (No. 186) regarding the working conditions of seafarers on ships.[5] The government's stated aim was to create 'a contemporary framework' for maritime safety and marine regulation by introducing 'greater flexibility' to allow the ILO amendments to be adopted and provide 'confidence and certainty for industry'. It consequently set up a process of consultation and invited responses from stakeholders, business, regulatory authorities, and unions.

The Maritime Union of Australia (MUA) responded, accepting that the legislation needed to be modernised but not on the grounds of allowing more flexibility for business. 'Regrettably, the term "flexibility for business" has come to mean a diminution of standards and a weakening of regulation, which is exactly the opposite of what is required in modernised maritime legislation'.[6] The Australian Shipowners Association (ASA) welcomed the possibility of benefits that might flow to the industry. The shipowners looked forward to having key shipping policy reforms enacted, the promise of having a new maritime regulatory regime to replace the existing 'cumbersome and complex legislation', a single national maritime jurisdiction, reduced uncertainty, removal of complexity and duplication, and 'a seamless transition from state to federal qualifications'.[7] A key proposal of the review was to replace eight separate state and territory jurisdictions with one federal regime.

The government's review (and subsequent introduction of the bill), however, provides a timely reminder of the importance of the Navigation Act to Australia's shipping industry history, and an opportunity to explore an example of federal regulation that is arguably as important in its impact on the maritime workforce as arbitration. Histories of Australia's industrial relations have not included

---

4   Australian Government, Department of Infrastructure, Transport, Regional Development and Local Government, Australian Maritime Safety Authority, *Navigation Act Discussion Paper, 3* (Navigation Act Discussion Paper) http://www.infrastructure.gov.au accessed 1 November 2011.

5   ibid.

6   Maritime Union of Australia (MUA), Response to Issues Raised on Department of Infrastructure, Transport, Regional Development/AMSA Navigation Act 1912 Discussion Paper, August 2010, http://www. infrastructure.gov.au/*maritime*/*paper*/files/MUA.pdf accessed 1 November 2011.

7   'Navigation Act under Review', *Ausmarine* 32, no. 9 (July 2010): 15.

discussions of the Navigation Act.[8] Yet, its history is rightfully considered along with the better-known measures for regulation of the workplace given to the federal government. The constitution under section 51 authorised, and also confined, the federal parliament's power to legislate on industrial matters to the power to make laws to settle industrial disputes, which, like bushfires and rabbits, could cross state borders. As is well known, the Commonwealth used this power to set up the Court of Conciliation and Arbitration in 1904, but the constitution also gave the Commonwealth parliament an instrument for more direct regulation of the workplace.

Under the provisions of s. 51(1) read in conjunction with s. 98, which gave the Commonwealth parliament the power to regulate its overseas and interstate trade, terms and conditions for the employment of the workforce in the maritime industry were laid down and monitored by federal regulation under the Navigation Act. The special nature of work at sea prompted specific legislative regulations. Maritime workers employed in the coastal shipping trade crossed state borders regularly. They had been at the centre of the industrial disputes of the 1890s, which led to the arbitration power being included in the constitution at the time of federation.[9] The mobility of this workforce, combined with the national economic (and defence) importance of merchant shipping to an island nation, produced a particular regulatory model as the two constitutional powers developed simultaneously as a conjunction of federal workplace regulation. Seafarers were regulated by both, and steered their course accordingly. The industrial importance of the Navigation Act cannot be underestimated, it is both historical and political.

Origins

The Australian statute's origins lay in the seventeenth century English Navigation Acts that were passed to develop English shipping by restricting the carriage of foreign trade to ships built, owned and crewed by English subjects, and reserving English coastal traffic for English shipping. This was the principle of cabotage. These acts, which were the foundation of the merchant marine and tied commerce and national defence together, were central as Britain rose to worldwide supremacy as a maritime power.[10] According to the current

---

8   An example is Greg Patmore, *Australian Labour History* (Melbourne: Longman Cheshire, 1991).
9   Stuart Macintyre and Richard Mitchell, eds, *Foundations of Arbitration* (Melbourne: Oxford University Press, 1989), 9–11.
10   Ernest Fayle, 'The Navigation Acts', *Edinburgh Review* 228, no. 465 (July 1918): 22–42.

government's discussion paper, 'These Acts covered a range of welfare and safety measures appropriate to the times to address the generally poor working conditions of seafarers and the high loss rate of both ships and lives'.[11]

The Australian colonies were empowered under this English legislation to regulate their coastal trade, although this was subject to restrictions under the United Kingdom (UK) *Merchant Shipping Act*, which controlled 'British possessions'. 'A wide field of subjects was regarded as an Imperial preserve and merchant shipping for economic and political reasons associated with Britain's worldwide supremacy was in that field'. Thus, merchant shipping 'was the Imperial subject par excellence'.[12]

The UK *Merchant Shipping Act 1869* and later, 1894, 'charted the boundaries of the Colonial powers of legislation': s. 736 allowed colonial parliaments to regulate 'the coasting trade' (not specifically defined) on condition the legislation was reserved and confirmed by the United Kingdom, treated all British ships in like manner, and preserved the treaty rights of foreign states. Under the terms of the Act, colonial legislatures could pass legislation for vessels registered in the colony, 'provided such legislation is not repugnant to the Merchant Shipping Act'.[13] Coasting vessels were not those trading on lakes, rivers or within a port; but those which traded along the coast and sometimes, of necessity, voyaged beyond three miles from the coastline, so colonial statutes were still binding on the masters, crew and passengers of those vessels. The colonial acts passed by the various Australian legislatures were not overturned by the enactment of federal legislation but they were narrowed in their application to ships trading between ports within the particular state.[14]

Australia's efforts to develop its own federal laws were slow and difficult. A Commonwealth bill to apply on the Australian coast in substitution for important sections of the UK *Merchant Shipping Act 1894* was originally drafted just a year after federation, in 1902, under the direction of Charles Cameron Kingston and, subsequently on his retirement, by Sir Harry Wollaston. It was introduced into the Senate in 1904, the same year as the Arbitration Act was passed, but then it was withdrawn and referred to a royal commission chaired by William (Billy) Hughes. In 1906, when a new UK Merchant Shipping Act was passed, the bill and the royal commission report were both presented to parliament and the next year were considered by an imperial Merchant Shipping Legislation conference that was held in London by representatives of the Australian, United Kingdom and New Zealand governments, along with British shipowners. The conference recommended 'that the coastal trade of the Commonwealth be reserved for ships

---

11   Navigation Act Discussion Paper.
12   Basil A. Helmore, 'Validity of State Navigation Acts', *Australian Law Journal* 27, (21 May 1953): 16.
13   ibid., 16.
14   ibid., 17.

… conforming to Australian conditions, and licensed to trade on the Australian coast'. The bill was then revised and reintroduced into the Senate in 1907, 1908, 1910 and finally passed late in 1912.[15]

The Bill was then reserved for the Royal Assent as required and, for many months in Britain and Australia, shipowners campaigned against its becoming law. British owners maintained that 'colonial' legislation ought not to apply to British ships. Australian owners objected that the Navigation Act would lead to an 'enormous increase' of their costs, for accommodation for each seaman would have to be almost doubled and compensation of sick and injured seamen would be greatly increased.[16] Consequently the Act was shelved until after the 1914 federal election, and the outbreak of war postponed it further as the British government requested its implementation be delayed.[17] Prime Minister Andrew Fisher announced it would be proclaimed in 1916, but it took until 1921 before the first sections, the Coasting Trade provisions, were proclaimed and it was not until 1923 that most of the other provisions were operative. At the time of the 1924 royal commission, 46 of 425 sections (most of them dealing with pilots and pilotage) still remained inoperative.

The purpose for passing the Navigation Act, 'which actuated the Parliament … and which lifted the subject to a plane of great importance above the ordinary considerations of party politics, was', in the view of royal commissioners J.H. Prowse and A.C. Seabrook, 'the desire to build an Australian Mercantile Marine'.[18] To do this, the commissioners said, Australian shipowners needed to be protected 'from subsidised foreign ships or poorly paid crews', so it was necessary to ensure all ships had the same manning scale, paid their crews Australian wage rates and provided them with the same accommodation. In order to achieve this 'the Australian coastal trade was to be reserved for Australian-owned ships, which were to be the source of a supply of skilled and trained Australian seamen in time of war'. Parliament regarded having an Australian Mercantile Marine as a matter of national security, of such national importance that higher freight rates was a price that had to be paid.[19]

This — applying the principle of cabotage — was in keeping with the spirit of the original British navigation acts, but it went further. According to Percy Clarey, former president of the Australian Council of Trade Unions (ACTU) and, by 1952, a Labor member of parliament, 'the Navigation Act was an earnest attempt on the part of the Australian parliament to give seamen reasonable

15   Royal Commission on the Navigation Act, 1924 (Royal Commission 1924), *Report* (Melbourne: Government Printer, 1924), 2.
16   Brian Fitzpatrick and Rowan Cahill, *The Seamen's Union of Australia, 1872–1972: A History* (Sydney: Seamen's Union of Australia, 1981), 47.
17   Royal Commission 1924, 2.
18   ibid.
19   ibid.

and decent conditions of employment, and make the maritime industry as safe as possible'. And, at the time it was passed, in 1912, he said, it was 'the best navigation act in the world ...'[20]

This Navigation Act, which specifically did not apply to the navy, applied only to 'British' ships, covered ships engaged in trade and commerce, taking on board and carrying passengers, or cargo, from and between ports in the Commonwealth and from there to foreign ports. The Act stipulated the number and nature of crews. All such ships had to have a duly certificated master and officers of differing grades (first mate, second mate, and engineers of various grades) who had to be British subjects and English-speaking. It included provisions relating to the qualifications of officers; the supply, engagement and discharge of crews; the payment of their wages, health and accident benefits, discipline and accommodation; as well as provisions as to safety, equipment, unseaworthy ships, and prevention of collisions.[21]

Division 4 on seamen applied to both British and foreign ships, covered methods of employment, apprenticeships, terms for becoming a rating (ABS or able bodied seaman after three years apprenticeship, and being 18 years old; an OS or ordinary seaman after one year at sea, minimum age 17 years old) all of which had to be verified with paperwork; a seaman could be 'disrated' by the master who had to record it in the logbook and provide the seaman with a copy; specified the number of crew to be employed; the procedures for establishing terms of agreement for employment and subsequent discharge from a ship; prohibited the payment of wages in advance; enabled the payment by 'allotment' of wages to family members; and procedures for deductions and payment on discharge. Division 12 of the *Navigation Act 1912* was on Discipline. 'Any master, seaman or apprentice who by wilful breach or neglect of duty or drunkenness' caused or failed to prevent damage or loss to the ship or its cargo was guilty of an indictable offence. Smuggling was an offence for seamen, assault was an offence if committed by an officer.[22]

Revisions and amendments

Just three years after it came into effect, in 1924, the government set up a royal commission to investigate whether the Navigation Act had succeeded in its purpose of developing an Australian merchant marine. The commissioners could not agree, so their report contained three different positions and three different sets of recommendations. The first report was produced by the chairman (J.H.

---

20 Australia, Parliament, *Hansard*, 1952, 3690.
21 Helmore, 17.
22 Australia, Statutes, *Navigation Act, 1912*, ss. 28–33; ss. 99–115.

Prowse, MP) and another commissioner (A.C. Seabrook, MP); the second by Labor parliamentarians Frank Anstey MP, Senator C.S. McHugh, and G.E. Yates MP; and the third by two Senators W.L. Duncan and H.E. Elliott.

Prowse and Seabrook were unequivocal that the Navigation Act had failed to develop an Australian merchant marine; Anstey, McHugh and Yates were equally sure that the attack on the Navigation Act from the Tariff Board alleging that the Act had caused Australian trade to suffer, was ill-founded; Duncan and Elliott argued that repeal of the Act would doubtless 'bring more foreign and non-British competition which would react very quickly against the wages and working conditions of our Australian seamen and against the best interests of Australia as a whole, unless some other form of protection be given'.[23] Put simply Australia, as an island continent, was heavily dependent on shipping, and could not afford to increase its dependence on foreign shipping for the marketing overseas of its primary products. Australian seafarers were necessarily protected because the merchant marine was nationally important both for economic and defence purposes. It was a principle written into law from the beginning, and which was subsequently maintained in later emendations. The two Labor MPs (Anstey and Yates) in their minority report recommended that official administration of the Act should be changed and the director (who was thought to be too sympathetic to shipowners) made directly responsible to a minister.[24]

While they waited for the Navigation Act to become law, the Seamen's Union of Australia (SUA) pushed their claims through the Arbitration Court where they won many of the same conditions as had been given to them in the Navigation Act.[25] When the Navigation Act finally became operational in the 1920s the SUA 'was jealous to see that its protective provisions were enforced': that Australian wages and conditions applied on ships trading on the Australian coast, that the provisions of the Act were sufficiently adhered to regarding unsafe practices, that damaged or overloaded ships, with improperly stowed cargo did not get clearances to sail from the Department of Navigation. When the SUA was de-registered in 1925 and no longer had an award under the Conciliation and Arbitration Court, the only safeguard the union had for their conditions was the Navigation Act, but shipowners refused to comply with the SUA demand that award conditions be incorporated into ships' articles of employment.[26] In 1925, this led to a three-month strike, which was part of a larger international industrial action. The 1930s were even tougher for seafarers, a huge strike in

---

23   Royal Commission, 1924, 78.
24   ibid., 65; see also Fitzpatrick and Cahill, 58.
25   Fitzpatrick and Cahill, 48.
26   ibid., 57–58.

1935 left the union devastated and led to a change in leadership.[27] Amendments made to the Navigation Act in that year, however, were not substantive in their impact on the workforce.

During the Second World War, the defence role of the merchant marine became crucial as Australian shipping carried troops and materials overseas and around the coast. Merchant shipping was administered by the Department of Supply, by which means the government chartered ships and shipowners acted as managers on the government's behalf. The SUA claimed its fight for seafarers' rights was 'just as fierce as any fight in warfare', but joined the war effort and cautioned members against sparking disputes over comparatively trivial issues which could strengthen shipowners and government opposition.[28] With the coming of war to the Pacific, in 1942 the Curtin Labor government, under the National Security Regulations, set up the Maritime Industry Commission (MIC) whose task was 'to secure the adequate and efficient manning of Australian merchant ships and the improvement and safeguarding' of their crews.[29] This was a tribunal authorised under special wartime conditions to deal with industrial matters that were traditionally covered within the jurisdiction of the arbitration system. It was chaired by former New South Wales industrial commissioner Justice de Baun, and consisted of representatives from each of the interested parties — three employer representatives for the shipowners, one nominee for the government, and four representatives from the several maritime unions, the Merchant Service Guild and the Australian Institute of Marine and Power Engineers which covered the officers; the Marine Cooks, Bakers and Butchers union which covered the catering crew and, for the deck crew, the Seamen's Union.[30]

The MIC had the power to make an order become law notwithstanding existing Commonwealth or state laws or awards of industrial tribunals, but it could not reduce the conditions of seafarers nor take actions that would impact negatively on the efficient, adequate manning of a ship.[31] The SUA welcomed the new commission. 'It is obvious the MIC has unlimited power — always keeping in mind it can only "improve and safeguard"', the *Seamen's Journal* reported. 'Marine unions can now avail themselves of the Commission to secure for their seamen the best living and working conditions in the world'.[32]

With this in mind, the SUA, through the MIC, was able during the war to gain for its members shorter working hours (from the 56-hour week to the 44-hour week)

---

27   ibid., 68–86; 99–113.
28   Editorial, *Seamen's Journal* 1, no. 2 (August 1941): 1.
29   Fitzpatrick and Cahill, 136.
30   ibid., 137.
31   ibid., 136.
32   *Seamen's Journal* 1, no. 5 (March 1942): 3.

they had been arguing for unsuccessfully in the Arbitration Court, increased wages to a level well above that of the regular navy, and improved accommodation — separate rooms for each watch, individual clothes lockers, change rooms, mess rooms with refrigerator — more improvements in one year than in the previous 25.[33] Their efforts to have meals and catering equivalent to that of the officers were less successful. The war years were turbulent as the SUA exerted its industrial strength and the MIC spent much time deciding misconduct cases and imposing disciplinary measures on seafarers held responsible for holding up shipping.[34] Nevertheless, these were years of comparative industrial peace and the SUA made gains without resorting to the procedures of arbitration. At the end of the war, under the Chifley Labor government, the MIC continued to deal with matters that would otherwise have gone to the Arbitration Court.[35] The SUA was successful in winning improvements to their conditions by actively disrupting the Australian post-war shipping trade with stoppages that, by the early 1950s, members of the Menzies conservative government claimed were both too frequent and unjustified. They used the machinery of the Navigation Act to force the unions back into the Arbitration Court.

When the Menzies government came to power in 1949, the maritime and stevedoring industries, in what Menzies called 'Australia's vital shipping industry', had the reputation for having the most troubled and difficult industrial relations records in Australia.[36] In the overheated and what historian Tom Sheridan describes as the 'miasma of Cold War propaganda', the reality of workplace disputes was often lost in charge and countercharge of class warfare and secret agendas.[37] At least one Arbitration Court judge saw seafarers as working in dreadful and degrading conditions that it was the court's task to improve, while the Menzies government saw industrial laws and arbitration court processes as a means to combat communists and clamp down on industrial militancy. These were less direct, more covert laws than the failed initiatives — the *Communist Party Dissolution Act 1950*, which was challenged in the High Court by the SUA, the Waterside Workers Federation (WWF) and several other unions, and found to be unconstitutional, and the subsequent referendum of 1951 which was also defeated by a narrow vote.[38] As the Cold War battle lines hardened, the government's agenda for dealing with communists was implemented through other less direct, more specifically targeted, measures.

---

33 Fitzpatrick and Cahill, 148–49.

34 ibid., 159

35 *Seamen's Journal* 4, no. 11 (February 1948: 4.

36 Tom Sheridan, *Australia's Own Cold War: The Waterfront under Menzies* (Melbourne University Press, 2006), 95.

37 ibid.

38 ibid., 96.

Penal sanctions were introduced into the Arbitration Act and amendments were made in 1952 to the Navigation Act, which others have claimed were 'a direct threat to communist power' in the leadership of the SUA.[39]

Understanding the Menzies government's amendments to the Navigation Act begins with the long-standing militancy of the Seamen's Union to win concessions from shipowners, now compounded in the post-war climate by a boom in shipping, an ageing fleet of ships, and the ideological battle lines of the Cold War. Led since 1941 by Eliot V. Elliott, described in the parliamentary debate as 'a self-confessed well-known Communist', the SUA was, like the WWF, held up as being Kremlin-dominated.[40] There is evidence that the government also recognised that much of the cause for disputation rested with the shipowners, 'the relative inefficiency of the private sector [which] rested on the twin historical handicaps of an ageing capital stock and a backward-looking management mindset which misjudged market trends'.[41] But, publicly and politically, this was never acknowledged.

In the 1950s Australian coastal shipping companies were, unlike overseas companies, protected from 'unfair' foreign competition by the relevant cabotage provisions of Australia's Navigation Act. However land transport was now a direct and growing competition, they also faced potential competition from the federal government-owned shipping line, while the militancy of the SUA was exerting pressure on their labour costs.[42] In this context, the Menzies government's free enterprise ideology pointed to a policy to prevent the government fleet from undermining the profits of the private shipping companies but, the inability of those companies to meet demand meant that the government had to expand its own fleet. Nevertheless, private shipowners were sheltered from the full impact of both market forces and the more profitable national shipping line as 'the government made every effort to prevent the publicly funded line from injuring private interests'.[43] As Sheridan says, 'unquestionably, coastal shipowners were fortunate that the Coalition government, and more particularly Prime Minister Menzies, remained in office'.[44]

With these economic considerations guiding policy, the government's alterations to the Navigation Act were consistent with the economic advantage that could be

---

39   Fitzpatrick and Cahill, 235.
40   *Hansard*, 1952, 3682; Sheridan, 89 et seq.
41   Tom Sheridan, 'Coastal Shipping and the Menzies Government 1950–1966', *Australian Economic History Review* 25 (March 1995): 3.
42   ibid., 3–4.
43   ibid., 4.
44   Sheridan, *Australia's Own Cold War*, 17.

gained by hobbling union militancy. The 1952 Bill proposed 'some revolutionary amendments' in the employment conditions of seafarers that Labor MPs claimed would 'not be in the best interests of Australia'.[45]

The essence of the 1952 Bill revolved around three key issues. Firstly, it abolished the MIC. For a decade, the MIC, consisting of representatives from the shipowners, the government and the unions, had handled disputes that would otherwise have gone to the Arbitration Court. In bringing the maritime industry within the general framework of the arbitration and conciliation system, the government's reform sought 'to tidy up a system of boards and commissions ... different rules and different interpretations of discipline applied to different industries' thereby imposing the same discipline on the maritime industry as the court imposed on other industries. It was bringing a 'new approach to discipline on the waterfront'.[46]

In Labor's or, more specifically, its leader, H.V. Evatt's, view, the MIC should have been strengthened instead of being disbanded.[47] Similarly, the MP Clyde Cameron pointed to the advantages of informality, the in-camera hearings, the trust and confidentiality of discussion conducted with 'common sense and amicable manner' within a committee framework. Experience suggested that industrial relations were best conducted around a table rather than in the adversarial formal proceedings of a courtroom.[48] Another MP reminded the parliament that 'the sailor is a human being' and should be treated as such.[49] To the government the MIC's task was not to settle industrial disputes nor had it been successful in doing so.[50] The fact that SUA Federal Secretary Elliott sat on the MIC meant critics and the government had easy ammunition to charge that 'communists sit on the MIC' thereby discrediting the MIC itself.[51] The Labor party pointed out that the government had introduced the measure without consultation with those in the industry: 'no responsible member of the MIC, no representative of the employees' organizations and ... no representative of the employers knew that this measure was to be introduced ...' and the bill contained 'nothing which in itself will provide a remedy for the evils which the Minister has mentioned'.[52]

Furthermore, in replacing the MIC, the Bill gave arbitration power to a single judge of the Conciliation and Arbitration Court and set up a separate committee to deal with issues of accommodation — both designed to reduce disputes

---

45   Clarey, *Hansard*, 1952, 3690.
46   Freeth, *Hansard*, 3679.
47   Evatt, *Hansard*, 1952, 3666.
48   Cameron, *Hansard*, 1952, 3675.
49   Haylen, *Hansard* 1952, 4316.
50   Holt, *Hansard*, 1952, 3423.
51   Howse, *Hansard*, 1952, 3682.
52   Evatt, *Hansard*, 1952, 3667.

generated by the maritime unions about their working conditions. The crew accommodation committee was to consist of trade union and shipowner representatives 'assisted by the expert advice of governmental shipping and shipbuilding officers' and was to 'be empowered to make orders' giving effect to its decisions.[53] By this means, the Act replaced a commission with a court, removed union representation from deliberations, and replaced committee decision-making with judicial power. Cameron said, 'If this bill is aimed at the Seamen's Union of Australia, although the Minister did not say so, that union will be no more co-operative with an arbitration court judge than it has been with the MIC'. He asked, reasonably, 'Why should it be?' and why could not the same power that was being given to a single judge instead be given to the MIC?[54] Removing the MIC and its union representation removed the important role that the SUA had played in the decision-making process affecting the workplace.

Most notably, the legislation tightened the 'disciplinary clauses to control seamen', by 'radically chang[ing] the definition of desertion' and increasing the penalty attached to being a 'deserter'.[55] Desertion by a seafarer was now defined as being absent from his ship for more than 48 hours without leave or reasonable excuse, even if the ship was in port for weeks.[56] This compared unfavourably with the previous definition, which made the intention of not returning to the ship the essence of the charge; that is, intention had to be proved for the charge of desertion to be maintained, which courts had difficulty doing. Now, absence in itself was held to be desertion, and the onus was placed on the seafarer to show he had a lawful or reasonable excuse for his absence.[57] The Bill also amended provisions relating to actions obstructing or interfering with officers 'and harbouring or secreting deserting seamen or apprentices'.[58] The SUA pointed out that 'the new law is aimed directly at every man who goes to sea regardless of rank or rating'.[59] 'Failure to obey' orders to take a ship to sea, subjected both 'officers and crew to a penalty of immediate dismissal, loss of repatriation to a home port, loss of accumulated leave, and a bad discharge which may mean exclusion from employment in the shipping industry'.[60]

Union officials could be held responsible for engaging seafarers as crew and punished with gaol for failure to obey, or for persuading seafarers to commit a breach of their agreement.[61] Furthermore, the Act gave power and responsibility to approve or refuse employment on board ship to a single individual ('a

53   Holt, *Hansard*, 1952, 3425.
54   Cameron, *Hansard*, 1952, 3676.
55   Clarey, *Hansard*, 1952, 3690, 3707.
56   'ACTU Back Maritime Unions' Protest on Act', *Seamen's Journal* 8, no.13 (November 1952): 4.
57   *Hansard*, 4314.
58   Holt, *Hansard*, 1952, 3425.
59   'Navigation Act Hits All Seamen', *Seamen's Journal* 8, no. 15 (December 1952): 4.
60   'A Challenge to All Seamen', *Seamen's Journal* 9, no. 1 (January 1953): 1.
61   'ACTU Back Maritime Unions' Protest on Act', 4.

superintendent') whose refusal may have no connection to any ship-related offence at all, something which had previously been decided by representatives of employers and employees meeting in conference in the MIC.[62] The government claimed it was preserving much of what the commission had done, especially in the area of discipline, but the Labor party saw it as contradictory to preserve the principles and practices while not preserving the commission itself.[63] Desertion meant a seaman was thus given a bad discharge from a ship and, under the new provisions, there was no provision for a seaman to appeal a bad discharge given by a master, yet three bad discharges excluded him from further employment. The Act took away the right to give a man a second chance, something the MIC had the power and discretion to do.[64] 'Let there be no doubt in anyone's mind that to refuse to take a ship to sea after being ordered to by the Master ... starts [a seafarer] on the way out of the industry', the SUA alerted their members, 'it is possible never to have received a bad discharge and yet to be excluded from the industry'. A 'very good conduct does not cancel out a report which is bad within the meaning of the Act'.[65]

The amended Navigation Act passed through parliament quickly and came into force early in 1953. A new industrial award, the Seamen's Award, followed in the Arbitration Court in 1955 which, when the SUA challenged it in the High Court in 1957, was upheld as valid.[66] Further amendments — 'far worse than the amendments which the ACTU strenuously opposed in 1952' — were made to the Navigation Act and rushed through parliament in 1958.[67] These amendments, again introduced into parliament without either the unions or the shipowners being given prior warning, imposed new and heavier penalties that deprived seamen of further rights. The government had held discussions on an earlier draft more than two years previously but when the bill was eventually introduced it included new provisions not contained in the 1955 draft, specifically 'vital clauses abolishing the rights of seamen'.[68] Despite a hastily organised deputation to the minister from all the seagoing unions (Merchant Service Guild, Marine Engineers, Radio Operators, Stewards, Cooks and SUA) which was neatly foiled by the minister being unavailable that particular day, combined with strong opposition from the Maritime Transport Council, and the Labor Party opposition on the floor of the House, the amended Act was hurriedly passed into law. The Maritime Transport Council considered the new clauses 'most dangerous' and that they would 'worsen the conditions

---

62   *Hansard*, 1952, 3665.
63   Holt, *Hansard*, 1952, 3423.
64   Cameron, *Hansard*, 1952, 3677.
65   'Let's Be Clear About This Act', *Seamen's Journal* 9, no. 15 (December 1953): 3.
66   High Court of Australia, *Queen v. Spicer and Others: Ex Parte Seamen's Union of Australia, Commonwealth Law Reports*, 96, 1957, 341–52.
67   *Seamen's Journal* 13, no. 3 (April 1958): 6.
68   'Navigation Act', *Seamen's Journal* 13, no. 5 (June 1958): 3.

of seamen'.[69] Indeed, in the campaign for a new award that the SUA waged between 1958–60, the penal provisions of the Navigation Act were frequently used against individual seafarers.[70] The SUA declared the Menzies government's refusal to listen to seafarers on the realities of their workplace conditions, even when presented through a committee of shipowner and union representatives established by the government itself, reflected an 'attitude of contempt towards the unions and all who work'.[71] With these two pieces of industrial relations law — the Arbitration Act and the Navigation Act — acting in tandem, all seafarers had their job security, conditions, wages and their safety jeopardised without addressing the inefficiencies of the shipowners. As a consequence, arguably and perhaps not coincidentally, the amended Navigation Act was instrumental in setting back the working conditions of ordinary seafarers for another 15 years. The SUA's agenda for stabilising and normalising their working conditions, which had been presented to shipowners as early as 1946, was not finally achieved until the mid 1960s.[72]

The Navigation Act 1912 has been amended many times since its inception but, from 1952, those changes were made consistently by Liberal Coalition governments, in conjunction with penal sanctions and more limitations being imposed on trade unions under the arbitration law. By 1979, when Prime Minister Malcolm Fraser was amending simultaneously both the Navigation Act and other industrial relations laws, seafarers were describing the Navigation Act as 'one of the most vicious pieces of legislation to be drawn up against a group of Australian workers'.[73] Calling it 'unjust and one-sided' with provisions that ought to have been rescinded years previously, union members found the most disturbing aspect of the penalties under the Act was the fact that seamen's rights of defence were very limited, indeed, in most instances were non-existent. 'When a seaman is fined and logged his only defence is his right of reply to the Master's log entry', the SUA pointed out, and appeals to the Marine Council were a waste of time. 'Very rarely does the Council alter or rescind any fine or log entry.' Consequently seafarers felt themselves to be powerless to prevent injustices, 'We have not got the right to refuse to pay a fine if we think we were dealt with unjustly ... [it just] can be deducted from your wages'.[74]

By the time of the Labor government's review in 2010, the regulatory regime of industrial relations had been restructured, enterprise bargaining and the *Fair Work Act* replaced the older machinery of arbitration, and the maritime

---

69   *Seamen's Journal* 13, no. 3 (April 1958): 6; 'Amended Navigation Act', *Seamen's Journal* 13, no. 5 (June 1958): 5.
70   Fitzpatrick and Cahill, 276.
71   'Navigation Act: Government Ignores Committee of Advice', *Seamen's Journal* 13, no. 5 (June 1958): 7–8.
72   Fitzpatrick and Cahill, 238.
73   H. Leonard, 'Navigation Act Vicious, Biased', *Seamen's Journal* 34, no. 8 (December 1979): 247.
74   ibid.

workforce was no longer a merchant marine based on the navy's models of hierarchy.[75] The Coalition government's review of the legislation reported in 2000 that 'there are several provisions in the legislation that address employment arrangements for seafarers that would more appropriately be addressed under modern company based employment arrangements governed by modern industrial relations legislation'.[76] Moves had begun to move employment aspects out of the Navigation Act but, significantly, this report saw safety of shipping as unconnected to workplace relations: 'In some cases, industrial and safety considerations have been intermingled. It is appropriate that these be separated to establish a clear focus on essential health and safety requirements in law, whilst enabling employers and employees greater freedom to negotiate on industrial matters'. Nevertheless the report also recognised that, 'Work at sea, however, presents some unique circumstances and it is appropriate that shipping law continue to provide for conditions that reflect safe operations and reflect particular industry characteristics'.[77] In other words, the maritime workplace continued to have its own very complex regulatory regime of which the Navigation Act is only one part.

Conclusion

The amendments and the debates over the Navigation Act are an insight in to what Sir Richard Kirby, former president of the Industrial Relations Commission, once called 'the very human problems bound up in industrial relations' that 'a scientific approach based on law, economics or any field of learning would not on its own solve'.[78] The history of the Navigation Act is a window on to this world. It follows a similar trajectory as the history of arbitration, as it moved from being 'the best Act in the world' protecting Australian industry, shipowners and maritime workers, to a mechanism for implementing punitive sanctions and reducing the bargaining power of the unions as companies trading on the coast faced increasing competition.

The review undertaken by the current Labor government, under Prime Minister Julia Gillard, was begun with the view that, a century later, Australia's international trade continues to be dependent on shipping, that coastal shipping is thus vital to the national economy, and a key segment of the transport industry.[79] The 2008 discussion paper made clear that the *Navigation*

---

75   For an account of the restructuring of Australia's seagoing workforce, see Diane Kirkby, *Voices From the Ships: Australia's Seafarers and Their Union* (Sydney: UNSW Press, 2008), 350–66.
76   Review of the Navigation Act 1912, Final Report, 2000, i.
77   ibid.
78   Richard Kirby, *A New Province for Law and Order* (Robert Garran Memorial Lecture: Canberra, 1968), 13.
79   Navigation Act Discussion Paper.

Act 1912 was now outdated, yet the government did not intend to rewrite its substantive provisions but rather, to modernise and clarify the current regulatory framework so changes would be 'predominantly of a technical nature'.[80] Prompted by the ILO and its MLC 2006 (no. 186) setting minimum requirements in the conditions of employment for seafarers to work on a ship, viz: 'hours of work and rest, accommodation, recreational facilities, food and catering, occupational health and safety protection, medical care, welfare and social security protection', the federal government set about establishing appropriate mechanisms for compliance, 'through formalised inspection and certification compliance procedures, shipowners' and shipmasters' supervision of conditions on ships, flag state jurisdiction and control over local ships, and port state inspection of foreign ships'. Put simply, the Navigation Act was being rewritten because it was 'the main legislative vehicle for implementing the MLC at the Commonwealth level'.[81]

Nevertheless, as the first Navigation Act to be amended by a Labor government since 1942, it constitutes a significant moment of Australian industrial lawmaking. While it remains to be seen what this current legislative rewriting brings to the revitalisation of Australian coastal shipping, it is a significant step in regulating the 'very human problems' of safety and security of its maritime workforce that are inherent, but not always acknowledged, in the employment relationship.

---

80   ibid., 5.
81   ibid., 13.

Parental 'Consent' to Child Removal in Stolen Generations Cases

Thalia Anthony and Honni van Rijswijk

Introduction: The problematic of consent in legal narratives

Consent, will and agency have problematic uses in the law.[1] Subjected groups are implicitly inferiorised through these concepts, such that their complicity to acts of the subjector is taken for granted. This complicity, Sadiya Hartman asserts, shrouds the 'condition of violent domination' that actually operates between subjector and subjected.[2] Writing about the legal context of racial subjugation during slavery and its aftermath in the United States of America, Hartman argues that consent became 'intelligible only as submission'.[3] In the Australian context, according to Ghassan Hage, non-'whiteness' has historically been a point of reference for structural inferiority.[4] Yet, the law nonetheless assumes consent as capable of being equally afforded by 'blacks' and 'whites'. The historical impossibility of consent in the context of forced subjection is usually not disentangled, explored, or even 'seen' by the courts.

In Stolen Generations cases, the subject of this chapter, assumptions that 'whites' could better care for children underlie the implication of complicity in the removal of children from Aboriginal[5] guardians. These assumptions were taught to and at times appropriated by Aboriginal parents — who were then seen as succumbing to the system's logic.[6] As Hartman suggests, power can become defined by these manipulations to present a picture of reciprocation, rather than

---

1 Sadiya V. Hartman, *Scenes of Subjection: Terror, Slavery, and Self-Making in Nineteenth-Century America* (New York: Oxford University Press, 1997), 40.

2 ibid., 85.

3 ibid.

4 'Whiteness' is a cultural historical construct (Ghassan Hage, *White Nation: Fantasies of White Supremacy in a Multicultural Society* (Sydney: Pluto Press 1998), 58–59), which involves 'both a European monopolisation of "civilised humanity" and a parallel monopolisation of Whiteness as its marker' (Hage, *Against Paranoid Nationalism: Searching for Hope in a Shrinking Society* (Sydney: Pluto Press, 2003), 49–50).

5 The term 'Aboriginal' rather than 'Indigenous' is used throughout the article, excepting quotes from other sources. While Torres Strait Islanders also experienced child removal, the cases discussed in this article are based on mainland Aboriginal people. The term 'Aboriginal' is also used because it is consistent with the term referred to in the legislation and cases that constitute the basis of this article.

6 Hartman, 88.

acts of domination.[7] The agency of the dominated in providing consent 'secures the fetters of subjection, while proclaiming the power and influence of those shackled and tethered'.[8] It allowed the state to be presented as a benevolent institution rather than a terrorising one. There is, however, a further sinister side to the domination, which is always on guard when manipulations falter. When parents failed to comply with the removal of their children, they would attract reprisals from state agents — with consequences that included being reported to police, losing employment or experiencing physical violence.[9] Hartman challenges the possibility that 'will' means anything when operating in such a state of subjection, because it is 'unrecognizable in a context in which agency and intentionality are inseparable from the threat of punishment'.[10] As Hartman explains in relation to the ability of slaves and ex-slaves in the United States to meaningfully consent to sexual activity, 'The issue of consent is framed by the law's negation of the captive will and the violent domination of slave relations'.[11]

Our reading of recent Stolen Generations cases, described below, argues that courts prior to *Lampard-Trevorrow*[12] treated consent as an individual act, freely and voluntarily given by a liberal subject. These readings are based on the texts of the judgments, rather than on analyses of the processes by which the texts were created — through the choice and shaping of facts, and the interpretation of evidence — which is the subject of research by Trish Luker.[13] Consent was seen as a legitimate factor that duly activated the powers of the legislation to bring about legal removal, according to Justice Maurice O'Loughlin in *Cubillo*.[14] In the previous Stolen Generations case of *Williams*, formal consent had barred false imprisonment and trespass on the basis that a child cannot be imprisoned if her mother consented to the removal.[15] This chapter goes further than simply suggesting that Aboriginal consent has been misread by the courts — which was clearly the situation until the case of *Lampard-Trevorrow*. It also proposes that consent was, and is still used in an underhanded way by the state to legitimise its actions and protect itself from liability. After all, most statutory creatures governing the Stolen Generations allowed for removal, irrespective of consent.

---

7   ibid., 89.

8   ibid.

9   *National Inquiry into the Separation of Aboriginal and Torres Strait Islander Children from Their Families, Bringing Them Home: Report of the National Inquiry into the Separation of Aboriginal and Torres Strait Islander Children from their Families* (Sydney: Human Rights and Equal Opportunity Commission, 1997), 6, 8, 56.

10   Hartman, 85–86.

11   ibid., 105.

12   *State of South Australia v Lampard-Trevorrow [2010] SASC 56*.

13   Trish Luker, 'Intention and Iterability in Cubillo v Commonwealth', *Journal of Australian Studies* 84, no. 1 (January 2005): 35–41.

14   *Cubillo v Commonwealth of Australia* (2000) 174 ALR 97, 262.

15   *Williams v The Minister, Aboriginal Land Rights Act 1983 and Anor* [1999] NSWSC 843. This finding was upheld on appeal: *Williams v The Minister Aboriginal Land Rights Act 1983 and New South Wales* [2000] NSWCA 255.

The state, nonetheless, sought to procure consent in order to rationalise the policy, facilitate removals, and shift the responsibility for removal from the state to Aboriginal parents.

The use of consent in this way turned the state's act of removal into a parental act, thereby transforming 'relations of violence and domination into those of affinity'.[16] It suggests that the powerless had agency and strength, and that there is an 'ostensible equality between the dominant and the dominated',[17] while at the same time concealing the actual powerlessness of the subjected. The fiction of consent suggests that Aboriginal people were placed in the same situations as, and had the same range of options available to, white people. Judicial narratives have mostly failed to illustrate the 'limited possibilities, constraint, despair, and duress'[18] that are masked by this narrative of consent. Further, the use of consent in organising child removal imputes that Aboriginal peoples are unwilling to care for their own children, and reaffirms the fiction that the caring and nurturing of children is the domain of 'whites', thereby undermining the role of the Aboriginal family. But, here, there is a further irony — that Aboriginal consent is predicated on the presumption of civility, and yet Aboriginal people are denied this virtue because of their role as neglectful parents.

Historical narratives in Stolen Generations cases

Historical narratives of the Stolen Generations in the 1997 report *Bringing them Home* revealed the hollow meaning of parental consent in child removal. Consent was often coerced and rarely informed. It was a veil for the forced removal of Aboriginal children. A Tasmanian Stolen Generations survivor described his mother's capacity to consent in the following way: '[Mum] could not read or write, and obviously would not have understood the implications of what she was signing'.[19] The report found that 'mothers who had just given birth were coerced to relinquish their newborn babies ... The Child Welfare Department did not check to ensure that Indigenous mothers understood they were being asked to agree to the permanent removal of their child'. The report identified that acquiring consent operated to circumvent official proof of neglect. *Bringing them Home* noted, 'If parents could be "persuaded" to consent to the removal of their children the Board did not have to show that a child was neglected or uncontrollable'.[20] When indigenous parents refused to consent, the Aboriginal

---

16   Hartman, 88.
17   ibid.
18   ibid., 104.
19   National Inquiry, 86, quoting 'Confidential evidence 384, Tasmania'.
20   National Inquiry, 40.

and Welfare Boards overpowered their agency. Parents 'were told they would have to leave the stations and would be denied rations'.[21] Police officers told young mothers that 'if they did not consent to the adoption of their babies the father of the child would be prosecuted for carnal knowledge'.[22] Alongside this was an ideological campaign to make parents feel guilty that they could not offer their children the opportunities of the 'outside world'.[23] This is despite contemporary evidence and theory that children who were not removed performed much better in life than those who were removed.

The issue of parental consent for the removal of Aboriginal children has been central to cases involving compensation for injuries arising out of the removal of Aboriginal children. In *Williams* (1999),[24] consent was key to whether Joy Williams's removal at birth constituted false imprisonment; in *Cubillo* (2000),[25] consent was not determinative to claims in negligence due to the broad scope of the statute granting the Welfare Board powers to remove children, but was nonetheless argued in defence by the government and, in the 2007 trial case of *Trevorrow*,[26] and the 2010 Appeal case of *Lampard-Trevorrow*,[27] consent was discussed both in relation to negligence and false imprisonment. Consent has been a central issue in Stolen Generations cases for two main reasons: first, it formed part of the factual archive due to the widespread practice of officials seeking parental consent to expedite the process of removal; and second, the state has used parental consent to bar actions in trespass or false imprisonment. Therefore, the procurement of consent has had a doubly wicked effect, because it was used to justify expedient removals and was subsequently put as a legal justification to deny compensation on the basis that the mother had given away her child.

Before the most recent Stolen Generations case of *Lampard-Trevorrow* (the first in which compensation was awarded), cases dealt inadequately with the historical operation of consent. In *Lampard-Trevorrow*, parental non-consent was important to both the factual and legal findings. Factually, the court found no consent had been given. Legally, non-consent became central to the court's interpretation of the state's failure to properly execute its statutory authority and assume control of Bruce Trevorrow, at the age of 13 months, without parental consent. We will argue that, in *Lampard-Trevorrow*, the court demonstrated a much more nuanced understanding of the operation of consent in historical

---

21   ibid., 51.
22   ibid., 56.
23   ibid., 7–8.
24   *Williams v The Minister, Aboriginal Land Rights Act 1983 and Anor* [1999] NSWSC 843. This finding was upheld on appeal: *Williams v The Minister Aboriginal Land Rights Act 1983 and New South Wales* [2000] NSWCA 255.
25   *Cubillo v Commonwealth of Australia* (2000) 174 ALR 97.
26   Trevorrow v State of South Australia [2007] SASC 285 (hereafter Trevorrow).
27   *State of South Australia v Lampard-Trevorrow* [2010] SASC 56.

circumstances, with mixed results. On one side, there was a departure from the earlier case of *Cubillo* in which a formalist reading of consent was ultimately accepted, and this departure allowed for a finding of negligence on the part of the state. The Appeal Court in *Lampard-Trevorrow*, however, did not go so far as to provide a finding in false imprisonment, continuing the courts' ahistorical reading of consent in the context of that legal issue. The court's approach in *Lampard-Trevorrow* is not unproblematic, and a key question we ask relates to the case's potential: does *Lampard-Trevorrow* provide a productive alternative and counter-narrative to past uses of consent in Stolen Generations litigation, or is it in fact traversing the same path as other litigation, where recognition depends on the existence of 'lucky' or atypical facts fitting within the dominant narrative, and which benefits a small number of survivors, while at the same time excluding many others?

Issue of consent in statutory interpretation: Taking the high ground in *Cubillo*

One of the first cases brought by a Stolen Generations survivor was *Cubillo and Gunner v The Commonwealth* in 2000.[28] Here, the Federal Court, presided over by Justice O'Loughlin, ultimately failed to acknowledge that the production of parental consent to child removal, which involved practices of bluff or deception on the part of the state, had any legal effect, despite the acceptance of evidence that established these practices as a matter of fact. The first plaintiff in this case, Lorna Cubillo, was born in 1938 and, at the age of seven, was forcibly removed by the Aborigines Inland Mission and the Native Affairs Branch to Retta Dixon Home in Darwin, where she remained until she was 18 years old. The second plaintiff, Peter Gunner, was born in 1948 on a pastoral station and was removed when he was about seven years old to St Mary's Church of England Hostel in Alice Springs. He remained there until he was 16 years of age. Before he was removed in 1956, the trial judge described him as having been 'part of a happy, healthy Aboriginal community and environment at Utopia Station'.[29] The issue of consent to removal was at the heart of the Commonwealth's legal argument against Lorna Napanangka Cubillo and Peter Gunner. Essentially, the Commonwealth sought to recharacterise the act of removal as consensual and thereby authorised by the parents. In Cubillo's case, the court found that the issue determining legislative authority to remove her under s. 6 of the Aboriginals Ordinance was not one of consent. Rather, it was whether the director of Native Affairs held the opinion that it was 'necessary or desirable' to

---

28   *Cubillo v Commonwealth of Australia* (2000) 174 ALR 97 (hereafter Cubillo).
29   ibid., 98.

undertake her 'care, custody or control'.[30] Ultimately, the court acknowledged that the director properly used his authority under the legislation. In Gunner's case, it was found that questions relating to consent, were not the 'correct question[s] to ask' in legally characterising the act of removal — rather, the key question was 'the reason for his removal' — so that 'it would not matter by what persons or by what means that removal was effected, if his removal was effected within the terms of ss 6 or 16 of the Aboriginals Ordinance'.[31] Nonetheless, parental consent was one factual matter that was taken into account in assessing whether the legislation had been properly applied. In referring to consent in his construction of compliance with s. 6, O'Loughlin J noted that 'there was no way of knowing whether the thumb mark on the "Form of Consent" was [Mr Gunner's mother's]; even on the assumption that it was, there was no way of knowing whether [she] understood the contents of the document'.[32] However, the court gave the government officers the benefit of doubt:

> But it is not beyond the realms of imagination to find that it was possible for a dedicated, well-meaning patrol officer to explain to a tribal Aboriginal such as [Mr Gunner's mother] the meaning and effect of the document. I have no mandate to assume that [Mr Gunner's mother] did not apply her thumb or that she, having applied her thumb, did not understand the meaning and effect of the document.[33]

Therefore, the documentary record was found to prevail over the context in which Aboriginal parents were made to give their consent for their children to be taken.

On his way to finding that the issue of consent did not go 'to the heart' of the trial,[34] O'Loughlin J rejected submissions made on behalf of the Commonwealth that some or all of the parents had initiated their children's removal by asking the Native Affairs Branch or Aborigines Inland Mission to provide their children with a better education and better standard of living.[35] The court found that evidence did not establish consent was generally obtained by the Native Affairs Branch in the removal of the children at Phillip Creek, of whom Cubillo was one.[36] Although making no formal finding on the matter, he found that the evidence (including the behaviour of the mothers, the evidence of three Tennant Creek women and the limited time available to explain the process of removal) suggested that 'some, if not all, of the children may well have been taken without

30   ibid., 262, 263.
31   ibid., 352.
32   ibid., 344.
33   ibid.
34   ibid., 262.
35   ibid., 263.
36   ibid., 251.

their mothers' consent'.[37] In fact, he was 'unable to make a finding that *any* of the mothers gave their informed consents to the removal of their children'.[38] Therefore, the judge rejected the Commonwealth's argument that consent had been generally given. Where there was documentary evidence of a thumbprint, however, he favoured the assumption that consent was informed, as in the case of Gunner's mother Topsy. Although the court demonstrated an appreciation of historical context, it was not applied to interpreting legal sources.

It is significant that the court examined the operation of consent more generally than the circumstances surrounding the particular plaintiffs, and demonstrated that 'consent' was not an untroubled concept. O'Loughlin J questioned the nature and quality of consent, and the power relationship that produced consent, by referring to evidence that showed that the practices of the director in obtaining consent included processes of 'educating and preparing mothers' for separation.[39] The implication here, of course, is that any final and formal consent can be seen as an end-effect of these processes of 'education'. O'Loughlin J questioned whether sufficient consent can be deemed to have been given by parents, considering the stringent time constraints under which the information was purportedly provided.[40]

Ultimately, however, the courts found that the documents reflected Topsy's informed consent. It took for granted that the relevant information was given in the correct language, and the effectiveness of a government education program in relation to removals. We will see later that, in *Lampard-Trevorrow*, the South Australian Court of Appeal, by contrast, expressed a distrust concerning the documentary record regarding consent, and used a practice of interpretation that considered general practices relating to consent (and its documentation) in evaluating the particular document at issue. In *Cubillo*, consent was made central to the narration of separation, as well as to the legal characterisation of this moment but, despite the fact that parental consent was discussed at length in the proceedings, it was rejected as a determining factor in law: it is a factor very much present in the text, but it ultimately appears in excess to the legal reasoning. It is thereby located strangely in the text, as a kind of haunting authority: the court found it impossible to narrate the separation of child from parent, or child from community, without considering the reactions of these parties; and the main way in which these reactions might matter in law is through the concept of consent. And yet, because these relationships are held to have no legal significance, the court told the story of this deeply problematic consent and then put that story aside.

---

37   ibid., 265.
38   ibid., 251, emphasis ours.
39   ibid., 179.
40   ibid., 265.

History meeting law in *Lampard-Trevorrow*

In 2010 the South Australian Court of Appeal in *Lampard-Trevorrow*[41] upheld a decision in 2007 to award Bruce Trevorrow over half a million dollars in compensation for the injuries he suffered following his removal from his family as a child. It was the first successful claim by a Stolen Generations litigant. The court's reasoning revealed a different historical reading of the facts and the policy context of the Stolen Generations from earlier cases. The finding of non-consent of his parents was fundamental. It enabled the court to portray the removal as forced and provided a basis for a breach of law. Therefore, not only was there forcible removal, but it was legally wrong.

The decided facts in *Lampard-Trevorrow* are that Trevorrow was taken by the Aborigines Protection Board (APB), without the consent of his parents, at the age of 13 months, while he was in hospital. The trial judge found that neither Joseph Trevorrow nor Thora Karpany, the natural parents, knew about or consented to the placement of Bruce Trevorrow with the Davies family. The court found that it was the state's failure to acknowledge the parents' authority (and therefore the lack of consent to Trevorrow's removal) that led, in part, to the state's liability. Unlike *Cubillo*, the court of appeal did not find that the ultimate authority concerning Trevorrow's removal lay elsewhere, such as with a statutory authority. The court found that s. 10 of the *Aborigines Act 1934* (SA), which provided that the APB was 'the legal guardian of every Aboriginal child' was ambiguous. It found that the legislation did not abrogate fundamental rights in the absence of the manifestation of a clear intention to do so. Therefore, s. 10 did not give the APB the power to foster an Aboriginal child without the consent of the child's parents.

Issue of consent in *Lampard-Trevorrow*

The state of South Australia submitted that the trial judge was wrong to find that neither parent consented to Bruce Trevorrow's placement with Mrs Davies, and here it relied mainly on missing documentation concerning the removal. The court of appeal acknowledged that documents were missing, but found that consent had not been given — significantly, in doing so, it relied on evidence concerning general practices concerning consent, as well as evidence concerning Trevorrow's particular case. While the court in *Cubillo* referred to similar general practices, its finding in relation to Gunner's mother's consent was based on the documentary evidence alone. The significance of the court's interpretation in *Lampard-Trevorrow* is that it is an acknowledgment of the

---

41   *State of South Australia v Lampard-Trevorrow* [2010] SASC 56 (hereafter *Lampard-Trevorrow*).

importance of context in the historical operation and legal interpretation of consent. It is significant that the court of appeal was willing to look critically at documents presented as evidence, and did not interpret the absence of documents as necessarily favouring the state's position. The court rejected the state's submission concerning a particular missing file, that it may have contained the records of the almoner testifying to the consensual removal of the plaintiff, arguing that the time constraints and role of the almoner made it unlikely that the records would include a document concerning consent.[42] On the question of privileging documentary evidence, the court held:

> There is no reason why, in principle, the documentary records should be preferred to the oral evidence. Everything depends upon the facts of the case. In the present case it needs to be borne in mind that documentary records are not to be assumed to be reliable.[43]

Based on an analysis of correspondence concerning other cases, the court found that 'the requirement to obtain parental consent was not always observed'.[44] The court based this conclusion on a number of documents. A letter dated 12 August 1958, from the secretary of the APB to the officer in charge at the Oodnadatta Police Station, stated:

> If the parents of these children have not already consented in writing for the United Aborigines Mission to care and control the children until a certain age, then I suggest that you endeavour to obtain the consent of the parents on the forms enclosed.
>
> In confidence, you will certainly realise that in any case this consent form is not a legal document, and should it be that the parents remove the children from the care of the Mission or the Board, no legal action could be taken to regain control of the children.[45]

Another document, a letter of 16 October 1958, written by the secretary of the APB to the superintendent of Aborigines welfare in Victoria, stated: 'Again in confidence, for some years without legal authority, the Board have taken charge of many aboriginal children'.[46] In a letter dated 19 May 1960, to Pastor Eckermann, the secretary of the APB stated:

---

42   ibid., 88.
43   ibid., 84.
44   ibid., 126.
45   ibid., 126.
46   ibid., 127.

> For your information only I have to inform you that legally, I have no right to remove a child from its parents. However, in such cases I do so and where deemed necessary we refuse to allow the child to be returned to its' [sic] parents without my consent.
>
> If you so desire you can inform the mother of the child that it has been placed in your Children's Home at my direction and cannot be released to the mother without my written consent. You should add that I will not likely consent to the children being released until such time as the mother is properly accommodated and able and willing to care for the child in a proper manner.[47]

Here the court concluded:

> the Secretary of the APB is informing Pastor Eckermann, 'off the record' that on occasions he has removed and will remove a child from its parents, without parental consent, and will subsequently refuse to allow the child to be returned to the parents, unless satisfied that the proposed living arrangements are suitable.[48]

The last paragraph quoted above 'contemplates a bluff being used to enable the APB to keep the child in question under its control'.[49]

It is in the context of this understanding that the court of appeal read a letter the APB sent to Thora Karpany in 1958, which was prepared in response to her inquiry about Bruce. The letter stated that Bruce was still undergoing medical treatment, and the court found this statement, and the implication that Bruce could therefore not be returned to her, 'dissembling'.[50] Even if Thora Karpany *had* consented to Bruce Trevorrow being fostered, such consent did not legally authorise Bruce's permanent removal — and the secretary of the APB knew of Thora's entitlement to have Bruce returned to her. Here we have the court explicitly acknowledging the problematic role of consent in the practice of removal — problems that were intimated in *Cubillo*, but which in *Lampard-Trevorrow* are labelled as 'a pretence of power'.[51]

Although the appeal court acknowledged the possibility that consent was obtained 'by one of the now unavailable witnesses, and ... placed in one of the missing files', the court found that the trial judge's conclusion of non-consent

---

47 ibid., 128.
48 ibid.
49 ibid.
50 ibid., 126.
51 ibid., 133.

was supported by significant evidence.[52] First, there was no documentation of consent in Bruce Trevorrow's file. Second, there was no reliable reference to consent being given in other documents. Third, there was evidence that:

> when necessary, in the perceived interests of a child, the [Board] would place a child in an institution or with a foster family without parental consent, using a pretence of power (which undoubtedly would have been effective) and, if appropriate, using an element of bluff or deception.[53]

This last point is significant since here, the South Australian Court of Appeal referred to the general context of practices and policies in which consent was made — taking a very different approach to interpretation from that used in *Cubillo*, where the Federal Court noted the evidence of general policies but, in making its findings, insisted on narrowing its focus to the particular circumstances of the applicants.[54] In contrast, the court of appeal found that, 'The reliance on medical advice in response to Thora Karpany's letter to the [Board] of 25 July 1958 is consistent with the use of a bluff to deflect her request'.[55]

Changing approach to false imprisonment: Turn from *Williams*

Consent was a central issue in the claim of false imprisonment in the first Stolen Generations case, *Williams v Minister, Aboriginal Land Rights Act 1983*, brought before the New South Wales Supreme Court in 1999.[56] False imprisonment is committed when someone 'directly subjects another to total deprivation of freedom of movement without lawful justification [or consent]'.[57] It is a powerful avenue for Stolen Generations litigants because it does not depend on the government acting negligently or breaching a statute. Rather, it arises because the plaintiff has his or her liberty restricted.

The facts of the *Williams* case were that Joy Williams was removed immediately after her mother had given birth and while being treated in hospital. Joy had stayed in children's homes until she was 18 years old. She was removed under s. 7(2) of the *Aborigines Protection Act 1909* (NSW), which gave the Aborigines Welfare Board the power to take Joy under circumstances where the mother

---

52   ibid., 132.
53   ibid., 133.
54   *Cubillo*, 179.
55   *Lampard-Trevorrow*, 133.
56   *Williams v The Minister, Aboriginal Land Rights Act 1983 and Anor* [1999] NSWSC 843 (*Williams*).
57   *Trevorrow*, 982.

consented. She claimed that the removal caused her physical and psychological harm and she brought a number of claims. However, it was false imprisonment in which the issue of consent was at the forefront.

The New South Wales Supreme Court emphasised the mother's consent to removal at the time of the birth of her daughter, although this was contested by Joy, and ruled against false imprisonment on that basis.[58] The court stated that there was no false imprisonment because the welfare board 'had lawful control over the plaintiff' due to the consent of the mother.[59]

In reviewing the case, the New South Wales Court of Appeal adverted to the problematic nature of consent, but chose to treat consent as proven by virtue of the documentary evidence of the application. The court held:

> One part of the plaintiff's case at trial depended on the proposition that she had been removed from her mother without her mother's consent. It was this which underlay the claims of false imprisonment ... This part of the case failed because ... the plaintiff was lawfully admitted to the control of the Board on the application of her mother ...[60]

The nature of the evidence of consent, and how consent was acquired, has been questioned by academics and legal practitioners. Anna Cody, who was a solicitor on the case, commented that Joy Williams 'was taken away from her mother when she was a few hours old. Any mother who's had a baby would question exactly how much she could consent to giving a baby away when she's just a few hours old'.[61] Chris Cunneen and Julia Grix argue that the court's comment that the mother may have forgotten whether she had consented reveal an 'extraordinary lack of insight into the issues of consent and the power of the [Board] over Aboriginal persons'.[62]

Another issue that was raised by the New South Wales Supreme Court to inculcate the mother in the removal was that the mother did not attempt to

58 The Supreme Court relied on s. 7(2) of the *Aborigines Protection Act 1909* provided: 'The board may on the application of the parent or guardian of any child admit such child to the control of the board' *Williams*, [26].
59 *Williams*, [142]. The court stated, 'My finding is that the AWB considered the mother's application to give up control of the plaintiff to its control, and having done so, admitted the child to its control. I find that there was not any removal by the Board to the plaintiff, in the sense of taking the child against the will of the mother. The plaintiff was taken into the AWB's control because the mother did not want the child, could not keep the child and asked the AWB to take control of her: see s 7(2)': *Williams*, [26].
60 *Williams v The Minister Aboriginal Land Rights Act 1983 and New South Wales* [2000] NSWCA 255 at [58].
61 Quoted in Annie White, 'Joy Williams loses her Stolen Generations Case', *The World Today*: ABC Local Radio, 26 August 1999, http://www.abc.net.au/worldtoday/stories/s46829.htm accessed on 1 October 2011.
62 Chris Cuneen and Julia Grix, *The Limitations of Litigation in the Stolen Generations Cases* (Canberra: AIATSIS Research and Discussion Paper, no. 15, 2004): 24.

release the child from foster care. This presumes that she was an informed liberal subject who had the capacity to pursue this avenue. It discounts the power of the state over Aboriginal people. The court stated:

> I further find as a fact that the plaintiff's mother at no time between 1942 and 1960 made application to the [Board] or, otherwise sought to have the plaintiff released from the [Board's] control, or sought her restoration to her care within the meaning of … the Act, nor was any discharge of the plaintiff sought at any time pursuant to … the Act.
>
> … [This] is consistent with a view that she did not wish the child's status or relationship viz the Board to change … nor did she wish to have the child returned to her care.[63]

False imprisonment in *Lampard-Trevorrow*

When false imprisonment was argued by Bruce Trevorrow, the Supreme Court of South Australia at trial accepted this on the basis that there was no parental or child consent. The court held:

> By being placed with [his foster mother], the plaintiff's will was completely overborne. Given the plaintiff's age at the time of the removal, he did not consent; neither did his parents. The plaintiff was imprisoned, and the State, through its agents and emanations, caused the imprisonment.[64]

However, the South Australian Court of Appeal in *Lampard-Trevorrow* overturned this finding through a narrow reading of 'imprisonment', which is anomalous to the broad contextual approach it took to other aspects of its reasoning — including consent. It held that the care and protection given by the carer of a child is not a deprivation of the child's liberty. The court of appeal reasoned that Bruce Trevorrow 'was able to move about (once he reached a certain age) as he wished subject only to the normal limits placed on children' and was 'not imprisoned within a defined area' by his foster parents beyond the normal control of parents.[65] The bench stated:

> It might be added that if this is a case of total restraint or total deprivation of freedom of movement, then all small children are, as a matter of

---

63   *Williams*, [179].
64   *Trevorrow*, 982.
65   *Lampard-Trevorrow*, 284.

fact, equally subject to the same restraint. ... Bruce Trevorrow, when fostered by Mrs Davies, had the same freedom of movement, or absence of freedom as the case may be, as other children of a like age.[66]

The court did not appreciate that non-Aboriginal children of Bruce Trevorrow's age would have had the freedom to be with their parents. It is only because of the policy of the Stolen Generations that Trevorrow was denied this freedom. The court drew unfitting analogies with restraint in childcare centres, stating, 'Most childcare centres have substantial fences and a gate that children cannot open'.[67] In this acontextual reading, the court was not addressing the liberty denied to Bruce Trevorrow to be with his parents due to the policy of Aboriginal child removal. In other words, an Aboriginal child's forcible restraint from his parents and against his parents' wishes was regarded as the same as a non-Aboriginal person who lived with his parents and was not subject to the Stolen Generations policy.

Conclusion

Consent generally implies an autonomous liberal agent who is invariably a white upper-class adult. The implications of this model do not auger well for Aboriginal subjects who do not have agency within a coercive policy of child removal. Nonetheless, the consent of the Aboriginal mother is referred to continuously by the state in attempting to defeat Stolen Generations cases. It was a powerful justification for the policy of removal, suggesting that not only did white officials and missionaries believe that removal was good for Aboriginal children, but so did their parents.

However, the historical record problematises the historical operation of Aboriginal consent in child removal. In *Cubillo*, the court alludes to these problems but it does not ultimately support the Aboriginal version of coerced consent or rely on it to affect the interpretation of the law underpinning removals. Justice Atkinson criticised the courts in *Williams* and *Cubillo* for not giving 'adequate recognition to the social and historical context of removal' in addressing the issue of consent.[68]

By contrast, the court in *Lampard-Trevorrow* explicitly acknowledged the problems with consent and this had legal effect. However, the court stopped short of recognising that non-consent to removal was a form of restraint on

---

66   ibid., 285.
67   ibid., 298.
68   The Hon Justice Roslyn Atkinson, 'Denial and Loss: Removal of Indigenous Australian Children from their Families and Culture', *QUT Law and Justice Journal* 5, no. 1 (2005): np, http://www.law.qut.edu.au/ljj/editions/v5n1/atkinson_full.jsp accessed on 1 October 2011.

the child, that is, a restraint to be with his or her parents. Ann Curthoys, Ann Genovese and Alexander Reilly in their book *Rights and Redemption: History, Law and Indigenous People* discuss the increasing role of historians as experts in indigenous litigation involving historical wrongs. They point to the importance of the disciplines of law and history to talk to one another in these cases.[69] The expertise of historians was drawn on, across the Stolen Generations cases discussed. It is only in *Lampard-Trevorrow*, however, that a contextualised historical understanding has legal effect. There we begin to see a true marriage of law and history. It is yet to be seen whether, in future cases, there will be a more contextual understanding of consent.

Our analysis of the narratives in Stolen Generations cases reveals deep tensions in the ways consent arises: the ways in which consent does and does not matter; and the ways in which, as narratives and legal issues become focalised through consent, counter-narratives arise that challenge the interpretation of consent. *Trevorrow* and *Lampard-Trevorrow* go some way to show the operation of consent institutionally in the removal of children — particularly the South Australian Supreme and appeal courts' selection/acceptance of evidence, which relies on an understanding of the institutional power that 'produced' consent and disguised both the state's coercion and families' resistance. The facts in *Lampard-Trevorrow* were held to indicate the absence of consent — in part this was due to the court's practices of interpretation, which acknowledged a different kind of history and evidence from early cases, but this was also partly due to Bruce Trevorrow's experience, which made him in many ways an 'ideal plaintiff'.[70] For mothers who gave their consent to the removal of their children, who were without choice or recourse in handing over consent, there continues to be no remedy.

The case leaves open a number of questions about how the legal narrative will continue to engage with historical accounts. Could future cases allow a claim in which formal consent is present, thus acknowledging the problematic operation of consent as a structural, historical practice? Or will *Lampard-Trevorrow* be confined to an exceptional status? How would Topsy's thumbprint be interpreted post-*Lampard-Trevorrow*? We know that, at the moment, litigants in South Australia and elsewhere are lining up to draw on the precedent in *Lampard-Trevorrow*. If the effect of *Lampard-Trevorrow* in future cases is to disavow the operation of meaningful consent in the context of Stolen Generations removals, this would go a long way in providing meaningful legal outcomes for Aboriginal plaintiffs. Under such an approach, the formal consent of Topsy's thumbprint

---

69   Ann Curthoys, Ann Genovese and Alexander Reilly, *Rights and Redemption: History, Law and Indigenous People* (Sydney: UNSW Press, 2008), 223–24.
70   Antonio Buti, 'The Stolen Generations Litigation Revisited', *Melbourne University Law Review* 32, no. 2 (2008): 420.

would be interpreted in the context of its historical production, and doubted as evidence of meaningful consent. A significant test will be how future courts confront documentary evidence of consent and how they handle competing historical evidence of the lack of choice facing an Aboriginal mother. *Lampard-Trevorrow* provides precedent for a more contextualised understanding of the removal of children. The courts, however, cannot be complacent about the legal discipline's role in addressing these matters, and will continue to need to rely on historians to unveil consent as a tool of disguise and a technique of force in particular circumstances.

Contributors

Jennifer Anderson has worked in the community legal sector and is now a PhD candidate in law at the University of Melbourne, researching the Children's Court Movement in Victoria, 1890–1910. She currently works as a solicitor at the Youth Legal Service (Children's Court section) at Victoria Legal Aid in Melbourne.

Thalia Anthony is Senior Lecturer in the Faculty of Law University of Technology Sydney. She has researched and written on remedies for Indigenous stolen wages, particularly in the Northern Territory and the legal basis of Australian colonisation and the place of Indigenous claims for sovereignty ('Sir William Blackstone's Commentaries on Colonialism' 2009). Her current project is on Indigenous sentencing in Australian higher courts over the past decade and criminalisation since the Northern Territory Intervention. She has worked on submissions to the United Nations Committee for the Elimination of Racial Discrimination and has been a volunteer for the Aboriginal Legal Service (NSW), the Cape York Land Council and the Public Interest Advocacy Centre.

Libby Connors is Senior Lecturer in History at the University of Southern Queensland. She is a co-author of three books and numerous articles on Australian and Queensland history. Her current research interests focus on Indigenous law and politics in Queensland in the early colonial period. She is a regular contributor to law and history conferences and is currently secretary of the Australian and New Zealand Law and History Society.

Shaunnagh Dorsett is Associate Professor in the Faculty of Law, University of Technology, Sydney. She researches at the intersections of property law, native title, jurisprudence and legal history. She is a member of the New Zealand Lost Cases project, which recovered decisions of the Supreme Court of New Zealand from 1841–1969 and Vice-President of the Australia New Zealand Law and History Society. Her most recent book, co-edited with Ian Hunter, is *Law and Politics in British Colonial Thought: Transpositions of Empire* (New York: Palgrave Macmillan, 2010).

Ann Genovese is an interdisciplinary law and history scholar who teaches at the University of Melbourne Law School. Her research focuses on the history and theory of the relationship between Australian law and political culture in the twentieth century. Some recent representative publications include *Rights and Redemption: Law, History, Indigenous Peoples* (UNSW Press, 2008), (with Ann Curthoys and Alexander Reilly); and, for *Feminist Review*, an edited collection of papers on the status of Australian feminism under neoliberalism, 'Mainstreamed or Muzzled' Issue 95, 2010.

Emily Haslam is a lecturer in international law at the University of Kent, where she teaches international law and international criminal law. She has published articles and book chapters on international criminal law and is currently working on a larger project dealing with legacies of nineteenth-century litigation on slavery and abolition in international criminal law.

Aleksandra Hadzelek is a lecturer in International Studies at the Faculty of Arts and Sciences, University of Technology, Sydney. She has been researching contemporary Spanish culture and society for over 20 years. Her current research interests include historical memory and the politics of memory and memorialisation in post-Franco Spain as well as post-Soviet countries of Central Europe. She is a member of the Social and Political Change Academic Group, and the Cosmopolitan Civil Societies Research Centre at UTS.

Anna Johnston is Associate Professor and Australian Research Council Queen Elizabeth II Fellow in the School of English, Journalism, and European Languages at the University of Tasmania, where she is also the Co-director of the Centre for Colonialism and Its Aftermath. Her recent books include *Reading Robinson: Companion Essays to Friendly Mission* (Quintus 2008, co-edited with Mitchell Rolls), *The Complete Indian Housekeeper and Cook* (OUP 2010, co-edited with Ralph Crane), and *The Paper War: Morality, Print Culture, and Power in Colonial New South Wales* (UWA Press 2011).

Diane Kirkby, FASAA, FAAH, is Professor of History at La Trobe University, a founding member and former president of the Australia New Zealand Law and History Society. She has previously edited *Sex Power and Justice: Historical Perspectives on Law in Australia* (1995) and with Cathy Coleborne, *Law History Colonialism: The Reach of Empire* (2001). She has won awards for her research from the Australian Historical Association and the Australian-American Educational (Fulbright) Foundation and is an elected Fellow of the Academy of the Social Sciences in Australia and the Australian Academy of the Humanities.

Stefan Petrow is an Associate Professor in the School of History and Classics at the University of Tasmania, where he lectures in Australian, British and European History. He is the author of *Policing Morals: The Metropolitan Police and the Home Office 1870-1914* (Oxford, 1994) and has published extensively on Australian legal and police history. Recent research has focused on how the law was used to protect animals from cruel practices and how effectively the law was enforced.

Debra Powell is a PhD candidate at the University of Waikato, New Zealand. Her research has a focus on child homicide cases tried in late-nineteenth and early twentieth century New Zealand and the cultural narratives that were utilised in the understanding of child murder. Her research endeavours to promote a deeper understanding of the record of child deaths by violence in New Zealand and her research interests include gender history, death studies, and histories of crime.

Honni van Rijswijk received her PhD from the University of Washington, where she was a Fellow in the Society of Scholars at the Simpson Center for the Humanities. She has taught at a number of universities in Australia and the United States and currently teaches Law and Literature, International Economic Law and Contracts at the University of Technology, Sydney. Her research focuses on the intersections between law and culture. She also has a wider background in the law of obligations, both through her LL.M. work at Trinity College Dublin, and through her work in private practice.

Bibliography

Juan Luis Abós, *La historia que nos enseñaron 1937–1975* (Madrid: Foca Ediciones, 2003).

Lynn Abrams, *The Orphan Country: Children of Scotland's Broken Homes from 1845 to the Present Day* (Edinburgh: John Donald, 1998).

Paloma Aguilar and Carsten Humlebaek, 'Collective Memory and National Identity in the Spanish Democracy. The Legacies of Francoism and the Civil War', *History and Memory* 14, no. 1/2 (2002): 121–64.

Sally Alexander and Anna Davin, 'Feminist History', *History Workshop* 1 (Spring 1976): 4–6.

Erik Allardt and Stein Rokkan, eds, *Mass Politics* (New York: The Free Press, 1970).

C.J.W. Allen, 'Bentham and the Abolition of Incompetence from Defect of Religious Principle', *The Journal of Legal History* 16 (1995): 172–88.

Judith Allen, *Sex and Secrets: Crimes Involving Australian Women Since 1880* (Melbourne: Oxford University Press, 1990).

Peter Anderson, 'Singling Out Victims: Denunciation and Collusion in the Post-Civil War Francoist Repression in Spain, 1939–1945', *European History Quarterly* 39, no. 7 (2009): 7–26.

Roger Anstey, *The Atlantic Slave Trade and British Abolition 1760–1810* (London and Basingstoke: Macmillan, 1975).

Hannah Arendt, 'The Modern Concept of History', *The Review of Politics* 20, no. 4 (1958): 570–90.

——, *Eichmann in Jerusalem: A Report on the Banality of Evil* (London: Penguin Books, 1994).

Christopher Arup, Peter Gahan, John Howe, Richard Johnstone, Richard Mitchell, Anthony O'Donnell, eds, *Labour Law and Labour Market Regulation: Essays on the Construction, Constitution and Regulation of Labour Market and Work Relationships* (Sydney: The Federation Press, 2006).

Harry Arthurs, *Without the Law: Administrative Justice and Legal Pluralism in Nineteenth-Century England* (University of Toronto Press, 1985).

Bain Attwood (with Helen Doyle), *Possession: Batman's Treaty and the Matter of History* (Melbourne: Miegunyah, 2009).

Constance Backhouse, 'Skewing the Credibility of Women: A Reappraisal of Corroboration in Australian Legal History', *Western Australian Law Review* 29 (2000): 79–107.

Mónica Zapico Barbeito, 'Investigating the Crimes of the Franco Regime: Legal Possibilities, Obligations of the Spanish State and Duties towards the Victims', *International Criminal Law Review* 10 (2010): 243–74.

Margaret Barbalet, *Far From a Low Gutter Girl: The Forgotten World of State Wards, South Australia 1887–1940* (Melbourne: Oxford University Press, 1983).

Andrew Barry, Thomas Osborne and Nikolas Rose, eds, *Foucault and Political Reason: Liberalism, Neoliberalism and Rationalities of Government* (University of Chicago Press, 1995).

Amy Bartholemew, ed., *Empire's Law: The American Imperial Project and the 'War to Remake the World'* (London: Pluto Press, 2006).

Jill Bavin-Mizzi, *Ravished: Sexual Violence in Victorian Australia* (Sydney: University of New South Wales Press, 1995).

Upendra Baxi, *The Future of Human Rights* (Oxford University Press, 2002).

George Behlmer, *Child Abuse and Moral Reform in England 1870–1908* (Stanford University Press, 1982).

Leslie Bethell, 'The Mixed Commissions for the Suppression of the Transatlantic Slave Trade in the Nineteenth Century', *Journal of African History* VII, 1 (1966): 79–93.

Sergio Gálvez Biesca, 'El proceso de la recuperación de la "memoria histórica" en España: Una aproximación a los movimientos socials por la memoria', *International Journal of Iberian Studies* 19, no. 1 (2006): 25–51.

Robin Blackburn, *The Overthrow of Colonial Slavery, 1776–1748* (London and New York: Verso, 1996).

Thom Blake, *A Dumping Ground: A History of the Cherbourg Settlement* (Brisbane: University of Queensland Press, 2001).

Lucy Bland, *Banishing the Beast: English Feminism and Sexual Morality, 1885–1914* (Harmondsworth: Penguin, 1995).

Peter Bolger, *Hobart Town* (Canberra: Australian National University Press, 1973).

Christine Bolt and Seymour Drescher, *Anti Slavery, Religion and Reform* (Kent: William Dawson and Sons, 1980).

Tim Bonyhady, *The Colonial Earth* (Melbourne: Miegunyah Press, 2000).

Wendy Brown, *Politics Out of History* (Princeton University Press, 2001).

Wendy Brown and Janet Halley, eds, *Left Legalism/Left Critique* (Durham; London: Duke University Press, 2002).

Thomas Brudholm, *Resentment's Virtue: Jean Amery and the Refusal to Forgive* (Philadelphia: Temple University Press, 2008).

Ramón Buckley, *La Doble Transición: Política y Literatura en la Espana de los Anos Setenta* (Madrid: Siglo Ventiuno, 1996).

Antonio Buti, 'The Stolen Generations Litigation Revisited', *Melbourne University Law Review* 32, no. 2 (2008): 382–421.

Barbara Caine, *Victorian Feminists* (Oxford University Press, 1992).

Natasha Campo, *From Superwomen to Domestic Goddesses: The Rise and Fall of Feminism* (Bern: Peter Lang, 2009).

Deborah Cao, *Animal Law in Australia and New Zealand* (Sydney: Law Book Co., 2010).

Raymond Carr, *Modern Spain 1875–1980* (Oxford and New York: Oxford University Press, 1980).

Antonio Cassese, Paola Gaeta and John R.W.D. Jones, eds, *The Rome Statute of the International Criminal Court: A Commentary*, vol. I (Oxford University Press, 2002).

Malcolm Caulfield, 'Live Export of Animals', in *Animal Law in Australasia*, eds, Peter Sankoff and Steven White (Sydney: Federation Press, 2009).

Ángela Cenarro, 'Matar, vigilar y delatar: la quiebra de la sociedad civil durante la guerra y la posguerra en España (1936–1948)', *Historia Social* no. 44 (2002): 65–86.

Dorothy E. Chunn, Susan B. Boyd and Hester Lessard, eds, *Reaction and Resistance: Feminism, Law, and Social Change* (Vancouver: UBC Press, 2007).

Inga Clendinnen, *Dancing with Strangers* (Melbourne: Text, 2003).

Libby Connors, 'Women on the South-East Queensland Frontier'. *Queensland Review* 15, no. 2 (2008): 19–37.

———, 'A Wiradjuri Child at Moreton Bay', *Queensland History Journal* 20, no. 13 (2010), 775–86.

Suzanne Corcoran, ed., *Law and History: A Collection of Papers Presented at the 1989 Law and History Conference* (University of Adelaide, 1989).

Robert Cover, *Justice Accused: Antislavery and the Judicial Process* (New Haven: Yale University Press, 1975).

Chris Cuneen and Julia Grix, *The Limitations of Litigation in the Stolen Generations Cases* (Canberra: AIATSIS Research and Discussion Paper, no. 15, 2004).

Ann Curthoys, 'Historiography and Women's Liberation', *Arena* 22 (1970): 35–40.

Ann Curthoys and John Docker, *Is History Fiction?* (Sydney: University of New South Wales Press, 2006).

Ann Curthoys, Ann Genovese and Alexander Reilly, *Rights and Redemption* (Sydney: University of New South Wales Press, 2008).

K.M. Dallas, *Horse Power* (Hobart: Fullers Bookshop, 1968).

Bronwyn Dalley, *Family Matters: Child Welfare in Twentieth Century New Zealand* (Auckland University Press, 1998).

Bronwyn Dalley and Margaret Tennant, eds, *Past Judgement: Social Policy in New Zealand History* (Otago University Press, 2004).

Kay Daniels, ed., *So Much Hard Work: Women and Prostitution in Australian Society* (Sydney: Fontana, 1984).

Huw T. David, 'Transnational Advocacy in the Eighteenth Century: Transatlantic Activism and the Anti-Slavery Movement', *Global Networks* 7, 3 (2007): 367–82.

David Brion Davis, *The Problem of Slavery in the Age of Revolution 1770–1823* (Ithaca and London: Cornell University Press, 1975).

Madeleine Davis, 'Is Spain Recovering its Memory? Breaking the Pacto del Olvido,' *Human Rights Quarterly* 27 no. 3 (August 2005): 858–80.

Marie-Bénédicte Dembour and Emily Haslam 'Silencing Hearings? Victim-Witnesses at the ICTY', *European Journal of International Law* 15, no. 1 (2004): 151–77.

John Dewar, 'The Normal Chaos of Family Law', *Modern Law Review* 61, no. 4 (July 1998): 467–85.

Alison Diduck, *Law's Families* (London: Lexis Nexis, 2003).

Jacques Donzelot, *The Policing of Families*, trans. Robert Hurley (New York: Pantheon Books, 1979).

Shaunnagh Dorsett, '"Sworn on the Dirt of Graves": Sovereignty, Jurisdiction and the Judicial Abrogation of Barbarous Customs in New Zealand in the 1840s', *The Journal of Legal History* 30 (2009): 175–97.

Shaunnagh Dorsett and Ian Hunter, eds, *Law And Politics In British Colonial Thought: Transpositions of Empire* (New York: Palgrave Macmillan, 2010).

Costas Douzinas, *Human Rights and Empire: The Political Philosophy of Cosmopolitanism* (Abingdon: Routledge-Cavendish, 2007).

Maria Drakopoulou, 'Women's Resolution of Lawes Reconsidered: Epistemic Shifts and the Emergence of the Feminist Legal Discourse', *Law & Critique* 11, no. 1 (2000): 47–71.

Maria Drakopoulou, 'Feminism, Governmentality and the Politics of Legal Reform', *Griffith Law Review* 14, no. 1 (2008): 330–56.

Ian Duncanson, *Historiography, Empire and the Rule of Law: Imagined Constitutions, Remembered Legalities* (Abingdon, Routledge, 2011).

Monica Dux and Zora Simic, *The Great Feminist Denial* (Melbourne University Press, 2008).

Elizabeth Elbourne, *Blood Ground: Colonialism, Missions, and the Context for Christianity in the Cape Colony and Britain, 1799–1852* (Montreal: McGill Queen's University Press, 2002).

M. Enders and B. Dupont, eds, *Policing the Lucky Country* (Sydney: Federation Press, 2001).

Norman Etherington, ed., *Missions and Empire* (Oxford University Press, 2005).

Julie Evans, Edward Eyre, *Race and Colonial Governance* (Dunedin: Otago University Press, 2005).

Carlos Jerez-Farrán and Samuel Amago, eds, *Unearthing Franco's Legacy. Mass Graves and the Recovery of Historical Memory in Spain* (University of Notre Dame Press, 2010).

Madoka Fatumura, *War Crimes Tribunals and Transitional Justice: The Tokyo Trial and the Nuremberg Legacy* (Abingdon: Routledge, 2008).

Ernest Fayle, 'The Navigation Acts', *Edinburgh Review* 228, no. 465 (July 1918): 22–42.

Paloma Aguilar Fernández, *Memoria y olvido de la Guerra Civil española* (Madrid: Alianza Editorial, 1996).

Carlos Jerez-Farrán and Samuel Amago, eds, *Unearthing Franco's Legacy: Mass Graves and the Recovery of Historical Memory in Spain* (University of Notre Dame Press, 2010).

Ofelia Ferrán, *Working through Memory: Writing and Remembrance in Contemporary Spanish Narrative* (Lewisburg, PA: Bucknell University Press, 2007).

Martha Fineman, *The Illusion of Equality: The Rhetoric and Reality of Divorce Reform* (The University of Chicago Press, 1990).

Rod Fisher *Brisbane: The Aboriginal Presence, 1824–1860* (Brisbane History Group Papers, 1992).

Brian Fitzpatrick and Rowan Cahill, *The Seamen's Union of Australia 1872–1972: A History* (Sydney: Seamen's Union of Australia, 1981).

Kathleen Fitzpatrick, *Sir John Franklin in Tasmania 1837–1843* (Melbourne University Press, 1949).

Sheila Fitzpatrick, 'New Perspectives on Stalinism', *Russian Review* 45, no. 4 (October 1986): 357–73.

Lisa Ford, *Settler Sovereignty: Jurisdiction and Indigenous People in America and Australia, 1788–1836* (Cambridge, Mass.: Harvard University Press, 2010).

Michel Foucault, *Discipline and Punish: The Birth of the Prison*, trans. Alan Sheridan (London: Penguin Books, 1977).

Katherine M. Franke, 'Gendered Subjects of Transitional Justice', *Columbia Journal of Gender and Law* 15 (2006): 813–28.

Monroe H. Freedman, 'Henry Lord Brougham — Advocating at the Edge for Human Rights', *Hofstra Law Review* 36 (2007): 311–22.

Christopher Fyfe, *A History of Sierra Leone* (Oxford University Press, 1962).

V.A.C. Gatrell, *The Hanging Tree: Execution and the English People, 1770–1868* (Oxford University Press, 1994).

Ann Genovese, 'Family Histories: John Hirst v Feminism, in the Family Court of Australia', *Australian Feminist Studies* 21 (2006): 173–96.

——, 'Writing The Past as Politics', *Lilith: A Feminist History Journal* 17 (2008): 1–5.

——, 'Worlds Turned Upside Down', *Feminist Review* 95 (2010): 69–74.

Abbott Gleason, 'Totalitarianism in 1984', *Russian Review* 43, no. 2 (April 1984): 145–59.

Gary Glover '"Going Mihinare", "Experimental Religion" and Maori Embracing of Christianity — A Reassessment', *Christian Brethren Research Fellowship Journal* 121 (1990).

Ben Golder and Peter Fitzpatrick, *Foucault's Law* (New York: Routledge, 2009).

Robert W. Gordon, 'Introduction: J. Willard Hurst and the Common Law Tradition in American Legal Historiography', *Law & Society Review* 10, no. 1 (Fall 1975), 9–56.

——, 'Critical Legal Histories', *Stanford Law Review* 36, no. 1/2 (January 1984): 57–125.

Helen Graham, 'Coming to Terms with the Past: Spain's Memory Wars', *History Today* 54, no. 5 (May 2004): 29–31.

Regina Graycar and Jenny Morgan, *The Hidden Gender of the Law* (Sydney: Federation Press, 1990).

Niel Gunson, ed., *Australian Reminiscences and Papers of L.E. Threlkeld, Missionary to the Aborigines, 1824–1859* (Canberra: AIAS, 1974).

Ghassan Hage, *White Nation: Fantasies of White Supremacy in a Multicultural Society* (Sydney: Pluto Press 1998).

——, *Against Paranoid Nationalism: Searching for Hope in a Shrinking Society* (Sydney: Pluto Press, 2003).

Catherine Hall, *Civilising Subjects: Metropole and Colony in the English Imagination, 1830–1867* (Cambridge: Polity, 2002).

——, 'Remembering 1807: Histories of the Slave Trade, Slavery and Abolition', *History Workshop Journal* 64 (2007): 1–5.

Jennifer A. Hamilton, *Indigeneity in the Courtroom: Law, Culture, and the Production of Difference in North American Courts* (New York and London: Routledge, 2009).

Brian Harrison, *Peaceable Kingdom: Stability and Change in Modern Britain* (Oxford: Clarendon Press, 1982).

Sadiya V. Hartman, *Scenes of Subjection: Terror, Slavery, and Self-Making In Nineteenth-Century America* (New York: Oxford University Press, 1997).

Pierre Hazan, *Justice in a Time of War: The True Story Behind the International Criminal Tribunal for the Former Yugoslavia* (Texas: A & M University Press, 2004).

Basil A. Helmore, 'Validity of State Navigation Acts', *Australian Law Journal* 27 (21 May 1953): 16–19.

Margaret Henderson, *Marking Feminist Times: Remembering the Longest Revolution in Australia* (Bern: Peter Lang, 1996).

Harry Hendrick, *Child Welfare: England 1872–1989* (London and New York: Routledge, 1994).

Les R. Hiatt, *Arguments about Aborigines: Australia and the Evolution of Social Anthropology* (Cambridge University Press, 1996).

Barry Hindess and Marian Sawer, eds, *Us and Them: Anti-Elitism in Australia* (Perth: API Network, 2004).

David Hirsh, *Law Against Genocide: Cosmopolitan Trials* (London: Glasshouse Press, 2003).

Adam Hochschild, *Bury the Chains: The British Struggle to Abolish Slavery* (Basingstoke and Oxford: Macmillan, 2005).

Robert Holden, *Orphans of History* (Melbourne: Text, 1999).

Damien Howard, Sue Quinn, Jenny Blokland and Martin Flynn, 'Aboriginal Hearing Loss and the Criminal Justice System', *Aboriginal Law Bulletin* 58 (1993).

Robert Hughes, *The Fatal Shore: A History of the Transportation of Convicts to Australia 1787–1868* (London: Pan Books, 1988).

Ann Hunter, 'The Origin and Debate Surrounding the Development of Aboriginal Evidence Acts in Western Australia in the Early 1840s', *University of Notre Dame Australia Law Review* 9 (2007): 115 -46.

Rosemary Hunter, ed., *Rethinking Equality Projects in Law: Feminist Challenges* (Oxford: Hart Publishing, 2008).

Samuel P. Huntington, *The Third Wave. Democratization in the Late Twentieth Century* (Norman, OK: Oklahoma University Press, 1991).

Louise A. Jackson, *Child Sexual Abuse in Victorian England* (London and New York: Routledge, 2000).

Philip Jamieson, 'Duty and the Beast: The Movement in Reform of Animal Welfare Law', *University of Queensland Law Journal*, 16 (1990–91): 238–45.

Anna Johnston, *Missionary Writing and Empire, 1800–1860* (Cambridge University Press, 2003).

——, *The Paper War: Morality, Print Culture, and Power in Colonial New South Wales* (Crawley: UWAP, 2011).

Anna Johnston and Mitchell Rolls, eds, *Reading Robinson: Companion Essays to Friendly Mission* (Hobart: Quintus, 2008).

Tony Judt, *Reappraisals: Reflections on the Forgotten Twentieth Century* (New York: Penguin Press, 2009).

Aristotle A. Kallis, '"Fascism", "Para-Fascism" and "Fascistization": On the Similarities of Three Conceptual Categories', *European History Quarterly* 33, no. 2 (2003): 219–49.

Grace Karskens, *The Colony: A History of Early Sydney* (Sydney: Allen and Unwin, 2010).

Hilda Kean, *Animal Rights: Political and Social Change in Britain Since 1800* (London: Reaktion, 1998).

Robert Kenny, *The Lamb Enters the Dreaming: Nathanael Pepper and the Ruptured World* (Melbourne: Scribe, 2007).

Bruce Kercher, *Outsiders: Tales from the Supreme Court of NSW, 1824–1836* (Melbourne: Australian Scholarly Publishing, 2006).

Holger Lutz Kern, 'Strategies of Legal Change: Great Britain, International Law, and the Abolition of the Transatlantic Slave Trade', *Journal of the History of International Law* 6 (2004): 233–58.

Kathleen Kete, ed., *A Cultural History of Animals in an Age of Empire* (Oxford: Berg, 2007).

Diane Kirkby, ed., *Sex, Power and Justice: Historical Perspectives on Law in Australia* (Melbourne: Oxford University Press, 1995).

———, *Barmaids: A History of Women's Work in Pubs* (Cambridge University Press, 1997).

———, *Dealing With Difference: Essays in Gender, History and Culture* (Melbourne University Press, 1997).

———, *Voices From the Ships: Australia's Seafarers and Their Union* (Sydney: UNSW Press, 2008).

Diane Kirkby and Catharine Coleborne, eds, *Law, History, Colonialism: The Reach of Empire* (Manchester University Press, 2001).

Paul Knaplund, *James Stephen and the British Colonial System 1813–1847* (Madison: University of Wisconsin Press, 1953).

Shino Konishi, '"Wanton with Plenty" Questioning Ethnohistorical Constructions of Sexual Savagery in Aboriginal Societies, 1788–1803', *Australian Historical Studies* 39, no. 3 (September 2008): 356–72.

Zoe Laidlaw, '"Aunt Anna's Report": The Buxton Women and the Aborigines Select Committee, 1835–37', *The Journal of Imperial and Commonwealth History* 32, no. 2 (2004): 1–28.

———, *Colonial Connections, 1815–45: Patronage, the Information Revolution and Colonial Government* (Manchester and New York: Manchester University Press, 2005).

Marilyn Lake, *Getting Equal: The History of Australian Feminism* (Sydney: Allen & Unwin, 1999).

Meredith Lake, 'Protestant Christianity and the Colonial Environment: Australia as a Wilderness in the 1830s and 1840s', *Journal of Australian Colonial History* 11 (2009): 21–44.

David Lambert, 'Sierra Leone and Other Sites in the War of Representation over Slavery', *History Workshop Journal* 64 (2007): 103–32.

David Lambert and Alan Lester, eds, *Colonial Lives across the British Empire* (Cambridge University Press, 2006).

Raeburn Lange, 'Indigenous Agents of Religious Change in New Zealand 1830–1860', *The Journal of Religious History* 24 (2002): 279–95.

Constance Larmour, *Labor Judge: The Life and Times of Judge Alfred William Foster* (Sydney: Hale & Iremonger, 1985).

John A. Lee, *The Children of the Poor* (Christchurch: Whitcoulls, 1973).

Alan Lester, *Imperial Networks: Creating Identities in Nineteenth-Century South Africa and Britain* (London and New York: Routledge, 2001).

José María Abad Liceras, *Ley de memoria histórica. La problemática jurídica de la retirada o mantenimiento de símbolos y monumentos públicos* (Madrid: Dykinson, 2009).

Trish Luker, 'Intention and Iterability in Cubillo v Commonwealth', *Journal of Australian Studies* 84, no. 1 (January 2005): 35–41.

Dominic McGoldrick, Peter Rowe and Eric Donnelly, eds, *The Permanent International Criminal Court: Legal and Policy Issues* (Oxford: Hart, 2004).

Randall McGowen, 'The Changing Face of God's Justice: The Debates over Divine and Human Punishment in Eighteenth-Century England', *Criminal Justice History* 9 (1988): 63–98.

John McGuire, 'Judicial Violence and the "Civilizing Process": Race and the Transition from Public to Private Executions in Colonial Australia', *Australian Historical Studies* 29, no. 111 (1998): 187–209.

Paul McHugh, *Aboriginal Societies and the Common Law: A History of Sovereignty, Status and Land* (Oxford University Press, 2004).

Stuart Macintyre and Richard Mitchell, eds, *Foundations of Arbitration* (Melbourne: Oxford University Press, 1989).

John McLaren, '"Men of Principle or Judicial Ratbags? The Trials and Tribulations of Maverick Colonial Judges in the 19th Century" or "A Funny Way to Run An Empire"', *Windsor Review of Legal & Social Issues* 27 (2009): 145–66.

Sally Maclean, 'Child Cruelty or Reasonable Punishment? A Case Study of the Operation of the Law and the Courts 1883–1903', *New Zealand Journal of History* 40, no. 1 (2006): 7–24.

Angela McRobbie, *The Aftermath of Feminism* (London: Sage Publications, 2009).

Shaun McVeigh, ed., *Jurisprudence of Jurisdiction*, ed. (Oxford: Routledge-Cavendish, 2007).

Frederick William Maitland, *Essays on the Teaching of English History* (Cambridge University Press, 1901).

Mahmood Mamdani, *Saviours And Survivors: Darfur, Politics and the War On Terror* (London: Verso, 2009).

Juan Marsal, *Pensar bajo el franquismo: Intelectuales y politica en la generacion de los años cincuenta* (Barcelona: Ediciones Península, 1979).

Karen L. Martin, 'Ways of Knowing, Ways of Being and Ways of Doing: A Theoretical Framework and Methods for Indigenous Re-search and Indigenist Research', *Journal of Australian Studies*, no. 76 (2003): 203–14.

Suzanne Miers, *Britain and the Ending of the Slave Trade* (London: Longman 1975).

Jane Millichamp, Judy Martin and John Langley, 'On the Receiving End: Young Adults Describe their Parents' Use of Physical Punishment and other Disciplinary Measures during Childhood', *Journal of the New Zealand Medical Association* 119, no. 1228 (27 January 2006): 1–143.

Roger Milliss, *Waterloo Creek: The Australia Day Massacre of 1838, George Gipps and the British Conquest of New South Wales* (Melbourne: McPhee Gribble, 1992).

Andrew Milner, Philip Thomson and Chris Worth, eds, *Postmodern Conditions* (New York: Berg Publishers, 1990).

Jeffrey Minson, *Genealogies of Morals: Nietzsche, Foucault, Donzelot and the Eccentricity of Ethics* (New York: St Martin's Press, 1985).

Will Mooney, 'Farmers' Foes or "Feathered Police"? Native Birds, Agriculture and the "Balance of Nature": Tasmania and Australia c. 1860 to 1920', *Tasmanian Historical Research Association Papers and Proceedings* 58, no. 2 (2011): 158–72.

Enrique Moradiellos, 'The Potsdam Conference and the Spanish Problem', *Contemporary European History* 10, no. 1 (March 2001): 82–89.

Gregorio Morán, *El precio de la transición* (Barcelona: Planeta, 1991).

Kenneth Morgan, *Slavery and the British Empire From African to America* (Oxford University Press, 2007).

Raúl Morodo, *La Transición Política* (Madrid: Tecnos, 1984).

Raúl Morodo, *Los orígenes ideológicos del franquismo: Acción Española* (Madrid: Alianza Editorial, 1985).

Meghan Morris, *Too Soon Too Late: History in Popular Culture* (Bloomington and Indianapolis: Indiana University Press, 1998).

Aileen Moreton-Robinson, ed., *Sovereign Subjects: Indigenous Sovereignty Matters* (Sydney: Allen and Unwin, 2007).

Arthur W. Moss, *Valiant Crusade: The History of the R.S.P.C.A.* (London: Cassell, 1961).

Jeremy Moss, ed., *The Later Foucault* (London: Sage Publications, 1998).

Makau Mutua, 'Terrorism and Human Rights: Power, Culture, and Subordination', *Buffalo Human Rights Law Review* 8 (2002): pp.1-14.

Ethan Nadelmann, 'Global Prohibition Regimes: The Evolution of Norms in International Society', *International Organisation* 44 (1990): 479–526.

Susana Narotzky and Gavin Smith, '"Being político" in Spain: An Ethnographic Account of Memories, Silences and Public Politics', *History and Memory* 14, no. 1/2 (2002): 189–228.

Friedrich Nietzsche, *On the Genealogy of Morality* (1887), ed., Keith Ansell-Pearson, trans., Carol Diethe (Cambridge University Press, 2007).

Mary E. Odem, *Delinquent Daughters: Protecting and Policing Adolescent Female Sexuality in the United States, 1885–1920* (Chapel Hill and London: University of North Carolina Press, 1995).

J.R. Oldfield, *'Chords of Freedom': Commemoration, Ritual and British Transatlantic Slavery* (Manchester University Press, 2007).

Diane Orentlicher, 'Settling Accounts: The Duty to Prosecute Human Rights Violations of a Prior Regime', *Yale Law Journal* 100 (1991): 2537–615.

Anne Orford, 'Commissioning the Truth', *Columbia Journal of Gender and Law* 15 (2006): 851–82.

Mark Osiel, *Mass Atrocity, Collective Memory and the Law* (New Jersey: Transaction Publishers, 2000).

José Antonio Álvarez Osés, Ignacio Cal Freire, María Carmen González Muñoz and Juan Haro Sabater, *La Guerra que aprendierion los espanoles: República y Guerra civil en los textos de Bachillerato (1938–1983)* (Madrid: Universidad Autónoma de Madrid, 2000).

Robert Paddle, *The Last Tasmanian Tiger: The History and Extinction of the Thylacine* (Cambridge University Press, 2000).

John Passmore, 'The Treatment of Animals', *Journal of the History of Ideas* 36 (1975): 195–218.

Greg Patmore, *Australian Labour History* (Melbourne: Longman Cheshire, 1991).

Stanley G. Payne, *The Franco Regime, 1936–1975* (Madison: University of Wisconsin Press, 1987).

——, *Spain: A Unique History* (Madison: University of Wisconsin Press, 2011).

Lachy Paterson 'Maori Conversion to the Rule of Law and Nineteenth-Century Imperial Loyalties', *Journal of Religious History* 32 (2008): 216–33.

Mark Peel, *The Lowest Rung: Voices of Australian Poverty* (Cambridge University Press, 2003).

Rachel Perkins and Marcia Langton, *First Australians* (Melbourne University Press, 2010).

Stefan Petrow, 'Arabs, Boys and Larrikins: Juvenile Delinquents and their Treatment in Hobart, 1860–1896', *Australian Journal of Legal History* 2 (1996): 37–59.

Stefan Petrow, 'Creating an Orderly Society: The Hobart Municipal Police 1880–1898', *Labour History*, no. 75 (1998): 175–94.

Peter Pierson, *The History of Spain* (Westport, CO and London: Greenwood Press, 1999).

David W. Pike, *Franco and the Axis Stigma* (New York: Macmillan, 2008).

Julio Rodríguez Puértolas, *Literatura fascista española* (Madrid: Akal, 1986).

António Costa Pinto, 'Elites, Single Parties and Political Decision-making in Fascist-era Dictatorships', *Contemporary European History* 11, no. 3 (2002): 429–54.

Paul Preston, 'Revenge and Reconciliation', *History Today* 39, no. 3 (March 1989): 28–33.

Paul Preston, *Franco: A Biography* (London: HarperCollins, 1993).

Paul Preston, *Juan Carlos: A People's King* (London: HarperCollins, 2004).

Paul Rabinow, ed., *The Foucault Reader* (New York: Pantheon Books, 1984).

Mike Radford, *Animal Welfare Law in Britain: Regulation and Responsibility* (Oxford University Press, 2001).

Vivienne Rae-Ellis, *Louisa Anne Meredith: A Tigress in Exile* (Hobart: St. David's Park Publishing, 1990).

Balakrishnan Rajagopal, *International Law from Below: Development, Social Movements and Third World Resistance* (Cambridge University Press, 2003).

Joan Ramon Resina, ed., *Disremembering the Dictatorship: The Politics of Memory in the Spanish Transition to Democracy* (Amsterdam and Atlanta: Rodopi).

Michael Richards, 'From War Culture to Civil Society: Francoism, Social Change and Memories of the Spanish Civil War', *History and Memory* 14, no. 1/2 (2002): 93–120.

Jane and James Ritchie, *Spare the Rod* (Sydney: Allen and Unwin, 1981).

David Rieff, *A Bed for the Night: Humanitarianism in Crisis* (London: Vintage, 2002).

Harriet Ritvo, *The Animal Estate: The English and Other Creatures in the Victorian Age* (Cambridge: Harvard University Press, 1987).

David A. Roberts, '"language to save the innocent": Reverend L. Threlkeld's Linguistic Mission', *Journal of the Royal Australian Historical Society* 94, no. 2 (2008): 107–25.

M.J.D. Roberts, *Making English Morals: Voluntary Associations and Moral Reform in England, 1787–1886* (Cambridge University Press, 2004).

Shirleene Robinson, *Something Like Slavery* (Melbourne: Australian Scholarly Publishing, 2008).

Lloyd Robson, *A Short History of Tasmania*, updated by Michael Roe, 2nd ed. (Melbourne: Oxford University Press, 1997).

Lionel Rose, *The Erosion of Childhood: Child Oppression in Britain 1860–1918* (London and New York: Routledge, 1991).

Christopher J. Ross, *Spain 1812–2004*, 2nd ed. (London: Arnold, 2004).

Nigel Rothfels, ed., *Representing Animals* (Bloomington: Indiana University Press, 2002).

B. Salter, 'Possess or Protect? Exploring the Legal Status of Animals in Australia's First Colonial Courts: Part 1, The Unnatural Theft and Murder', *Australian Animal Protection Law Journal* 2 (2009): 35–48.

Kay Saunders and Ray Evans, eds, *Gender Relations in Australia: Domination and Negotiation* (London: Harcourt Brace Jovanovich, 1992).

Dorothy Scott and Shurlee Swain, *Confronting Cruelty: Historical Perspectives on Child Protection in Australia* (Melbourne University Press, 2002).

Joan Scott, *Gender and Politics of History* (New York: Columbia University Press, 1988) .

Rodolfo Serrano, *La España de Cuéntame cómo pasó : el final de los años sesenta* (Madrid: Aguilar, 2004).

K. Sharman, 'Sentencing Under Our Anti-Cruelty Statutes: Why Our Leniency Will Come Back to Bite Us', *Current Issues in Criminal Justice* 13 (2002): 333–38.

Tom Sheridan, 'Coastal shipping and the Menzies Government 1950–1966', *Australian Economic History Review* 25 (March 1995): 3–39.

——, *Australia's Own Cold War: The Waterfront under Menzies* (Melbourne University Press, 2006).

Marika Sherwood, *After Abolition: Britain and the Slave Trade since 1807* (London: I. B. Tauris, 2007).

F.O. Shyllon, *Black Slaves in Britain* (London: Oxford University Press, 1974).

Gerry Simpson, 'Didactic and Dissident Histories in War Crimes Trials', *Albany Law Review* 60 (1996–97): 841-60.

——, *Law, War and Crime* (Cambridge: Polity Press, 2007).

Russell Smandych, 'Contemplating The Testimony of "Others": James Stephen, The Colonial Office, and The Fate of Australian Aboriginal Evidence Acts, circa 1839–1849', *Australian Journal of Legal History* 8 (2004): 237–84.

Carol Smart, *The Ties that Bind: Law, Marriage, and the Reproduction of Patriarchal Relations* (London; Boston: Routledge & Kegan Paul, 1984).

——, *Feminism and the Power of Law* (London; New York: Routledge, 1989).

Keith Vincent Smith, *King Bungaree: A Sydney Aborigine Meets the Great South Pacific Explorers, 1799–1830* (Sydney: Kangaroo Press, 1992).

——, *Bennelong: The Coming in of the Eora: Sydney Cove 1788–1792* (Sydney: Kangaroo Press, 2001).

——, *Wallumedegal: An Aboriginal History of Ryde* (Sydney: Ryde City Council, 2005).

Maya Steinitz, 'The Milošević Trial Live!', *Journal of International Criminal Justice* 3 (2005): 203–46.

Michael Sturma, 'Death and Ritual on the Gallows: Public Executions in the Australian Penal Colonies', *OMEGA* 17, no. 1 (1986): 89–100.

D.B. Swinfen, *Imperial Control of Colonial Legislation, 1813–1865: A Study of British Policy Towards Colonial Legislative Powers* (Oxford: Clarendon Press, 1970).

Ruti Teitel, *Transitional Justice* (Oxford University Press, 2000).

Hugh Thomas, *The Slave Trade: The History of the Atlantic Slave Trade 1440–1870* (London and Basingstoke: Picador, 1997).

Margaret Thornton, *Dissonance and Distrust: Women in the Legal Profession* (Oxford University Press, 1996).

Margaret Thornton, ed., *Romancing the Tomes: Popular Culture, Law and Feminism* (London; Sydney: Cavendish Publishing, 2002).

Margaret Thornton, 'Neoliberal Melancholia: The Case of Feminist Legal Scholarship', *The Australian Feminist Law Journal* 20 (2004): 7–22.

Margaret Thornton, ed., *Sex Discrimination in Uncertain Times* (Canberra: ANU E Press, 2010).

Christopher Tomlins, 'Law's Disciplinary Encounters: A Historical Narrative', *Law and Society Review* 34 (2000): 911–72.

David S. Trigger, *Whitefella Comin': Aboriginal Responses to Colonialism in Northern Australia* (Cambridge University Press, 1992).

David Turley, *The Culture of English Antislavery, 1780–1860* (London and New York: Routledge, 1991).

Javier Tusell, 'La Transición política: un planteamiento metodológico', in *Historia de la transición 1975–1986*, eds, Javier Tusell and Álvaro Soto (Madrid: Alianza Editorial, 1996).

Universo de Micromundos, eds, Carmelo Romero and Alberto Sabio (Zaragoza: Institución Fernando el Católico, 2009), 47–62.

Mariana Valverde, 'Specters of Foucault in Law and Society Scholarship', *American Review of Law and Society* 6 (2010): 45–59.

Mariana Valverde, *The Age of Light, Soap, and Water: Moral Reform in English Canada, 1885–1925* (Toronto: McClelland and Stewart, 1991).

Dacia Viejo-Rose, *Reconstructing Spain. Cultural Heritage and Memory after Civil War* (Brighton, Portland and Toronto: Sussex Academic Press, 2011).

Teresa Vilarós, *El mono del desencanto: una crítica cultural de la transición espanola (1973–1993)* (Madrid: Siglo Veintiuno, 1998).

Elizabeth Kowaleski Wallace, *The British Slave Trade and Public Memory* (Chichester: Columbia University Press, 2006).

James Walvin, *Black Ivory: A History of British Slavery* (London: Harper Collins, 1992).

Damen Ward, 'Legislation, Repugnancy and the Disallowance of Colonial Laws: The Legal Structure of Empire and Lloyd's Case (1844)', *Victoria University of Wellington Law Review* 41 (2010): 381–402.

Joanne Watson, *Palm Island: Through a Long Lens* (Canberra: Aboriginal Studies Press, 2010).

Hayden White, 'The Abiding Relevance of Croce's Idea of History', *Journal of Modern History* 37 (June 1963) 109–24.

Howard J. Wiarda and Margaret MacLeish Mott, *Catholic Roots and Democratic Flowers: Political Systems in Spain and Portugal* (Westport, CO and London: Praeger, 2001).

William Wiecek, 'Somerset: Lord Mansfield and the Legitimacy of Slavery in the Anglo-American World', *University of Chicago Law Review* 42 (1974–75): 86–146.

Howard Hazen Wilson, 'Some Principal Aspects of British Efforts to Crush the African Slave Trade, 1807–1929', *The American Journal of International Law* 44 (1950): 505–26.

Jay Winter and Emmanuel Sivan, eds, *War and Remembrance in the Twentieth Century* (Cambridge University Press, 2000).

Steven Wise, *Though the Heavens May Fall* (Cambridge, MA: Da Capo Press, 2005).

Beth Wood, Ian Hassall and George Hook, *Unreasonable Force: New Zealand's Journey Towards Banning the Physical Punishment of Children* (Wellington: Save the Children New Zealand, 2008).

David Young, *Sporting Island: A History of Sport and Recreation in Tasmania* (Hobart: Sport and Recreation, Tasmania, 2005).

Ralph Zacklin, 'The Failings of Ad Hoc International Tribunals', *Journal of International Criminal Justice* 2 (2004): 541–45.

Viviana Zelizer, *Pricing the Priceless Child: The Changing Social Value of Children* (New York: Basic Books, 1985).

www.ingramcontent.com/pod-product-compliance
Lightning Source LLC
Chambersburg PA
CBHW061245270326
41928CB00041B/3420